Directory of Points and Landings on Rivers and Bayous Mississippi Watershed

Louis A. Adam

Heritage Books
2025

HERITAGE BOOKS
AN IMPRINT OF HERITAGE BOOKS, INC.

Books, CDs, and more—Worldwide

For our listing of thousands of titles see our website
at
www.HeritageBooks.com

A Facsimile Reprint
Published 2025 by
HERITAGE BOOKS, INC.
Publishing Division
5810 Ruatan Street
Berwyn Heights, MD 20740

Originally published:
New Orleans
W. L. Murray, Publisher
1877

International Standard Book Number
Paperbound: 978-0-7884-7770-6

ADAM'S
DIRECTORY

—OF—

Points and Landings

—ON—

RIVERS AND BAYOUS

IN THE STATES OF

ALABAMA, ARKANSAS, FLORIDA, GEORGIA
INDIANA, ILLINOIS, KENTUCKY, IOWA,
LOUISIANA, MINNESOTA, MISSISSIPPI,
MISSOURI, NEBRASKA, OHIO,
TENNESSEE, TEXAS AND
WISCONSIN.

By LOUIS A. ADAM,
RIVER CLERK OF THE FACTORS' AND TRADERS' INSURANCE CO.

FIVE DOLLARS PER COPY.

NEW ORLEANS.
W. L. MURRAY, Publisher, No. 61 Camp Street.
1877.

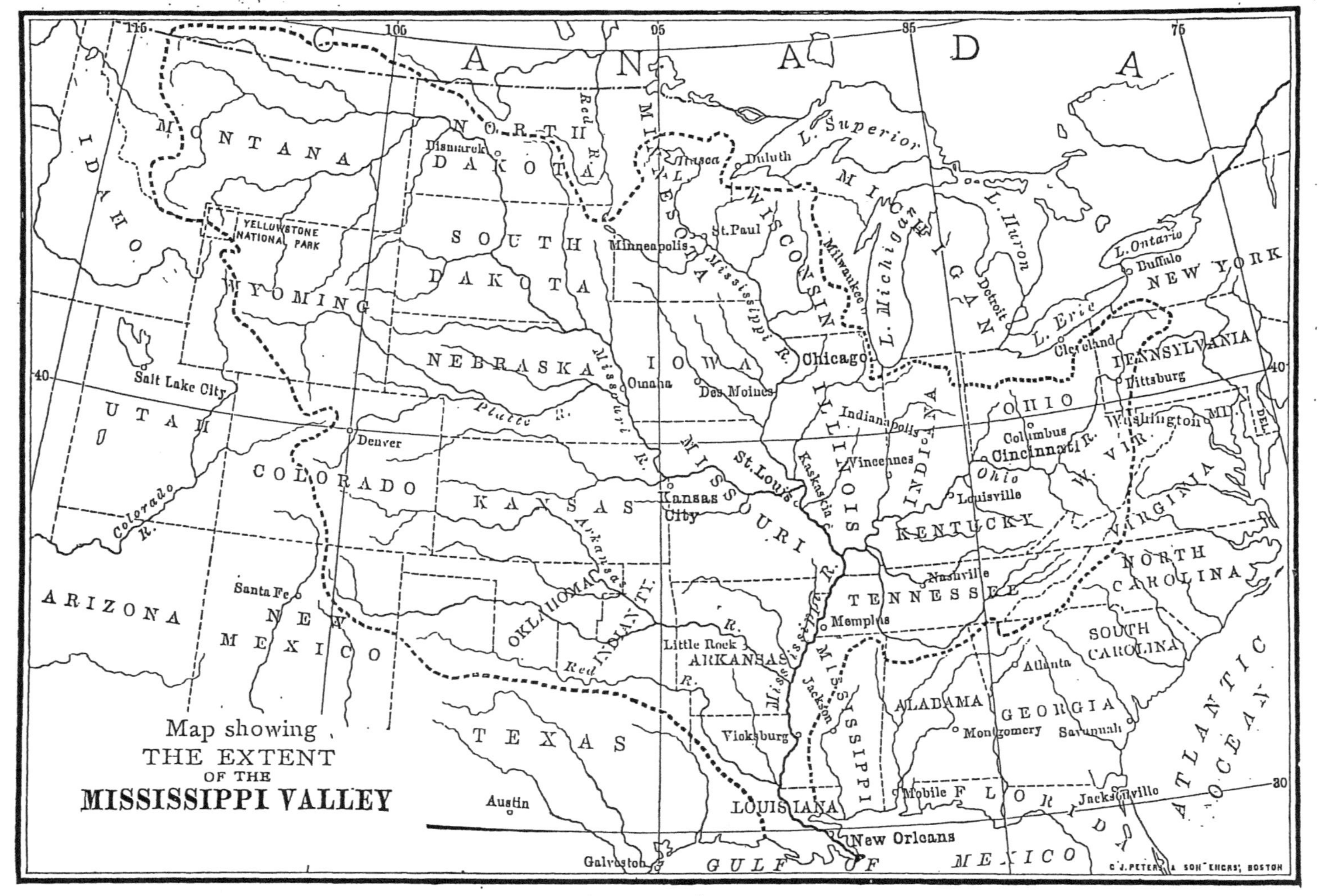

Map showing
THE EXTENT
OF THE
MISSISSIPPI VALLEY

REVISED REGISTER

—OF—

Points and Landings.

A

AARON LANDING.—Tallahatchie river, not above Cassidy's Bayou.

ABBEVILLE, *La.*—20 miles from New Iberia.

ABBEVILLE, *Miss.*—Tallahatchie river, above Belmont.

ABERDEEN, *Miss.*—Tombigbee river, above Columbus, not above Cotton Gin Port.

ABERDEEN, *O.*—Ohio river, 594 miles above its mouth, above Cincinnati.

ABERDEEN, *Ark.*—White river, 125 miles from its mouth, below the junction of Black river.

ABERCROMBIE, *Ark.*—Mississippi river, above Greenville, not above Memphis.

ABEY'S (Dr.) LANDING.—Ouachita river, not above Trenton.

ABEYDOS.—Yazoo river, not above Yazoo City.

ABNEY'S LANDING, *La.*—Red river, above Grand Ecore, not above Shreveport.

ABNEY'S.—Red river, above Shreveport and not above foot of Raft.

ACHARD'S LANDING, *Ark.*—Arkansas river, 207 miles above Napoleon, above Pine Bluff, not above Little Rock.

ACKER'S LANDING, *Ala.*—Tombigbee river, not above Demopolis.

ACKER'S WOODYARD, *Ala.*—Alabama river, not above Selma.

ACKLAND'S LANDING, *La.*—Black river, not above Harrisonburg.

ACKLEN'S (Col.) or ANGOLA LANDING, *La.*—Mississippi river, 204 miles above New Orleans, above Bayou Sara, not above Grand Gulf.

ADAMS' FERRY, *Tex.*—Trinity river, above Smithville, not above Magnolia Landing.

ADAMS' LANDING, *Ala.*—Tombigbee river, not above Demopolis.

ADAMS' BLUFF, *Ark.*—White river, 105 miles above its mouth, below the junction of Black river.

ADAMS' LANDING, *Ark.*—Arkansas river, 272 miles above Napoleon, above Pine Bluff, not above Little Rock.

ADAM LANDING, *Miss.*—Above Grand Gulf, not above Greenville

ADAMS.—Yazoo river, not above Yazoo City.

ADAMS.—Red river, above Fulton, not above Lanesport.

ADDISON, *Ohio.*—Ohio river, 742 miles above its mouth, above Cincinnati.

ADDLE (Mrs. S.)—Red river, above Grand Ecore, not above Shreveport.

ADGER, J. E, or MOLTRIES.—Red river, above Shreveport, not above foot of Raft.

ADKINS, WIDOW (New Hope).—Red river, above Grand Ecore not above Shreveport.

ADKINSON LANDING.—Mississippi river, above Greenville, not above Memphis.

AFRICA, *Miss.*—121 miles up Sunflower river.

AGEE'S LANDING, *Ala.*—Alabama river, not above Selma.

AIKEN'S (Mrs.) LANDING, *Ark.*—Little Red river, a tributary to White river, below the junction of White and Black rivers.

AITKIN'S, GRANNY, *Ark.*—Little Red river, 23 miles above its mouth, below the junction of White and Black rivers.

AIKENS, Col.—Mouth of Pecan Bayou, Red River, above Lanesport, not above Mound City.

AKERVILLE, *Ark.*—Arkansas river, above Fort Smith.

ALABAMA LANDING.—111 miles up Bœuf river, above Thomas' Landing.

ALABAMA, *Tex.*—Trinity river, above Smithville, not above Magnolia Landing.

ALABAMA LANDING, *La.*—Ouachita river, 340 miles from the mouth of the old river, above Trenton.

ALBAN (Little Pass).—Red river, above Shreveport, not above Carolina Bluff.

ALBAN'S GUT, or STANTON'S.—Red river above foot of Raft, not above Fulton.

ALBANY, *La.*—Lake Caddo.

ALBANY, *La.*—Red river, 17 miles above Shreveport, not above mouth of Black Bayou.

ALBANY, *Geo.*—Flint river, above Newtown.

ALBEMARLE.—Mississippi river, above Grand Gulf, not above Greenville.

ALBINO INNO.—Yazoo river, above Yazoo City, not above Leflore.

ALBION CITY.—Red river, above Rowland and Mound City.

ALBION, G. N.—Red river, 487 miles above Shreveport, above Mound City.

ALDERBROOK, *Ark.*—White river, not above Batesville.

ALLEN'S FERRY.—St. Francis river, above Philips' Bayou.

ALLEN'S LANDING, *Ala.*—Warrior river, not above Tuscaloosa.

ALLEN, J. D. (Palmetto Plantation.)—Red river, above Alexandria, not above Cane river.

ALEXANDRIA, *La.*—Red river, 360 miles from New Orleans.

ALEXANDRIA, *O.*—Ohio river, 644 miles above its mouth, above Cincinnati.

ALEXANDRIA, *Mo.*—Mississippi river, 210 miles above St. Louis, above Alton, not above first Rapids.

ALEXANDRIA (Mrs.)—Red river, not above Alexandria.

ALEXANDER (Dr.)—136 miles up Bœuf river, above Thomas' Landing.

ALEXANDER'S.—Bayou Bartholomew, above Point Pleasant, not above Arkansas line.

ALEXANDER LANDING.—Big Deer Creek, not above Yazoo City.

ALFRED WILLIAMS.—Big Deer Creek.

ALL RIGHT LANDING, *La.*—Mississippi river, above Grand Gulf, not above Greenville.

ALL NUT'S LANDING, *La.*—Bayou Macon, 110 miles from its mouth, not above Monticello.

ALLIGATOR.—Thompson's, Yazoo river, not above Yazoo City.

ALLIGATOR BLUFF.—Bayou Bartholomew, above Arkansas line, not above Portland.

ALLIGATOR BAYOU.—Red river, not above Alexandria.

ALLIGATOR.—Ouachita river, above Harrisonburg, not ab. Trenton.

ALPHIA, *Ky.*—Ohio river, above Paducah, not above Cincinnati.

ALTERA.—Yazoo river, above Yazoo City, not above Leflore.

ALTO.—Bœuf river, 128 miles up, above Thomas Landing.

ALTO, *La.*—Mississippi river, not above Bayou Sara.

ALTON'S LANDING, *La.*—Black river, La.

ALTON, *Ills.*—Mississippi river, 20 miles above St. Louis.

ALTON, *Ind.*—Ohio river, 305 miles above its mouth, above Paducah, not above Cincinnati.

ALTON, *Tenn.*—Tennessee river, not above Eastport.

AMAZONIA, *Ind.*—Missouri river, above Iatan.

AMERICUS, *Ind.*—Wabash river, above the Rapids, not above Terre Haute.

AMERICA, *Ills.*—Ohio river, 9 miles from its mouth, not ab. Paducah.

AMITE, *La.*—Jackson railroad, 68 miles from New Orleans.

AMSTERDAM, *Miss.*—Big Black river.

AMSTERDAM, *O.*—Ohio river, 326 miles above its mouth, above Paducah, not above Cincinnati.

AMSTERDAM, *Ind.*—Wabash river, above the Rapids, not above Terre Haute.

ANCHOR WOODYARD.—Red river, above Grand Gulf, not above Shreveport.

ANCHORAGE, or CAPT. CARTER'S.—Red river, above Shreveport, not above foot of Raft.

ANCHORAGE PLACE.—Mississippi river, not above Bayou Sara.

ANCHOR PLANTATION, *La.*—Tensas river, 41 miles from Trinity, not above the mouth of Bayou Macon.

ANDALUSIA, *Ills.*—Mississippi river, 1508 miles above New Orleans, above the foot of First Rapids, not above the foot of Second Rapids.

ANDERSON, *Miss.*—Mississippi river, above Greenville, not above Memphis.

ANDERSON'S BLUFF, *Ark.*—White river, 85 miles from its mouth, below the junction of Black river.

ANDERSON'S LANDING, *Miss.*—119 miles up Big Deer Creek.

ANDERSON, A. L.—Bayou Bartholomew, not above Pt. Pleasant.

ANDERSON, J. M.—Bayou Bartholomew, above Pt. Pleasant, not above Arkansas Line.

ANDERSON RIVER, *Ind.*—Ohio river, 255 miles above its mouth, above Paducah, not above Cincinnati.

ANDREWS, or IXUDIN, *Miss.*—Yazoo river, above Yazoo City, not above Leflore.

ANGELINA RIVER.—Above Bevilport.

ANGOLA LANDING, *Miss.*—Mississippi river, above Bayou Sara, not above Grand Gulf.

ANGUILLA, *Miss.*—122 miles up Big Deer Creek.

ANNADALE, *Miss.*—Yazoo river, not above Yazoo City.

ANSILL, J. J. (Boutlet's Bluff).—Red river, above Grand Ecore, not above Shreveport.

ANTONEY'S.—Red river, above foot of Raft, not above Fulton.

ANTIOCH, *Ind.*—Wabash river, not above the Rapids.

ANTOINE RAPIDS.—Missouri river, 2967 miles from St. Louis, above Iatan.

APPANOOSE, *Ills.*—Mississippi river, 1400 miles above New Orleans, above Alton, not above foot of First Rapids.

APPLE CREEK, *Ills.*—Illinois river, not above Beardstown.

APPLE CREEK, *Mo.*—Mississippi river, above the mouth of the Ohio, not above Alton.

ARAGO.—Missouri river, 647 miles from St. Louis, above Iatan.

ARCOLA, *Ala.*—Warrior river, not above Tuscaloosa.

ARCOLA, *Miss.*—165 miles up Big Deer Creek.

ARCHULA.—Tallahatchie river, not above Cassidy Bayou.

ARCHERLETTA.—Yazoo river, above Yazoo City, not above Leflore.

ARGYLE.—Mississippi river, above Greenville, not above Memphis.

ARKADELPHIA, *Ark.*—Ouachita river, 607 miles from the mouth of Old river, above Ross's Landing, not above Arkadelphia.

ARKAPOLA, *Ark.*—White river, 172 miles from its mouth, below the junction of Black river.

ARKANSAS, *Ark.*—White river, below the junction of Black river.

ARKANSAS LINE, *Ark.*—Mississippi river, above Memphis, not above the mouth of the Ohio.

ARKANSAS POST, *Ark.*—Arkansas river, 58 miles above Napoleon.

ARKANSAS CITY.—Mississippi river, above Greenville, and not above Memphis.

ARKAPOLIS.—Same place as Arkansas City (see above.)

ARKANSAS LINE.—Bayou Bartholomew, above Pt. Pleasant, not above Louisiana line.

ARGENTA, *Ark.*—Opposite Little Rock.

ARLINGTON, *La.*—Mississippi river, not above Bayou Sara.

ARMORS, MRS —Red river, above foot of Raft, not above Fulton.

ARMSTEAD, B. F.—Red river, above Grand Ecore, not above Shreveport.

ARMSTEAD, JNO. W.—Red river, above Grand Ecore, not above Shreveport.

ARMSTEAD, R. H.—Red river, above Grand Ecore, not above Shreveport.

ARMSTEAD, W. (Cabin Point).—Red river, above Grand Ecore, not above Shreveport.

ARMSTEAD, R.—Red river, above Grand Ecore, not above Shreveport.

ARMONIA, *La.*—Bayou Macon, 112 miles from its mouth, not above Monticello.

ARMSTRONG, *Ind.*—Wabash river, above the rapids, not above Terre Haute.

ARMSTRONG'S LANDING, *Ark.*—Arkansas river, above Pine Bluff, not above Little Rock.

ARNET'S, MRS., LANDING, *Ark.*—Arkansas river, 380 miles above Napoleon, above Little Rock, not above Norristown.

ARNOE, JNO. B., LANDING.—Red river, not above Alexandria.

ARRICK PLACE.—Yazoo river, above Yazoo City, not above Leflore.

ARRINGTON'S LANDING, *Ark.*—Warrior river, not above Tuscaloosa.

ARROW RIVER.—Missouri river, 2007 miles from St. Louis, above Iatan.

ARROW ROCK, *Mo.*—Missouri river, 218 miles above its mouth, above Jefferson City, not above Lexington.

ASH PLANTATION, *La.*—Red river, above Grand Ecore, not above Shreveport.

ASHWOOD, *La.*—Tensas river, not above the mouth of Bayou Macon.

ASCENSION, *La.*—Above Donaldsonville, not above Bayou Sara.

ASESTOS.—Yazoo river, not above Yazoo river.

ASHCOTT, *La.*—Black river, not above Harrisonburgh.

ASH FLAT.—Red river, above Shreveport, not above foot of Raft.

ASHLEY.—Tallahatchie river, not above Cassidy Bayou.

ASHLEY.—Ouachita river, above Alabama Landing, not above Camden.

ASHLEY'S LANDING.—Arkansas river, above Arkansas Post, not above Pine Bluff.

ASHLEY'S LANDING, *Miss.*—Mississippi river, above Bayou Sara, not above Grand Gulf.

ASHLY ISLAND.—Missouri river, 1721 miles from St. Louis, above Iatan.

ASHTON'S FERRY, *Texas.*—Sabine river, above Hamilton.

ASHBURN, *La.*—Red river, above Alexandria, not above Cotile Landing.

ASHFORD LANDING, *Ark.*—White river, 120 miles from its mouth, below the junction of Black river.

ASHLAND, *Miss.*—Mississippi river, above Grand Gulf, not above Greenville.

ASHPORT, *Tenn.*—Mississtppi river, 918 miles above New Orleans, above Greenville, not above the mouth of the Ohio.

ASHTON, *La.*—Mississippi river, 497 miles above New Orleans, above Grand Gulf, not above Greenville.

ASKEE'S LANDING, *Ark.*—Mississippi river,. above Greenville, not above the mouth of the Ohio river.

ASPINWALL.—Missouri river, 671 miles from St. Louis, above Iatan.

ASSUMPTION, *La.*—Bayou Lafourche.

ASTON, *Ill.*—Mississippi river, 1326 miles above New Orleans, above Alton, not above Foot of First Rapids.

ASHWOOD, *Miss.*—Yazoo river, above Yazoo City, not above Leflore.

ASHWOOD PLANTATION, *La.*—Red river, above Grand Ecore, not above Shreveport.

ASHWOOD, L.—Mississippi river, above Grand Gulf, not above Greenville.

ASHBOURN (Dr. Luckett's).—Red river, above Alexandria, not above mouth of Cane river.

ASHWOOD LANDING, *Miss.*—Mississippi river, 578 miles above New Orleans, above Greenville, not above Memphis.

ASHLAND STORE·—Mississippi river, not above Bayou Sara.

ASHLAND (B. W, Marston).—Red river, above Grand Ecore, not above Shreveport.

ASHLAND.—Yazoo river, above Yazoo City, not above Leflore.

ASH POINT, *La.*—Red river, above Grand Ecore, not above Shreveport.

ASHTON.—Yazoo river, above Yazoo City, not above Leflore.

ATKIN'S, WIDOW (NEW HOPE).—Red river, above Grand Ecore, not above Shreveport.

ATHENS, *La.*—Claiborne Parish, inland, five miles east of Minden.

ATCHAFALAYA RIVER. *La.*

ATCHINSON, *Kan.*—Missouri river, 465 miles above its mouth, above Iatan.

ATCHISON'S LANDING, *Ala.*—Tombigbee river, not above Demopolis.

ATHENS, *Ark.*—White river, 322 miles from Mississipi river, above Batesville.

ATHERTON'S LANDING, *Ill.*—Mississippi river, above the mouth of the Ohio, not above Alton.

ATKINSON'S LANDING, *La.*—Red river, above Grand Ecore, not above Shreveport.

ATKINSON'S LANDING, *Ala.*—Alabama river, not above Selma.

ATLANTA, *Geo.*—7 miles southeast of Chattahootchie river.

ATTICA, *Ind.*—Wabash river, above the Rapids, not above Terre Haute.

ATWELL'S LANDING, *La.*—Ouachita river, above Trenton, not above Alabama Landing.

AUBURN LANDING, *Ark.*—Arkansas river, 96 miles above Napoleon, above Arkansas Post, not above Pine Bluff.

AUGUSTA, *Ark.*—White river, 282 miles from the Mississippi river below the junction of Black river.

AUGUSTA, *Ky.*—Ohio river, 575 miles above its mouth, above Cincinnati.

AUSTIN & HEBERT, *La.*—87 miles up Bœuf river, above Thomas' Landing.

AUBURN LANDING,, *Miss.*—Mississippi river, above Grand Gulf, not above Greenville.

AUGUSTE PERRE.—Ouachita river, above Alabama Landing, not above Camden.

AUGUSTA, *Miss.*—Back of Mississippi City.

AUGUSTA, *Mo.*—Missouri river, 58 miles above its mouth, not above Jefferson City.

AURORA, *La.*—Red river, above Grand Ecore, not above Shreveport.

AURORA, *Texas.*—Sabine river, above Sabine City, not above Belgrave.

AURORA, *Ind.*—Ohio river, 514 miles above its mouth, above Paducah, not above Cincinnati.

AUSTIN, *Miss.*—Mississippi river, 750 miles above New Orleans, above Greenville, not above Memphis.

AUSTELL'S LANDING, *Ala.*—Tombigbee river, not above Demopolis.

AUSTRALIA, *Miss.*—Mississippi river, above Greenville, not above Memphis.

AVERA LANDING, *La.*—Ouachita river, above Trenton, not above Alabama Landing.

AVERY'S.—Ouachita river, above Alabama Landing, not above Camden.

AVOCA.—Yazoo river, not above Yazoo City.

AVOCA (Capt. Mead).—Red river, above Alexandria, not above Cane river.

AVOYELLES, *La.*—Red river, below Alexandria.

AWOOKER'S LANDING, *La.*—Red river, above Alexandria, not above Cane river.

B

B. PLACE, *La.*—Red river, above Grand Ecore, not above Shreveport.

B. STORE.—Red river, above Grand Ecore, not above Shreveport.

BABIN'S LANDING, *La*—Red river, 290 miles from New Orleans, below Alexandria.

BACON'S BLUFF, *Texas*—Sabine river.

BADLEY, JNO.—Red river, above Grand Ecore, not above Shreveport.

BAD AXE RIVER, *Wis.*—Mississippi river, 1711 miles above New Orleans, above Galena.

BADEN.—Ohio river, 982 miles above its mouth, above Cincinnati.

BADGETT'S LANDING, *Ark.*—Arkansas river, 271 miles above Napoleon, above Pine Bluff, not above Little Rock.

BAGLEY'S LANDING, *La.*—Red river, above Grand Ecore, not above Shreveport.

BAILEY, L. (Rock Island).—Red river, above Cane river, not above Grand Ecore.

BAILEY'S.—Yazoo river, above Yazoo City, not above Leflore.

BAILEY'S, or JONESBORO.—Red river, above Rowland and Mound City.

BAILEY'S.—93 miles up Bœuf river, above Thomas' Landing.

BAILEY'S.—Tallahatchie river, not above Cassidy's Bayou.

BAILEY'S STORE, *Miss.*—149 miles up Big Deer Creek.

BAIRFIELD, *Ala.*—Alabama river, not above Selma.

BAILEY'S LANDING, *Mo.*—Mississippi river, 1123 miles above New Orleans, above the mouth of the Ohio, not above Alton.

BAINBRIDGE, *Mo.*—Mississippi river, 1096 miles above New Orleans, above the month of the Ohio, not above Alton.

BAMBRICK'S LANDING.—Ouachita river, above Harrisonburg, not above Trenton.

BAKSTER'S LANDING, *Tenn.*—Cumberland river, not above Nashville.

BAKER'S (ED.) LANDING.—123 miles up Sunflower river.

BAKER'S (W. H.) LANDING.—Ouachita river, above Trenton not above Alabama Landing.

BAKER'S (JOE) LANDING).—Ouachita river, above Trenton, not above Alabama Landing.

BALDWIN'S BLUFF, *Ala.*—Tombigbee river, not above Demopolis.

BALIZE, *La.*—Mississippi river, 102 miles below New Orleans.

BALDWINSVILLE, *Mo.*—Mississippi river, 982 miles above New Orleans, above Memphis, not above the mouth of the Ohio.

BALE SHED.—Mississippi river, above Grand Gulf, not above Greenville.

BALLOU'S LANDING.—Black river, La., not above Trinity.

BALLARD & GROVER'S.—Mississippi river, above Grand Gulf, not above Greenville.

BALLAND'S.—Mississippi river, above Grand Gulf, not above Greenville.

BALLARD, FK.—Ouachita river, above Harrisonburg, not above Trenton.

BALL'S, W. L. (Moore's.)—Red river; above Grand Ecore, not above Shreveport.

BANKHEAD'S LANDING, *Ark.*—Arkansas river, 129 miles above Napoleon, above Arkansas Post, not above Pine Bluff.

BANKSMITH LANDING.—Ouachita river, above Trenton, not above Alabama Landing.

BANGS.—Ouachita river, above Alabama Landing, not above Camden

BARDSTOWN, *Ky.*—Ohio river, 368 miles above its mouth, above Paducah, not above Cincinnati.

BARNES, G. LANDING, *Ala*—Tombigbee river, not above Demopolis.

BARNEY'S LANDING, *Ala.*—Tombigbee river, not above Demopolis.

BARNEY'S UPPER PLACE, *Ala.*—Tombigbee river, not above Demopolis.

BARAQUE'S LANDING, *Ark.*—Arkansas river, 228 miles above Napoleon, above Pine Bluff, not above Little Rock.

BAREFIELD'S (SAM.) LANDING, *Miss.*—150 miles up Big Deer Creek.

BARBER, TOM—Bayou Bartholomew, not above Point Pleasant.

BARBIN'S LANDING.—Red river, not above Alexandria.

BAREHOUSE POINT.—Bayou Bartholomew, not above Point Pleasant.

BARENAU.—Tallahatchie river, not above Cassidy Bayou.

BARGOU BENOIST, or G. Y. GRAY.—Red river, above Shreveport, not above foot of Raft.

BARKER'S LANDING.—Black river, La., not above Trinity.

BARKHOW'S (Mrs.) or McBEE'S LANDING.—Yazoo river, above Yazoo City, not above Leflore.

BARGE TOWN.—Red river, above foot of Raft, not above Fulton.

BARNARD'S (WM.) LANDING, *Miss.*—121 miles up Big Deer Creek.

BARNARD, *Ark.*—Mississippi river, above Grand Gulf, not above Greenville.

BARNEY'S LANDING, *Ark.*—Mississippi river, 646 miles above New Orleans, above Greenville, not above Memphis.

BARNETT.—194 miles up Sunflower river.

BARRON PORT.—Mississippi river, not above Bayou Sara.

BARRINGER'S.—Bayou Bartholomew, above Arkansas Line, not above Portland.

BARRAS, L.—Ouachita river, above Harrisonburg, not above Trenton

BARRO.—Red river, above Shreveport, not above foot of Raft.

BARRY'S, W. S.—Tallahatchie river, not above Cassidy Bayou.

BARRY'S LANDING, *Miss.*—Tombigbee river, above Columbus, not above Cotton Gin Port.

BARRY'S (Dr.) LANDING, *Ark.*—Mississippi river, above Greenville, not above Memphis.

BARRY'S LANDING, *Ark.*—Arkansas river, 385 miles above Napoleon, above Little Rock, not above Norristown.

BARS.—Red river, above Shreveport, not above Carolina Bluffs.

BARTLETT'S LANDING, *La*—Red river, above Cane river, not above Grand Ecore.

BARTLETT'S LANDING.—Ouachita river, above Trenton, not above Alabama Landing.

BARTLETT'S (T. G.) LANDING.—Red river, above Cane river, not above Grand Ecore.

BARTONIA.—Yazoo river, above Yazoo City, not above Leflore.

BASLEY, J. R.—Red river, above Grand Ecore, not above Shreveport.

BASTROP, PIERRE.—Red river, above Cane river, not above Grand Ecore.

BASS,' L., LANDING, *Miss.*—Mississippi river, above Grand Gulf, not above Greenville.

BASTROP, *La.*—Near Bayou Bartholomew.

BASS,' H., LANDING, *Ala.*—Tombigbee river, not above Demopolis.

BASSETT'S LANDING, *Ala.*—Tombigbee river, not above Demopolis.

BASSON LANDING. (Wood Yard.)—Red river; not above Alexandria.

BASSORA, *Mo.*—Missouri river, 65 miles above its mouth, not above Jefferson City.

BACHELOR'S MISERY, or DR. W. C. VANCE.—Red river, above Shreveport, not above foot of Raft.

BATES, R. L.—Yazoo river, above Yazoo City, not above Leflore.

BATES, G. G. (Sixteenth Sec.)—Red river, above Grand Ecore, not above Shreveport.

BATES, CICERO.—Red river, above Grand Ecore, not above Shreveport.

BATES POINT.—(Rube White.)—Red river, above Grand Ecore, not above Shreveport.

BATES HOMESTEAD.—Red river, above Grand Ecore, not above Shreveport.

BATTAILLE PLACE.—Yazoo river, above Yazoo City, not above Leflore.

BATTIES, JOHN.—Red river, above Shreveport, not above foot of Raft.

BATES' LANDING, *La.*—Red river, above Grand Ecore, not above Shreveport.

BATES' PLACE, *La.*—Red river, above Grand Ecore, not above Shreveport.

BATEMAN'S LANDING, *Tenn.*—Mississippi river, above Memphis, not above the mouth of the Ohio river.

BATON ROUGE, *La.*—Mississippi river, 130 miles above New Orleans, not above Bayou Sara.

BATTLE GROUND, *La.*—Mississippi river, 6 miles below New Orleans.

BATESVILLE, *Ark.*—White river, 265 miles from the Mississippi.

BATESVILLE, *Ind.*—Ohio river, 352 miles above its mouth, above Paducah, not above Cincinnati.

BATCHELOR'S BEND, *Miss.*—Mississippi river, 547 miles above New Orleans, above Grand Gulf, not above Greenville.

BATTERY ROCK, *Ills.*—Ohio river, 116 miles above its mouth, above Paducah, not above Cincinnati.

BATH, *Ills.*—Illinois river, 114 miles above its mouth, above Beardstown, not above the mouth of Fox river.

BATTLEFIELD, *Wis.*—Mississippi river, 1709 miles above New Orleans, above Galena.

BATTLE'S (H. I.) LANDING, *Ark.*—Red river, 162 miles above Shreveport, above Carolina Bluff, not above Fulton.

BATTLE'S (Thos.) LANDING, *Ark.*—Red river, 218 miles above Shreveport, above Carolina Bluff, not above Fulton.

BATTLE'S (J. W.) LANDING, *Texas.*—Red river, 313 miles above Shreveport, above Carolina Bluff, not above Fulton.

BAYOU SARA, *La.*—Mississippi river, 165 miles above New Orleans.

BAYOU PIERRE, *Miss.*—Mississippi river, 331 miles above New Orleans, above Grand Gulf, not above Greenville.

BAYOU MACON, *La.*—Not above Monticello.

BAYOU LAFOURCHE, *La.*—Mississippi river, 82 miles above New Orleans.

BAYOU D'ARBONNE, *La.*—Red river, not above Farmersville.

BAYOU GOULA, *La.*—Mississippi river, 96 miles above New Orleans, below Bayou Sara.

BAYOU BARTHOLOMEW, *La.*—Above Portland.

BAYOU CANE, *La.*—Red river, 394 miles above New Orleans, not above Grand Ecore.

BAYOU DES ALLEMANDS, *La.*—Morgan Railroad, 48 miles from New Orleans.

BAYOU BŒUF, *La.*—Morgan Railroad, 73 miles from New Orleans.

BAYOU ROUGE, *La.*—Parish of Avoyelles, La.

BAYOU SALINE, *La.*—Red river, 280 miles above New Orleans, below Alexandria.

BAYOU PIERRE, *La.*—Red river, 660 miles from New Orleans, above Grand Ecore, not above Shreveport.

BAYOU DES GLEIZES, *La.*—(Mouth of) not above Simmsport.

BAYOU MARIE.—Red river, not above Alexandria.

BAYOU LARTO (Little and Big).—Red river, not above Alexandria.

BAYOU PAUL.—Mississippi river, not above Bayou Sara.

BAYOU ROW GULLY.—Red river, above Alexandria, not above Cane river.

BAYOU SANDY.—Red river, not above Alexandria.

BAYOU WINSEY.—Red river, above Grand Ecore, not above Shreveport.

BEALES (J. S.) LANDING, *Ala.*—Warrior river, not above Tuscaloosa.

BEACH HILL.—Ouachita river, above Alabama Landing, not above Camden.

BEARDS, JNO. (or Eureka).—Red river, above Grand Ecore, not above Shreveport.

BEARDS, W. C.—Red river, above Grand Ecore, not above Shreveport.

BEARDS, W.—Black river, La., not above Trinity.

BEARDS, JNO.--Red river, above Grand Ecore, not above Shreveport.

BEARD'S (W. J.) STORE.—Red river, above Grand Ecore, not above Shreveport.

BEARD, A. W. (Elder Grove), *La.*—Red river, above Grand Ecore, not above Shreveport.

BEAD, ALLIN.—Red river, above foot of Raft, not above Fulton.

BEARDSTOWN, *Ills.*—Illinois river, 89 miles above its mouth, not above the mouth of Fox river.

BEARD'S (A.) LANDING, *La.*—Red river, above Grand Ecore, not above Shreveport.

BEARD'S FERRY LANDING, *La.*—Red river, above Grand Ecore, not above Shreveport.

BEAVER CREEK, *Ala.*—Tombigbee river, not above Demopolis.

BEASLEY'S LANDING, *Ala.*—Tombigbee river, not above Demopolis.

BEAVER DAM, *Ark.*—Arkansas river, 309 miles above Little Rock, not above Norristown.

BEAVER, *Tenn.*—Ohio river, 975 miles above its mouth, above Cincinnati.

BEAUREGARD, *La.*—Jackson railroad, 139 miles above New Orleans.

BEACH HILL, *La.*—Ouachita river, 471 miles from Old river, above Alabama Landing, not above Camden.

BEAUMONT, *Texas.*—(Not above) on the Neches river.

BEAR FIELD LANDING, *Ark.*—Mississippi river, 842 miles above New Orleans, above Greenville, not above Memphis.

BECK'S F. K. LANDING, *Ala.*—Alabama river, not above Selma.

BECK'S T. H. LANDING, *Ala*—Alabama river, not above Selma.

BECK'S A. J. LANDING, *Ala.*—Alabama river, not above Selma.

BECK'S W. K. LANDING, *Ala*—Alabama river, not above Selma.

BECKHAM'S LANDING, *Ala.*—Tombigbee river, not above Demopolis.

BEDFORD, *Ills.*—Illinois river, not above Beardstown.

BEDFORD, *Tenn.*—Mississippi river, above Memphis, not above the mouth of the Ohio.

BEE'S NEST LANDING, *Ala.*—Tombigbee river, above Demopolis, not above Gainesville.

BEE LAKE.—Yazoo river, above Yazoo City, not above Leflore.

BEESLEY, DR.—Bayou Bartholomew, not above Point Pleasant.

BELLARD'S.—Mississippi river, above Grand Gulf, not above Greenville.

BELLE AIR LANDING.—Atchafalaya, not below Simmsport.

BELAIR LANDING.—Ouachita river, not above Trenton.

BELL PLANTATION.—Ouachita river, above Alabama Landing, not above Camden.

BELL, S. S.—Bayou Bartholomew, above Arkansas line, not above Portland.

BELL, JOE.—Bayou Bartholomew, above Arkansas line, not above Portland.

BELL, JAMES.—Bayou Bartholomew, above Point Pleasant, not above Arkansas line.

BELLE POINT.—Ouachita river, above Alabama Landing, not above Camden.

BELLE ISLE.—Yazoo river, not above Yazoo City.

BELMONT.—Yazoo river, above Yazoo City, not above Leflore.

BELLE PRAIRIE.—Yazoo river, above Yazoo City, not above Leflore.

BELL'S LANDING.—Yazoo river, above Yazoo City, not above Leflore.

BELL'S WOODYARD.—Red River, above Cane river, not above Grand Ecore.

BELLE BOSCOE.—Ouachita river, above Harrisonburgh, not above Trenton.

BELLE HOPE.—Ouachita river, above Trenton, not above Alabama Landing.

BELLE POINT, *Tenn.*—Mississippi river, above Memphis, not above the mouth of the Ohio.

BELLE POINT, *La.*—Mississippi river, not above Bayou Sara.

BELLE TOWER, *Tenn.*—Cumberland river, not above Nashville.

BELLEVUE, *Ark.*—Mississippi river, above Greenville, not above Memphis.

BELMONT PLANTATION, *La.*—Mississippi river, not above Bayou Sara.

BELMONT, *Miss.*—Tallahatchie river, (not above).
Do do. (above).

BELMONT, *Ky.*—Ohio river, 559 miles above its mouth, above Cincinnati.

BELT'S, DR., LANDING, *Ala.*—Alabama river, not above Selma.

BELGRADE, *Ills.*—Ohio river, 40 miles above its mouth, not above Paducah.

BELGRADE, *Texas.*—Sabine river, not above Hamilton.

BELLEVUE, *Ky.*—Ohio river, 501 miles above its mouth, above Paducah, not above Cincinnati.

BELLEVUE, *La.*—Lake Bodeau—Goods shipped to Shreveport, thence into Lake Bistenau.

BELLEVUE, *Nebr.*—Missouri river, 665 miles above its mouth, above Iatan.

BELLEVUE, *La.*—Mississippi river, 1601 miles above New Orleans, above the foot of the second Rapids, not above Galena.

BELLEFONTAINE, *Mo.*—Missouri river, not above Jefferson City.

BELLE FONT, *Ala.*—Tennessee river, above Florence, not below Eastport.

BELLEVILLE, *Va.*—Ohio river, 805 miles above its mouth, above Cincinnati.

BELPRE, *Ind*—Ohio river, 823 miles above its mouth, above Cincinnati.

BELLAIR, *Ohio.*—Ohio river, 907 miles above its mouth, above Cincinnati.

BELL'S LANDING, *Ala.*—Alabama river, 136 miles above Mobile, not above Selma.

BENNETT'S B. B. LANDING—Alabama river, not above Selma.

BENTON'S LANDING, *Ala.*—Alabama river, above Selma, not above Wetumpka.

BENNETT'S LANDING, *Ark.*—Arkansas river, 44 miles above Napoleon, not above Arkansas Post.

BELLE SARA, or BONNEY PLACE, *Miss.*—86 miles up Sunflower river.

BELLE VIEW.—Tallahatcie river, not above Cassidy Bayou.

BELZORIA.—Sabine river, Texas.

BELZONIA.—Yazoo river, above Yazoo City, not above Leflore.

BEND WOODYARD (G. HOLSTEIN).—Red river, not above Alexandria.

BENDY'S BLUFF.—Neches river, Texas.

BENNETT'S.—Tallahatchie river, not above Cassidy Bayou.

BENSON BLAKE (GASKIN).—Yazoo river, not above Yazoo City.

BENTON (R. L. LIVINGSTON).—Bayou Bartholomew, above Pt. Pleasant, not above Arkansas line.

BENTON.—Red river, above Shreveport, not above Carolina Bluffs.

BERMUDA.—Yazoo river, above Yazoo City, not above Leflore.

BERNARD, *Ark.*—Mississippi river, above Grand Gulf, not above Greenville.

BETTERY & CO. F. LANDING—Red river, not above Alexandria.

BEULAH LANDING.—130 miles up Bœuf river, above Thomas' Landing.

BEULAH GIN.—131 miles up Bœuf river, above Thomas Landing.

BEULAH.—Tallahatchie river, not above Cassidy Bayou.

BEVERLY.—Tallahatchie river, not above Cassidy Bayou.

BEN THOMPSON, *Miss.*—Mississippi river, above Grand Gulf, not above Greenville.

BENTON, *La.*—Cypress Lake, 30 miles below Jefferson.

BENTON, *Ala*—Alabama river, above Selma, not above Wetumpka.

BERLIN, *La.*—Red river, not above Alexandria.

BERWICK'S BAY, *La.*—80 miles from New Orleans, by Morgan's railroad.

BESTAIR'S LANDING, *Ala.*—Tombigbee river, not above Demopolis.

BETHIER'S LANDING, *Ala.*—Alabama river, not above Selma.

BETHLEHEM, *Ind.*—Ohio river, 437 miles above its mouth, above Paducah, not above Cincinnati.

BETHLEHEM, *Iowa.*—Missouri river, 652 miles above its mouth, above Iatan.

BETHEL, *Ala.*—Alabama river, not above Selma.

BETTISE'S LANDING, *Ala.*—Tombigbee river, not above Demopolis.

BEULAH, *Miss.*—Mississippi river, 622 miles above New Orleans, above Greenville, not above Memphis.

BEVIL PORT, *Texas.*—Angelina river.

BIDWELL MASTERSON.—Red river, above Grand Ecore, not above Shreveport.

BICKERS, J. W.—Arkansas river, above Arkansas Post, not above Pine Bluff.

BIENVEST, DR.—Red river, above Grand Ecore, not above Shreveport.

BIENVILLE PLAT.—Red river, above Shreveport, not above foot of Raft.

BIG BAYOU LARTO.—Red river, not above Alexandria.

BIG CREEK.—61 miles up Bœuf river, not above Thomas' Landing.

BIG EDDY BEND, or DILLARD'S.—Red river, above Lanesport, not above Mound City.

BIG BEND LANDING.—Bayou Des Glaises.

BIG DEER CREEK.—Yazoo river, not above Yazoo City.

BIG DEER CREEK LANDING, *Miss.*—110 miles from Vicksburg.

BIG JOHN TOE HEAD.—107 miles up Bœuf river, above Thomas' Landing.

BIG SPRING.—175 miles up Sunflower river.

BIBB'S, DICK LANDING, *Ark.*—Mississippi river, above Greenville, not above Memphis.

BIBB'S, J. B. LANDING, *Ala.*—Alabama river, not above Selma.

BICKLEY'S LANDING, *Ala.*—Tombigbee river, not above Demopolis.

BIDDELL'S POINT, *Mo.*—Mississippi river, above Memphis, not above the mouth of the Ohio.

BIENVILLE LANDING, *La.*—Red river, above Grand Ecore, not above Shreveport.

BIG SUNFLOWER, *Miss.*—Yazoo river, 60 miles above Vicksburg, below Yazoo City.

BIG BLACK RIVER, *Miss.*—Any point.

BIG PRAIRIE.—Mississippi river, 780 miles above New Orleans, above Greenville, not above Memphis.

BIG CANE, *La.*—Parish of St. Landry.

BIG BONE LICK CREEK, *Ky.*—Ohio river, 486 miles above its mouth, above Paducah, not above Cincinnati.

BIG SANDY RIVER, *Ky.*—Ohio river, 686 miles above its mouth, above Cincinnati.

BENTON, *Minn.*—Mississippi river, 1938 miles above New Orleans, above Galena.

BIG RACOON CREEK, *Ohio.*—Ohio river, 729 miles above its mouth, above Cincinnati.

BIG GRAVE CREEK, *Va.*—Ohio river, 398 miles above its mouth, above Cincinnati.

BIG CREEK, *Ark.*—White river, 72 miles from mouth, below junction of Black river.

BIG BLACK ISLAND, *La*—Ouachita river, not above Harrisonburg.

BIG EDDY BEND, *Texas.*—Red river, 416 miles above Shreveport, above Lanesport, not above Mound City.

BINSON'S LANDING, *Ala.*—Alabama river, above Selma, not above Wetumpka.

BIRD'S POINT, *Mo.*—Mississippi river, 1040 miles above New Orleans, opposite Cairo.

BIRCH'S, J. B. LANDING, *Ark.*—Arkansas river, 34 miles above Napoleon, above Arkansas Post, not above Pine Bluff.

BIRMINGHAM, *Ala.*—Tennessee river, above Florence.

BIZZEL'S LANDING, *Ark.*—Red river, 307 miles above Shreveport, above Lanesport.

BIZZEL'S UPPER PLACE, *Texas.*—Red river, 228 miles above Shreveport, above Carolina Bluff, not above Fulton.

BIG SPRING (J. Broadwell's).—Red river, above Cane river, not above Grand Ecore.

BISMARCK.—Missouri river, 1614 miles from its mouth, above Iatan.

BIZZELL, HENRY.—Red river, above Fulton, not above Lanesport.

BILOXI, *Miss.*—Mobile Railroad.

BLACK'S, JNO. LANDING, *Ala.*—Alabama river, not above Selma.

BLACK BLUFF, *Ala.*—Tombigbee river, not above Demopolis.

BLACKWELL'S, *Ala.*—Alabama river, not above Selma.

BLACKWELL'S LANDING, *Ala.*—Tombigbee river, not above Demopolis.

BLADEN'S LANDING, *Ala.*—Tombigbee river, not above Demopolis.

BLEWET'S LANDING, *Miss.*—Tombigbee river, above Gainesville, not above Columbus.

BLOOM'S LANDING, *Ill.*—Illinois river, not above Beardstown.

BLOUNT'S LANDING, *Ala.*—Tombigbee river, not above Demopolis.

BLACK RIVER, *Minn.*—Mississippi river, 1738 miles above New Orleans, above Galena.

BLACK RIVER, *La.*—250 miles from New Orleans.

BLACK RIVER, *Ark.*—A tributary of White river.

BLACK BAYOU, *La.*—Red river (Lake Clear).

BLACK ROCK, *Ark.*—Arkansas river, 588 miles, above Napoleon, above Fort Smith, not above Fort Gibson.

BLACK BAYOU.—Tallahatchie river, not above Cassidy Bayou.

BLACK HILLS LANDING.—Missouri river, 1330 miles from its mouth, above Iatan.

BLACK'S WOODYARD.—Ouachita river, above Alabama Landing, not above Camden.

BLAIR, COL. J. D.—Red river, above Grand Ecore, not above Shreveport.

BLAKE'S S. B. (Redwood).—Yazoo river, not above Yazoo City.

BLAKE, BENSON (Gaskins).—Yazoo river, not above Yazoo city.

BLOODSWORTH POINT.—Red river, above Cane river, not above Grand Ecore.

BLAITON'S BLUFF.—Red river, above foot of Raft, not above Fulton.

BLANCHE, J. B.—Red river, above Grand Ecore, not above Shreveport.

BLANC, JOS. D.—Red river, above Cane river, not above Grand Ecore.

BLANKS, R. A. LANDING.—Ouachita river, above Harrisonburg, not above Trenton.

BLEDSOE, or ROSEDALE.—Tallahatchie river, not above Cassidy Bayou.

BLACK CREEK.—Yazoo river, above Yazoo City, not above Leflore.

BLOOMER, L.—Bayou Bartholomew, above Arkansas line, not above Portland.

BLOOM'S STORE, *Miss.*—134 miles up Big Deer Creek.

BLUFF, JAMES.—Red river, not above Alexandria.

BLUFF SPRINGS —Yazoo river, above Yazoo City, not above Leflore.

BLUE CANE.—Black river, La., not above Trinity.

BLUE SACK.—Yazoo river, above Yazoo City, not above Leflore.

BLYTHE.—Tallahatchie river, not above Cassidy Bayou.

BOAT SLOUGH.—Yazoo river, not above Yazoo City.

BOGUE PHOLIA.—158 miles up Sun Flower river.

BOLAND, W.—Red river, above Grand Ecore, not above Shreveport.

BOND, J., or CRESCENT, *La.*—Red river, above Grand Ecore, not above Shreveport.

BONNETT LAKE.—Tallahatchie river, not above Cassidy Bayou.

BONNER (Lower).—Bayou Bartholomew, above Point Pleasant, not above Arkansas line.

BONNER (Gin).—Bayou Bartholomew, above Point Pleasant, not above Arkansas line.

BONNER, DR.—Bayou Bartholomew, above Point Pleasant, not above Arkansas line.

BLANDERHASSETT, *Ind.*—Ohio river, 821 miles above its mouth, above Cincinnati.

BLAKESVILLE, *Ind.*—Ohio river, 323 miles above its mouth, above Paducah, not above Cincinnati.

BLAIR'S LANDING, *La.*—Red river, 500 miles above New Orleans, above Grand Ecore, not above Shreveport.

BLANDERSBURG, *Ohio.*—Ohio river, 753 miles above its mouth, above Cincinnati.

BLANTON'S LANDING, *Ark.*—Red river, 103 miles above Shreveport, above Carolina Bluff, not above Fulton.

BLACK BLUFF, *Ala.*—Alabama river, 185 miles above Mobile, below Selma.

BLACKHAWK, *La.*—Mississippi river, above Bayou Sara, not above Grand Gulf.

BLADSOE'S LANDING, *Ark.*—Mississippi river, above Greenville, not above Memphis.

BLUE RIVER, *Ky.*—Ohio river, 327 miles above its mouth, above Paducah, not above Cincinnati.

BLUES POINT, *Ark.*—Mississippi river, 711 miles above New Orleans, above Greenville, not above Memphis.

BLUFF PORT, *Mo.*—Missouri river, 212 miles above its mouth, above Jefferson City, not above Lexington.

BLUE LAKE LANDING, *Texas.*—Red river, 325 miles above Shreveport, above Fulton, not above Lanesport.

BOB CUNNINGHAM'S LANDING, *Ark.*—Arkansas river, 372 miles above Napoleon, above Little Rock, not above Norristown.

BŒUF RIVER, *La.*—Not above Thomas' Landing.

BOGUE CHITTO, *La.*—Jackson railroad, 119 miles from New Orleans.

BOHANNON'S LANDING, *Ala.*—Tombigbee river, above Demopolis, not above Gainesville.

BOLIVIA, *Miss.*—Mississippi river, 638 miles above New Orleans, above Greenville, not above Memphis.

BOLIVAR, *Tenn.*—Hatchee river.

BOLIVAR, *Miss.*—Mississippi river, 605 miles above New Orleans, above Greenville, not above Memphis.

BOLIVAR, *Ala.*—Tennessee river, above Florance, not below Eastport.

BONNELL'S FERRY, *Ala.*—Alabama river, above Selma, not above Wetumpka.

BONNET CARRE, *La.*—Mississippi river, 42 miles above New Orleans, below Bayou Sara.

BON HARBOR, *Ky.*—Ohio river, 224 miles above its mouth, above Paducah, not above Cincinnati.

BONJURANT LANDING, *La.*—Mississippi river, 350 miles above New Orleans, above Bayou Sara, not above Grand Gulf.

BONNEVILLE, *Mo.*—Missouri river, 202 miles above its mouth, above Jefferson City, not above Lexington.

BOOTH'S, JOS., LANDING, *Ala.*—Alabama river, not above Selma.

BOOTH, T. J., LANDING, *Ala.*—Alabama river, not above Selma.

BOOKER'S & BEADLEY'S LANDING, *Ark.*—Red river, 146 miles from Shreveport, above Carolina Bluff, not above Fulton.

BOONE, *Ky.*—Ohio river, above Paducah, not above Cincinnati.

BOONESVILLE, *Ills.*—Mississippi river, 1323 miles above New Orleans, above Alton, not above foot of the first Rapids.

BOONSBORO, *Mo*—Missouri river, above Jefferson City, not above Lexington.

BOSSIER'S LANDING, *La.*—Red river, above Grand Ecore, not above Shreveport.

BOUTTE STATION, *La.*—Morgan railroad, 32 miles from New Orleans.

BOULARD'S LANDING, *Ark.*—Mississippi river, above Greenville, not above mouth of the Ohio river.

BOWLAND'S LANDING, *La.*--Red river, above Grand Ecore, not above Shreveport.

BOWLAND'S BLUFF, *La.*—Red river, not above Alexandria.

BOWLING GREEN, *Tenn.*—Cumberland river, not above Nashville.

BOWLING HALL, *Ala.*—Alabama river, above Selma, not above Wetumpka.

BOWIE'S POINT, *Miss.*—Mississippi river, above Greenville, not above Memphis.

BOWLING'S LANDING, *La.*—Red river, not above Alexandria.

BOYD'S H. C. LANDING, *Ark.*—Red river, 192 miles from Shreveport, above Carolina Bluffs, not above Fulton

BOYD'S LANDING, *Texas*—Red river, 381 miles above Shreveport, above Lanesport, not above Mound City.

BOYAL'S LANDING, *Ala.*—Warrior river, not above Tuscaloosa.

BONNEY PLACE, or BELLE SARA, *Miss.*—86 miles up Sunflower river.

BONNETT, J. J. LANDING.—Red river, not above Alexandria.

BOOMERANG.—Black river, La.

BOOKER'S, ED.—Red river, above foot of Raft, not above Fulton.

BOONVILLE.—Missouri river, above Jefferson City, not above Lexington.

BOON FORD.—Bayou Bartholomew, above Point Pleasant, not above Arkansas line.

BORDELON, ST. JAMES.—Red river, not above Alexandria.

BORDELON'S (Woodyard).—Red river, not above Alexandria.

BOSTON PLACE.—Yazoo river, above Yazoo City, not above Leflore.

BOUCHETTE, R. J.—Bayou Bartholomew, not above Pt. Pleasant.

BOUCHE'S GRAVE.—Missouri river, 2267 miles from its mouth, above Iatan.

BOUTLET'S BLUFF (J. J. Ansill).—Red river, above Grand Ecore, not above Shreveport.

BOUTROE'S (or Gibson's).—Red river, above Cane river, not above Grand Ecore.

BOWER'S, MRS.—Mississippi river, above Grand Gulf, not above Greenville.

BOWMAN'S.—Ouachita river, above Harrisonburg, not above Trenton.

BOWMAN'S LANDING.—Tensas river, not above Bayou Macon.

BOYCE, M.—Red river, above Grand Ecore, not above Shreveport.

BOYCE, WILLIE.—Red river, above Lanesport, not above Mound City.

BOYCE, MRS, or MOUTH OF MILL CREEK.—Red river, above Lanesport, not above Mound City.

BOYCE, JESSIE, or EPPERSON PLANTATION.—Red river, above Lanesport, not above Mound City.

BOYCE PLACE (Cotile).—Red river, above Alexandria, not above mouth of Cane river.

BOYCE'S LANDING.—334 miles up Sunflower river.

BOYD'S LANDING.—Ouachita river, above Harrisonburg, not above Trenton.

BOYER'S MILLS.—184 miles up Sunflower river.

BOSLEY, H. S. (or Telegram).—Red river, above Grand Ecore, not above Shreveport.

BORDELEON, L. F.—Red river, above Grand Ecore, not above Shreveport.

BORDELEON, A.—Red river, above Grand Ecore, not above Shreveport.

BOSSIER'S, MAD.—Red river, above Grand Ecore, not above Shreveport.

BOUSQUET PLANTATION.—Mississippi river, not above Bayou Sara.

BRANNON, HARRY'S LANDING.—65 miles up Sunflower river.

BRAZEALE STORE (C. Green).—Red river, above Grand Ecore, not above Shreveport.

BRAZEALE, W. W.—Red river, above Grand Ecore, not above Shreveport.

BRAZEALE, WIDOW.—Red river, above Grand Ecore, not above Shreveport.

BRADWAY.—Ouachita river, above Harrisonburgh, not above Trenton.

BRADIN'S, SAM.—Yazoo river, not above Yazoo City.

BRADLEY'S FERRY.—Ouachita river, above Alabama Landing, not above Camden.

BRADY'S LANDING.—170 miles up Sunflower river.

BRANCH PLACE, *Miss.*—116 miles up Big Deer Creek.

BRANDIN, JOHN.—87 miles up Bœuf river, above Thomas' Landing.

BRANDIN, L.—85 miles up Bœuf river, above Thomas' Landing.

BRANDIN, PAUL.—82 miles up Bœuf river, above Thomas' Landing.

BRANDIN, S.—82 miles up Bœuf river, above Thomas' Landing.

BRANNON'S LANDING.—Bayou Bartholomew, not above Point Pleasant.

BRAY GIN.—Bayou Bartholomew, above Point Pleasant, not above Arkansas line.

BRAZILLE, W. O. (Hauronet's).—Red river, above Cane river, not above Grand Ecore.

BREEDLOVE.—207 miles up Sunflower river.

BRES, JEROME LANDING.—Ouachita river, above Harrisonburg, not above Trenton.

BRESTON LANDING.—Ouachita river, above Harrisonburg, not above Trenton.

BRIARLY, JOE.—Red river, above Lanesport, not above Mound City.

BRIARLY, R. T., JR.—Red river, above Rowland and Mound City.

BRIANS, MOSES E.—Ouachita river, above Harrisonburg, not above Trenton.

BRIDGER, R. D.—Ouachita river, above Harrisonburg, not above Trenton.

BRIDGER, JR., LANDING.—Ouachita river, above Harrisonburg, not above Trenton.

BRIGDER, SR., LANDING.—Ouachita river, above Harrisonburg, not above Trenton.

BOYLE, M. LANDING, *Ala.*—Alabama river, not above Selma.

BOYCE, M. LANDING, *La.*—Red river, above Grand Ecore, not above Shreveport.

BOZMAN'S LANDING, *Ala.*—Alabama river, not above Selma.

BRACKETT'S LANDING, *Ala.*—Tombigbee river, above Gainesville, not above Columbus.

BRACKENRIDGE, *Ala.*—Tombigbee river, not above Demopolis.

BRADLEY'S LANDING, *Ala.*—Alabama river, not above Selma.

BRADLEY'S, COL. LANDING, *Ark.*—Mississippi river, above Greenville, not above Memphis.

BRADFORD'S LANDING, *La.*—On Little river.

BRADFORD, *Ohio.*—Ohio river, 640 miles above its mouth, above Cincinnati.

BRAGG'S BLUFF, *Ala.*—Tombigbee river, above Demopolis, not above Gainesville.

BRANDENBURG, *Ky.*—Ohio river, 342 miles above its mouth, above Paducah, not above Cincinnati.

BRASHEAR, *La.*—Morgan railroad, 80 miles from New Orleans.

BRAZIL'S BAR, *La.*—Red river, 518 miles from New Orleans, above Grand Ecore, not above Shreveport.

BRENT'S LANDING, *Ark.*—Arkansas river, 121 miles above Napoleon, above Arkansas Post, not above Pine Bluff.

BREMEN, *Mo.*—Mississippi river, 1184 miles above New Orleans, above the mouth of the Ohio, not above Alton.

BREESEVILLE, *Ills.*—Mississippi river, 1067 miles above New Orleans, above the mouth of the Ohio, not above Alton.

BRITTE'S LANDING, *Tenn.*—Tennessee river, not above Eastport.

BRICCOURT'S LANDING, *Miss.*—Mississippi river, above Grand Gulf, not above Greenville.

BRIDGEPORT, *Ind.*—Ohio river, 379 miles above its mouth, above Paducah, not above Cincinnati.

BRIDGEPORT, *Ill.*—Illinois river, 43 miles above its mouth, not above Beardstown.

BRIDGEPORT, *Ohio.*—Ohio river, 911 miles above its mouth, above Cincinnati.

BRIDGEPORT, *Mo.*—Missouri river, 94 miles above its mouth, not above Jefferson City.

BRIDGEPORT, *Ala.*—Alabama river, 227 miles from Mobile, not above Selma.

BRIDGEPORT, *Tenn.*—Tennessee river, above Florence.

BRIKLEY, *Ark.*—Black river, above junction of White river.

BRIGG'S LANDING, *Ill.*—Illinois river, not above Beardstown.

BRINKLEY'S LANDING, *Miss.*—Mississippi river, above Greenville, not above mouth of the Ohio.

BROTHER'S POINT, *Tenn.*—Mississippi river, above Greenville, not above mouth of the Ohio.

BROWN'S, DANIEL, LANDING, *La.*—Red river, above Grand Ecore, not above Shreveport.

BROWN'S, MARY, LANDING, *La.*—Red river, above Grand Ecore, not above Shreveport.

BROWN'S, JOHN, LANDING, *La.*—Red river, above Grand Ecore, not above Shreveport.

BROWN'S LANDING, *Ark.*—Arkansas river, 345 miles above Napoleon, above Little Rock, not above Norristown.

BROOKHAVEN, *Miss.*—Jackson railroad, 129 miles from New Orleans.

BROOKLYN, *Ky.*—Ohio river, 536 miles above its mouth, above Cincinnati.

BROOKLYN, *Minn.*—Mississippi river, 1732 miles above New Orleans, above Galena.

BROWNSVILLE, *Minn.*—Mississippi river, 1722 miles above New Orleans, above Galena.

BROWN'S, SALLY, LANDING, *La.*—Red river, above Grand Ecore, not above Shreveport.

BROWN'S, SAM'L, LANDING, *Ala.*—Alabama river, not above Selma.

BROWN'S, J. H., LANDING, *Ala.*—Tombigbee river, above Demopolis, not above Gainesville.

BROWN'S LANDING, *Ala.*—Warrior river, not above Tuscaloosa.

BROWN'S LANDING, *Ark.*—Arkansas river, above Little Rock, not above Norristown.

BROWN'S LANDING, *Tenn.*—Mississippi river, above Memphis, not above mouth of the Ohio.

BROWN'S BLUFF, *Ala.*—Warrior river, not above Tuscaloosa.

BROWN'S LANDING, *Ills.*—Illinois river, above Beardstown, not above mouth of Fox river.

BROWNSVILLE, *Neb.*—Missouri river, 602 miles above its mouth, above Iatan.

BRUINSBURG, *La.*—Mississippi river, above Bayou Sara, not above Grand Gulf.

BRUNSWICK, *Mo.*—Missouri river, 261 miles above its mouth, above Jefferson City, not above Lexington.

BRUSSVILLE, *Ills.*—Mississippi river, above mouth of the Ohio, not above Alton.

BRYAN'S WOODYARD, *Ala.*—Alabama river, not above Selma.

BRYAN'S, WM., GIN, *Ala.*—Alabama river, not above Selma.

BUCKSTON'S LANDING, *La.*—Red river, 425 miles from New Orleans, above Cane river, not above Grand Ecore.

BRINGHURST (or NEW HOPE).—Red river, not above Alexandria.

BROADWELLS, J. (BIG SPRING).—Red river, above Cane river, not above Grand Ecore.

BROWN, W. B., *Miss.*—110 miles up Big Deer Creek.

BROWN, JOHN, *Miss.*—124 miles up Big Deer Creek.

BROWN, J. T. L., LANDING.—124 miles up Big Deer Creek.

BROOKS LANDING.—Mississippi river, above Grand Gulf, not above Greenville.

BROOKS LANDING.—Ouachita river, above Harrisonburg, not above Leflore.

BROOKS, (MRS.) LANDING.—115 miles up Sunflower river.

BROOKLYN.—Yazoo river, not above Leflore.

BROWN'S.—Red river, above Grand Ecore, not above Shreveport.

BROWN'S, PAT.—Tallahatchie river, not above Cassidy Bayou.

BROWN'S, J. W.—Red river, above Grand Ecore, not above Shreveport.

BROWNSVILLE.—Red river, mouth of Bayou Pierre, above Grand Ecore, not above Shreveport.

BRUCE'S LANDING.—Black river, La., not above Harrisonburg.

BRUSHLEY LANDING,—Ouachita river, not above Harrisonburg.

BRUNSWICK POINT.—Mississippi river, above Grand Gulf, not above Greenville.

BRYANT'S LANDING.—Ouachita river, above Harrisonburg, not above Trenton.

BRYES' LANDING.—Ouachita river, above Harrisonburg, not above Trenton.

BUCKNER, E. P., LANDING, *Miss.*—171 miles up Big Deer Creek.

BUCK SNORT.—Yazoo river, above Yazoo City, not above Leflore.

BROWN'S, WESLEY.—Red river, above Grand Ecore, not above Shreveport.

BROWN'S, DAN.—Red river, above Grand Ecore, not above Shreveport.

BROWN'S, MRS. MARY.—Red river, above Grand Ecore, not above Shreveport.

BRULE AGENCY.—Missouri river, 1223 miles from its mouth, above Iatan.

BRULE CITY.—Missouri river, 1192 miles above its mouth, above Iatan.

BRULENSBURG.—Mississippi river, above Bayou Sara, not above Grand Gulf.

BUCKNER.—Mississippi river, above Grand Gulf, not above Greenville.

BURLEIGH LANDING.—Mississippi river, above Grand Gulf, not above Greenville.

BUCK'S GIN.—122 miles up Sunflower river.

BUCK HALL, or DR. S. W. VANCE.—Red river, above Shreveport, not above foot of Raft.

BUCKHORN LANDING.—Ouachita river, above Harrisonburg, not above Trenton.

BUCKHORN.—Mississippi river, above Grand Gulf, not above Greenville.

BUCKHORN, or G. POOLE'S.—Red river, above Grand Ecore, not above Shreveport.

BUCK RIDGE.—Mississippi river, above Grand Gulf, not above Greenville.

BUNKER HILL.—Ouachita river, above Harrisonburg, not above Trenton.

BURCH PLACE.—284 miles up Sunflower river.

BURCH, UPPER.—285 miles up Sunflower river.

BURDETT'S LANDING, *Miss.*—176 miles up Big Deer Creek.

BURDETT'S MARSH.—183 miles up Big Deer Creek.

BURLING'S, GEO., LANDING.—Red river, not above Alexandria.

BURNS' LANDING, MRS.—Black river, La., not above Trinity.

BURNS.—96 miles up Bœuf river, above Thomas' Landing.

BURNS, *La.* (or RIVER VIEW.)—Mississippi river, above Grand Gulf, not above Greenville.

BURNS' BLUFF.—Neches river, Texas.

BURNHAM'S LANDING, *Texas.*—Sabine river, above Stark's, not above Toledo.

BURNLY.—Mississippi river, above Grand Gulf, not above Greenville.

BUCKRIDGE, *Miss.*—Mississippi river, above Greenville, not above Memphis.

BUCKLEY'S LANDING, *Ark.*—Little Red river, below junction of White and Black rivers.

BUCKHORN, *La.*—Red river, above Grand Ecore, not above Shreveport.

BUCK ISLAND, *Miss.*—Mississippi river, above Greenville, not above Memphis.

BUCK'S LANDING. *Ark.*—Red river, 352 miles from Shreveport, above Fulton, not above Lanesport.

BUENA VISTA, *Ark.*—White river, 180 miles from its mouth, below junction of Black river.

BUENA VISTA, *Iowa.*—Mississippi river, 1649 miles above New Orleans, above Galena.

BUENA VISTA, *La.*—Mississippi river, not above Bayou Sara.

BUENA VISTA, *Ala.*—Tombigbee river, not above Demopolis.

BUENA VISTA, *Ark.*—Mississippi river, above Greenville, not above Memphis.

above Magnolia Landing.

BUFORD'S LANDING, *Ala.*—Alabama river, not above Selma.

BUFORD'S LAKE, *Ark.*—Mississippi river, above Greenville, not above Memphis.

BUFFALO, *Ark.*—Ouachita river, above Alabama Landing, not above Camden.

BUFFALO, *Iowa.*—Mississippi river, 1508 miles above New Orleans, above foot of second Rapids, not above Galena.

BULLARD'S LANDING, *Ala.*—Alabama river, not above Selma.

BULL PENN., *Ala.*—Tombigbee river, not above Demopolis.

BULLITT'S FERRY, *Miss.*—Mississippi river, above Grand Gulf, not above Greenville.

BULLITT'S BLUFF, *La.*—Red river, above Grand Ecore, not above Shreveport.

BULLITT'S BAYOU, *La.*—Mississippi river, above Bayou Sara, not above Grand Gulf.

BUNKER HILL, *Ark.*—Arkansas river, 343 miles above Napoleon, above Little Rock, not above Norristown.

BUNKER HILL, *Ky.*—Cumberland river, above Gainsboro.

BUNKER HILL, *Ark.*—Ouachita river, above Alabama Landing, not above Camden.

BUNCH'S BEND, *La.*—Mississippi river, 470 miles above New Orleans, above Grand Gulf, not above Greenville.

BURNAN'S LANDING, *Ark.*—Arkansas river, 418 miles above Napoleon, above Norristown, not above Fort Smith.

BURN'S LANDING, *Ala.*—Tombigbee river, not above Demopolis.

BURN'S LANDING, *Ala.*—Tombigbee river, not above Demopolis.

BURT'S LANDING, *Miss.*—Tombigbee river, above Columbus, not above Cotton Gin Port.

BURTON'S BLUFF, *Ala.*—Tombigbee river, not above Demopolis.

BURROW'S LANDING, *Ark.*—Arkansas river, 517 miles above Napoleon, above Norristown, not above Fort Smith.

BURLINGTON, *Ohio.*—Ohio river, 913 miles above its mouth, above Cincinnati.

BURLINGTON, *Ohio.*—Ohio river, 690 miles above its mouth, above Cincinnati.

BURLINGTON, *Iowa.*—Mississippi river, 1420 miles above New Orleans, above the foot of second rapids, not above Galena.

BURKEVILLE, *Ky.*—Cumberland river, above Gainsboro.

BUSH ISLAND, *Mo.*—Mississippi river, above mouth of the Ohio, river, not above Alton.

BUSSETT'S LANDING, *La.*—Red river, above Cane river, not Grand Ecore.

BUSH'S, DR., LANDING, *La.*—Red river, above Alexandria, not above Cane river.

BUSH'S, DR., LANDING, *Ala.*—Tombigbee river, not above Demopolis.

BUTLER'S, DR., LANDING, *La.*—Red river, above Cane river, not above Grand Ecore.

BUTLER'S LANDING, *Miss.*—Tombigbee river, above Gainesville, not above Columbus.

BUVARD'S LANDING, *Ala.*—Alabama river, above Selma, not Wetumpka.

BUZZARD'S BLUFF, *Ark.*—Red river, 232 miles above Shreveport, above Carolina Bluff, not above Fulton.

BYRD'S LANDING, *Ark.*—Red river, 305 miles above Shreveport, above Fulton, not above Lanesport.

BYRAN, *Miss.*—Jackson railroad, 174 miles from New Orleans.

BURR'S FERRY, *Texas.*—Sabine river, above Stark's, not above Toledo.

BURNS, WM., LANDING.—Red river, above Cane river, not above Grand Ecore.

BURNETT'S, *Ark.*—Arkansas river, not above Arkansas Post.

BURWELL BAYOU.—262 miles up Sunflower river.

BUSH, WILLIAM Mouth Darro).—Red river, above Alexandria, not above Cane river.

BUTLER'S, MRS. (or E. LEWIS.)—Red river, above foot of Raft, not above Fulton.

BUTLER'S, M., LANDING.—Ouachita river, above Harrisonburg, not above Trenton.

BUTLER'S, T. M.—Red river, above Shreveport, not above foot of Raft.

BUTLER'S, JOHN.—Ouachita river, above Harrisonburg, not above Trenton.

BUTLER'S.—Ouachita river, above Harrisonburg, not above Trenton.

BUXTON'S LANDING—Red river, above Cane river, not above Grand Ecore.

BYR'S LANDING, MRS.—Ouachita river, above Harrisonburg, not above Trenton.

C

CABIN POINT, (W. ARMSTEAD).—Red river, above Grand Ecore, not above Shreveport.

CABIN PLANTATION, *La.*—Red river, above Grand Ecore, not above Shreveport.

CABINTEELE (or MARSHALL).—Mississippi river, above Grand Gulf, not above Greenville.

CACHE MARCEAUX, *Ark.*—Ouachita river, above Ross' Landing, not above Arkadelphia.

CADE'S, T. J., LANDING, *Ala.*—Alabama river, not above Selma.

CADRON'S LANDING, *Ark*—Arkansas river, 328 miles above Napoleon, above Little Rock, not above Norristown.

CAHAWBA, *Ala.*—Alabama river, 26 miles above Mobile, not above Selma.

CADDO BANK —Red river, above Grand Ecore, not above Shreveport.

CALIFORNIA PLANTATION, or J. McCLINTOCK.—Red river, above foot of Raft, not above Fulton.

CALHOUN'S SAW-MILL.—Red river, above Alexandria, not above mouth of Cane river.

CALHOUN'S, W. S. (MIRBEAU).—Red river, above Alexandria, not above mouth of Cane river.

CALHOUN'S.—Red river, above Shreveport, not above foot of Raft.

CALHOUN, W. S. (SMITHFIELD).—Red river, above Cane river, not above Grand Ecore.

CALHOUN, S. L. (DIXIE PLACE).—Red river, above Grand Ecore, not above Shreveport.

CALHOUN'S PLACE.—Bayou Bartholomew, above Arkansas line, not above Portland.

CALLS.—Ouachita river, above Harrisonburg, not above Trenton.

CALLAO.—151 miles up Sunflower river.
CALVERT, W. N.—Red river, not above Alexandria.
CALVERT, MRS.—Red river, not above Alexanhria.
CALWELL.—Yazoo river, above Yazoo city not above Leflore.
CAMMACK'S, J. C.—Red river, above Cane river, not above Grand Ecore.
CAMPBELLSVILLE, or MOUTH OF SILVER CREEK.—83 miles up Sunflower river.
CAMPBELL'S, F. L., *La.*—Black river, not above Harrisonburg.
CAHOKIA, *Mo.*—Mississippi river, above the mouth of the Ohio, not above Alton.
CAIN'S LANDING, *Ala.*—Alabama river, above Selma, not above Wetumpka.
CAIRO, *Ills.*—At the mouth of the Ohio river, on the Mississippi river, 1040 miles above New Orleans.
CAIRO, *Tenn.*—Cumberland river, above Nashville, not above Gainsborough.
CALHOUN, *Miss.*—Jackson railroad, 199 miles above New Orleans.
CALEDONIA, *Ills.*—13 miles from the mouth of the Ohio, not above Paducah.
CALEDONIA, *Ark.*—Arkansas river, 326 miles above Napoleon, above Little Rock, not above Norristown.
CALIFORNIA, *Ohio.*—Ohio river, 539 miles above its mouth, above Cincinnati.
CALIFORNIA CITY, *Iowa.*—Missouri river, 658 miles above its mouth, above Iatan.
CALDWELL'S LANDING, *Texas,*—Red river, 509 miles above Shreveport, above Mound City.
CALEDONIA, *Ark.*—Bayou Macon, 250 miles above its mouth, above Monticello.
CALIFORNIA WOODYARD, *Ala.*—Alabama river, not above Selma.
CALDWELL'S, MRS., *Ark.*—Arkansas river, 221 miles above Napoleon, above Pine Bluff, not above Little Rock.
CALDWELL'S LANDING, *La.*—Black river, La.
CALHOUN'S FERRY, *La.*—Bayou Bartholomew, above Point Pleasant, not above Arkansas line.

CALHOUN'S FERRY, *Texas.*—Trinity river, above Smithville, not above Magnolia Landing.

CALHOUN'S LANDING, *La.*—Red river, not above Shreveport, not above foot of Raft.

CALLOWAY'S LANDING, *La.*—Bayou Macon, 28 miles above its mouth, not above Monticello.

CAMPTE, *La.*—Red river, 500 miles above New Orleans, above Grand Ecore, not above Shreveport.

CAMPBELLSVILLE, *La.*—Mississippi river, 412 miles above New Orleans, above Grand Gulf, not above Greenville.

CAMPBELL'S LANDING, *Ark.*—Arkansas river, 524 miles above Napoleon, above Norristown, not above Fort Smith.

CAMDEN, *Ark.*—Ouachita river, 501 miles from the mouth of Old river, not above Ross' Landing.

CAMDEN, *Mo.*—Missouri river, 350 miles above its mouth, above Lexington, not above Iatan.

CAMDEN, *Tenn.*—Mississippi river, above Memphis not above mouth of the Ohio.

CAMDEN, *Tenn*—Tennessee river, not above Eastport.

CAMDEN, *Ala.*—Alabama river, not above Selma.

CAMDEN, *Ind.*—Wabash river, above the Rapids, not above Terre Haute.

CAMPBELL'S LANDING, *Ala.*—Tombigbee river, not above Demopolis.

CAMMACK'S LANDING, *Miss.*—Mississippi river, 467 miles above New Orleans, above Grand Gulf, not above Greenville.

CAMMACK'S LANDING, *La.*—Red river, not above Alexandria.

CAMANCHE, *Iowa.*—Mississippi river, 1554 miles above New Orleans, above the foot of second Rapids, not above Galena.

CAMBRIDGE, *Mo.*—Missouri river, 241 miles above its mouth, above Jefferson City, not above Lexington.

CANE RIVER, *La.*—Natchitoches.

CANE LANDING, *Ark.*—Red river, 332 miles above Shreveport, above Fulton, not above Lanesport.

CANTON, *Miss.*—Jackson railroad, 206 miles from New Orleans.

CANTON, *Ky.*—Cumberland river, 72 miles from its mouth, below Nashville.

CANTON, *Ala.*—Alabama river, 211 miles above Mobile, not above Selma.

CANNELTON, *Ind.*—Ohio river, 262 miles above its mouth, above Paducah, not above Cincinnati.

CANNELTON AND HAWKSVILLE, *Ky.*—Ohio river, above Paducah, not above Cincinnati.

CANADIAN SHOALS, *Ark.*—Arkansas river, 623 miles above Napoleon, above Fort Smith, not above Fort Gibson.

CANADIAN'S LANDING, *Ark.*—Arkansas river, 628 miles above Napoleon, above Fort Smith, not above Fort Gibson.

CAPE GIRARDEAU, *Mo.*—Mississippi river, 1082 miles above New Orleans, above the mouth of the Ohio, not above St. Louis.

CAMPOBELLO.—Red river, above Grand Ecore, not above Shreveport.

CAMDEN.—Sabine river, Texas, above Grand Bluff.

CANE POINT.—Red river, above Shreveport, not above Carolina Bluffs.

CAMPTON'S, PETER B., LANDING.—Red river, not above Alexandria.

CAMPTON'S, SAM L., LANDING.—Red river, not above Alexandria.

CAMPTON, T. G.—Red river, not above Alexandria.

CANDLER'S, DR., or HOWARD'S.—Red river, above foot of Raft, not above Fulton.

CANTHORN'S.—Red river, above foot of Raft, not above Fulton.

CANNIE, MARY.—Ouachita river, above Alabama Landing, not above Camden.

CANNSBORO.—Bayou D'Arbonne, not above Farmsville.

CAPE HORN.—Ouachita river, above Alabama Landing, not above Camden.

CARDIFF.—Yazoo river, not above Yazoo City.

CAREYVILLE.—Ouachita river, above Alabama Landing, not above Camden.

CARLOCK, MRS.—Bayou Bartholomew, above Arkansas line, not above Portland.

CAROLINA.—Ouachita river, above Harrisonburg, not above Trenton.

CARNAHAN'S.--Red river, above Alexandria, not above mouth of Cane river.

CARROLL, E. A., WIDOW.—Red river, above Grand Ecore, not above Shreveport.

CARROLLS, DR.—Yazoo river, above Yazoo City, not above Leflore.

CARO PLANTATION.—Red river, above Shreveport, not above foot of Raft.

CAROLINA BLUFF (or FOOT OF RAFT).—Red river.

CAPT. TAYLOR'S LANDING, *Ark.*—White river, 201 miles above its mouth, below the junction of Black river.

CARROLLVILLE, *Ala.*—Tennessee river, 185 miles above its mouth, not above Eastport.

CARROLLTON, *La.*—Mississippi river, 6 miles above New Orleans, below Bayou Sara.

CARR'S LANDING, *La.*—Mississippi river, above Bayou Sara, not above Grand Gulf.

CARPENTER'S LANDING, *La.*—Black river.

CARPENTER'S LANDING, *Ala.*—Tombigbee river, above Gainesville, not above Columbus.

CARPENTER'S WOODYARD, *Ala.*—Alabama river, above Selma, not above Wetumpka.

CARROLLTON, *Ky.*—Ohio river, 452 miles above its mouth, not above Cincinnati.

CARROLL'S LANDING, *Ark.*—Arkansas river, 358 miles above Napoleon, above Little Rock, not above Norristown.

CARONDELET, *Mo.*—Mississippi river, 1233 miles above New Orleans, above mouth of the Ohio, not above Alton.

CARROLL'S LANDING, *Ark.*—Red river, 153 miles above Shreveport, above Carolina Bluff, not above Fulton.

CARO EPPERSON'S LANDING, *Texas.*—Red river, 404 miles above Shreveport, above Mound City.

CARSON'S LANDING, *Ark.*—Arkansas river, above Arkansas Post, not above Pine Bluff.

CARSON'S LANDING, *Texas.*—Red river, 330 miles above Shreveport, above Fulton, not above Lanesport.

CARSON'S LANDING, *Miss.*—Mississippi river, above Greenville, not above Memphis.

CAROLINA LANDING, *Miss.*—Mississippi river, above Grand Gulf, not above Greenville.

CAROLINA BLUFF, *La.*—Red river, 50 miles above Shreveport, not above the mouth of Black Bayou.

CARRINGTON, *Ark.*—Red river, 373 miles above Shreveport, above Lanesport, not above Mound City.

CARUTHERSVILLE, *Mo.*—Mississippi river, above Memphis, not above the mouth of the Ohio.

CARTHAGE, *Ohio.*—Ohio river, 138 miles above its mouth, above Paducah, not above Cincinnati.

CARTHAGE, *Miss.*—Mississippi river, above Grand Gulf, not above Greenville.

CARTHAGE, *Tenn.*—Cumberland river, above Nashville, not above Gainsboro.

CARDIFF, *Miss.*—Yazoo river, not above Yazoo City.

CAROLINA LANDING, *Texas.*—Trinity river, above Smithville not above Magnolia Landing.

CARR'S LANDING. *Tenn.*—Mississippi river, above Greenville, not above the mouth of the Ohio.

CARROLLTON, *Ind.*—Wabash river, above the Rapids, not above Terre Haute.

CARROLL'S, M., LANDING, *La.*—Red river, above Grand Ecore, not above Shreveport.

CARINGTON LANDING, *La.*—Onachita river, above Harrisonburg, not above Trenton.

CARTHAGE, *Texas.*—Sabine river, above Hamilton.

CARNEY'S WOODYARD, *Ala.*—Tombigbee river, not above Demopolis.

CARNEY'S BLUFF, *Ala.*—Tombigbee river, not above Demopolis.

CARSON'S, J., LANDING. *Ala.*—Warrior river, not above Tuscaloosa.

CARSON'S LANDING, *Ala.*—Alabama river, not above Selma.

CARSTAPHNEY'S WOODYARD, *Ala.*—Alabama river, not above Selma.

CARSTER'S LANDING, *Ala.*—Alabama river, not above Selma.

CAREYVILLE, *Ark.*—Ouachita river, 410 miles above the mouth of Old river, above Alabama Landing, not above Camden.

CASPIANA, *La.*—Red river, 630 miles above New Orleans, above Grand Ecore, not above Shreveport.

CAS COE, *Ark.*—White river, 115 miles above its mouth, below the junction of Black river.

CARTER'S, CAPT. (ANCHORAGE.)—Red river, above Shreveport, not above foot of Raft.

CARTER'S.—Ouachita river, above Harrisonburg, not above Trenton.

CARSON'S.—Bayou Bartholomew, above Pt. Pleasant, not above Arkansas line.

CARSON'S.—Arkansas river, above Arkansas Post, not above Pine Bluff.

CARTER'S PLACE.—Bayou Bartholomew, above Arkansas line, not above Portland.

CASH, P. B—Red river, above Grand Ecore, not above Shreveport.

CASH, P. B., GIN.—Red river, above Grand Ecore, not above Shreveport.

CASEBOW.—Yazoo river, above Yazoo City, not above Leflore.

CAUSHATTA.—Red river, above Shreveport.

CASSIQUE.—Yazoo river, above Yazoo City, not above Leflore.

CASH POINT, or PICKETS.—Red river, above Shreveport, not above foot of Raft.

CASSANDRIA.—Red river, not above Alexandria.

CASSIDY BAYOU.—Tallahatchie river, not above Cassidy.

CASTLE, DR. (or COLONY PLANTATION.—Red river, above Alexandria, not above Cane river.

CAT ISLAND.—Red river, above Shreveport, not above foot of the Raft.

CAWLEY BLUFF.—Bayou Bartholomew, above Point Pleasant, not above Arkansas line.

CEDAR BLUFF (or MARK'S).—Red river, above foot of Raft, not above Fulton.

CEDAR BLUFF (A. MANFERT).—Red river, above Shreveport, not above Carolina Bluffs.

CENTER'S, DR.—Arkansas river, above Norristown, not above Roseville.

CETTER'S, F., LANDING.—Red river, above Shreveport, not above Carolina Bluffs.

CASEYVILLE, *Ky.*—Ohio river, 126 miles from its mouth, above Paducah, not above Cincinnati.

CASEYVILLE, *Ills.*—Ohio river, 118 miles above its mouth, above Paducah, not above Cincinnati.

CASSVILLE, *Wis.*—Mississippi river, 1645 miles above New Orleans, above Galena.

CASTOR'S LANDING, *La.*—Bayou Bartholomew, above Pt. Pleasant, not above Arkansas line.

CASON'S, JAS., LANDING, *La.*—Atchafalaya river, below Simmsport.

CASTOR'S LANDING, *La.*—Ouachita river, above Harrisonburg, not above Trenton.

CASH LANDING, *La.*—Red river, above Grand Ecore, not above Shreveport.

CASSANDRA LANDING, *La.*—Red river, 305 miles from New Orleans, not above Alexandria.

CAT FISH POINT, *Miss.*—Mississippi river, above Greenville, not above Memphis.

CATAHOMA LANDING, *Ala.*—Tombigbee river, not above Demopolis.

CATO'S, MRS. LANDING, *Ala.*—Tombigbee river. not above Demopolis.

CATLETT'S BURG, *Ky.*—Ohio river, 686 miles above its mouth, above Cincinnati.

CAT ISLAND, *Ark.*—Mississippi river, above Greenville, not above Memphis.

CAVE IN ROCK, *Ills.*—Ohio river, 98 miles above its mouth, not above Cincinnati.

CEDAR BLUFF, *Ala.*—Tombigbee river, above Demopolis, not above Gainesville.

CEDAR POINT, *Tenn.*—Mississippi river, above Memphis, not above the mouth of the Ohio.

CEDAR SPRINGS, *Texas.*—Trinity river, above Magnolia Landing.

CEDAR CREEK, *Ala.*—Tombigbee river, not above Demopolis.

CEDAR CREEK, *Ala.*—Alabama river, not above Selma.

CELINA RESERVOIR, *Ohio.*—Wabash river, not above the Rapids.

CENTRE PORT, *La.*—Atchafalaya river, below Simmsport.

CENTER, *Ohio.*—Ohio river, 821 miles above its mouth, above Cincinnati.

CENTERVILLE, *La.*—Bayou Teche.

CENTERPOINT, *Tenn.*—Cumberland river, above Gainsboro.

CHARLESTON, *Ky.*—Ohio river, 587 miles above its mouth, above Cincinnati.

CHARLESTON LANDING, *Ind.*—Ohio river, 406 miles above its mouth, above Paducah, not above Cincinnati.

CHALFUNT, C. LANDING, *La.*—Atchafalaya river, above Simmsport.

CHAPPEL'S, MRS. LANDING, *Ark.*—Red river, 250 miles above Shreveport, above Fulton, not above Lanesport.

CHARLESTON LANDING. *La.*—Ouachita river, above Harrisonburg, not above Trenton.

CHANDLER'S LANDING. *La.*—Bayou Macon, 30 miles from its mouth, not above Monticello.

CHACK BLUFF, *Tenn.*—Tennessee river, not above Eastport.

CHACK BACK, *Ky.*—Mississippi river, above Memphis, not above mouth of the Ohio.

CHASTANG'S BLUFF. *Ala*—Tombigbee river, not above Demopolis.

CHANEY'S, W. T. LANDING, *Ala.*—Tombigbee river, not above Demopolis.

CHANEY'S, W. P. LANDING, *Ala.*—Tombigbee river, not above Demopolis.

CHASTANG'S BLUFF, *Ala.*—Alabama river, not above Selma.

CHANEY'S BLUFF, *Ala.*—Tombigbee river, above Gainesville, not above Columbus.

CHANEY'S GIN, MRS. *Ala.*—Tombigbee river, not above Demopolis.

CHAPMAN'S BLUFF, *Ala.*—Tombigbee river, not above Demopolis.

CHAPMAN'S LANDING, *Ala.*—Alabama river, not above Selma.

CHARISTON RIVER, *Mo.*—Missouri river, 236 miles above mouth, above Jefferson City, not above Lexington.

CHAMPAGNOLLE, *Ark.*—Ouachita river, above Alabama Landing, not above Camden.

CHAPPELL'S FERRY, *La.*—Red river, above Shreveport, not above Fulton, not above Lanesport.

CHAMBER'S LANDING, *Ark.*—White river, 285 miles above its mouth, not above junction Black river.

CHESTER, *Mo.*—Mississippi river, 1141 miles above New Orleans, above the mouth of the Ohio, not above Alton.

CHESTER, *Ills.*—Mississippi river, 1193 miles above New Orleans, above the mouth of the Ohio, not above St. Louis.

CHEATHAM'S LANDING, *Ark.*—Red river, 267 miles above Shreveport, above Lanesport, not above Mound City.

CHESHIRT, *Ohio.*—Ohio river, 745 miles above its mouth, above Cincinnati.

CHEVRETTEVILLE, *La.*—Bayou Lafourche.

CHEROKEE BAY, *Ark.*—Currant river, a tributary of White and Black rivers.

CHESTERFIELD LANDING, *La.*—Bayou Macon, 95 miles from its mouth, not above Monticello.

CHERRY LANDING, *Ala.*—Tombigbee river, not above Demopolis.

CHARLESTON.—Ouachita river, above Harrisonburg, not above Trenton.

CHAPPLES.—Red river, above Grand Ecore, not above Shreveport.

CHAMBERS, J. W. (WOODYARD).—Red river, not above Alexandria.

CHAMBERS, JOE (ASHTON PLACE).—Red river, not above Alexandria.

CHAYTOR'S, JOE, CAPT. (OLD PAXTON PLACE).—Red river, above Fulton, not above Lanesport.

CHENIER.—Ouachita river, above Harrisonburg, not above Trenton.

CHEOAS (LODI YAZOO).—Yazoo river, above Yazoo City, not above Leflore.

CHEUF MENTEUR STATION.—20 miles from New Orleans, on the Mobile railroad.

CHEMIN-EN-HAUT BAYOU.—Bayou Bartholomew, above Point Pleasant, not above Arkansas line.

CHEYENNE AGENCY.—Missouri river, 1371 miles from its mouth, above Iatan.

CHICKASAW BAYOU (WM. LAKE).—Yazoo river, not above Yazoo City.

CHILDERS, O. B.—Red river, above Grand Ecore, not above Shreveport.

CHICOPE.—Yazoo river, above Yazoo City, not above Leflore.

CHINA GROVE (J. GREGG'S).

CHICOT, *Ark.*—Mississippi river, above Greenville, not above Memphis.

CHOCTAW, *Miss.*—102 miles up Sunflower river.

CHICOSA.—167 miles up Sunflower river.

CHOCTAW BAYOU.—Red river, not above Alexandria.

CHOTARD.—Mississippi river, above Grand Gulf, not above Greenville.

CHRISTMAS.—Mississippi river, above Grand Gulf, not above Greenville.

CHRISTIANI.—Red river, above Grand Ecore, not above Shreveport.

CHURCH.—83 miles up Bœuf river, above Thomas' Landing.

CHURCH.—Bayou Bartholomew, not above Point Pleasant.

CHERY BLUFF, *Ala.*—Tombigbee river, above Demopolis, not above Gainsville.

CHEET'S LANDING, *Ala.*—Warrior river, not above Tuscaloosa.

CHENEVILLE, *La.*—Bayou Bœuf.

CHICANINA CUT-OFF, *Ark.*—Red river, 171 miles from Shreveport, above Carolina Bluff, not above Fulton.

CHICKASAW, *Ala.*—Tennessee river, above Eastport, not above Florence.

CHICKASAW BLUFF, *Ark.*—White river, below the junction of Black river.

CHIPPEWA RIVER, *Wis.*—Mississippi river, 1786 miles above New Orleans, above Galena.

CHIPPEWA, *Ills.*—Mississippi river, 1196 miles above New Orleans, above the mouth of the Ohio, not above Alton.

CHILLICOTHE, *Ills.*—Illinois river, 196 miles above its mouth, above Beardstown, not above the mouth of Fox river.

CHILDER'S LANDING, *Ala.*—Tombigbee river, above Gainesville, not above Columbus.

CHILES FERRY, *Ala.*—Warrior river, not above Tuscaloosa.

CHINA GROVE, *La.*—Red river, above Grand Ecore, not above Shreveport.

CHOCTAW, *Ala.*—Warrior river, not above Tuscaloosa.

CHOCTAW BLUFF, *Ala.*—Alabama river, not above Selma.

CHOCUMA, *Miss.*—Yazoo river, above Yazoo City, not above Leflore.

CHOCTOWATCHEE RIVER.—Not above Geneva.

CHUCKAHOULA, *La.*—Morgan railroad, 62 miles from New Orleans.

CHURCHILL'S LANDING, *Ark.*—Arkansas river, 274 miles above Napoleon, above Pine Bluff, not above Little Rock.

CHURCH HILL, *Miss.*—Mississippi river, above Bayou Sara, not above Grand Gulf.

CHURCHVILLE, *La.*—Atchafalaya river, 25 miles below Simmsport.

CINCINNATI, *Texas.*—Trinity river, above Smithville, not above Magnolia Landing.

CINCINNATI, *Ohio.*—Ohio river, 1505 miles above New Orleans.

CINCINNATI, *Wis.*—Mississippi river, 1665 miles above New Orleans, above Galena.

CLARK, SAM'L, LANDING, *La.*—Red river, above Grand Ecore, not above Shreveport.

CLARE LANDING, *Ark*—Mississippi river, above Greenville, not above Memphis.

CLARK'S, DR., LANDING.—336 miles up Sunflower river.

CLARK, E.—Big Deer Creek, Miss., 110 miles from Vicksburg.

CLARK'S.—Tallahatchie river, not above Cassidy Bayou.

CLARK'S.—Bayou Bartholomew, above Portland.

CLARK'S.—Bayou Bartholomew, above Portland.

CLARK'S MILLS.—Bayou Bartholomew, above Arkansas line, not above Portland.

CLARK'S.—Ouachita river, above Harrisonburg, not above Trenton.

CLARKSVILLE, *Tenn.*—Cumberland river, 148 miles from the Ohio, not above Nashville.

CLARKSVILLE, *Miss.*—Mississippi river, above Grand Gulf, not above Greenville.

CLARKSVILLE, *Mo.*—Mississippi river, above Alton, not above foot of first Rapids.

CLARKSVILLE, *Ark.*—Landing at Spadra, on Arkansas river.

CLARINGTON, *Ohio*.—Ohio river, 883 miles above its mouth, above Cincinnati.

CLAYBORNE, *Ala*.—Alabama river, 114 miles above Mobile, not above Selma.

CLARENDON, *Ark*.—White river, 135 miles above its mouth, below the junction of Black river.

CLAYTON, *Ind*.—Mississippi river, 1663 miles above New Orleans, above Galena.

CLAYSVILLE, *Ala*.—Tennessee river, above Florence.

CLEAR LAKE.—Any point.

CLEAR CREEK, *Ills*.—Mississippi river, 1085 miles above New Orleans, above the mouth of the Ohio, not above St. Louis.

CLEAR CREEK LANDING, *Ills*.—Mississippi river, above the mouth of the Ohio, not above Alton.

CLEVELAND, *Ala*—Alabama river, not above Selma.

CLIFTON, *Ala*.—Alabama river, not above Selma.

CLINGENHOIFER'S LANDING, *Ark*.—Arkansas river, 378 miles above Napoleon, above Little Rock, not above Norristown.

CLIFTON, *Mo*.—Mississippi river, 1151 miles above New Orleans, above the mouth of the Ohio, not above Alton.

CLIFTON, *Tenn*.—Tennessee river, not above Eastport.

CLIFDALE, *Mo*.—Mississippi river, above the mouth of the Ohio, not above Alton.

CLINTON, *Ind*.—Wabash river, above the Rapids, not above Terre Haute.

CLINTON, *La*.—Landing at Port Hudson, or Bayou Sara, on the Mississippi river.

CLINTON, *Texas*.—Red river, near Jefferson, Texas.

CLOSEAU PLANTATION, *La*.—Red river, above Grand Ecore, not above Shréveport.

CLOVERSPORT, *Ky*.—Ohio river, 270 miles above its mouth, above Paducah, not above Cincinnati.

CLOVER BEND, *Ark*.—Black river, above the junction of White river.

CLARKSDALE, *Miss*.—342 miles up Sunflower river.

CLARKSON'S.—Red river, above Fulton, not above Lanesport.

CLAVERIE, FRANK (NIGGER POINT).—Red river, not above Alexandria.

CLAYTON'S LANDING, *Miss.*—149 miles up Big Deer Creek.

CLENENGERS.—132 miles up Bœuf river, above Thomas' Landing.

CLIFFORD.—Yazoo river, above Yazoo City, not above Leflore.

CLEMENT'S LANDING.—Red river, not above Alexandria.

CLERES PRIAUX.—Red river, above Grand Ecore, not above Shreveport.

CLOWEN —Mississippi river, above Grand Gulf, not above Greenville.

COLT'S LANDING.—266 miles up Sunflower river.

COCKERHAN'S, J. W. LANDING.—Red river, above Cane river, not above Grand Ecore.

COCK'S POINT.—Yazoo river, above Yazoo City, not above Leflore.

CODY'S.—Ouachita river, above Harrisonburg, not above Trenton.

COFFEE'S POINT.—Mississippi river, above Grand Gulf, not above Greenville.

COLES, DR.—Ouachita river, above Harrisonburg, not above Trenton.

COLEMAN'S LANDING, *Miss.*—147 miles up Big Deer Creek.

COLE, ISAAC, and P. SCRIBER.—Bayou Bartholomew, not above Point Pleasant.

COLFAX.—Red river, above mouth of Cane river, not above Grand Ecore.

COLLEGE POINT.—Mississippi river, not above Bayou Sara.

COLLINS, OWEN.—Red river, above foot of Raft, not above Fulton.

COLLINGSBURG (BOSSIER PH., La.)—Red river, above Shreveport, not above Jefferson.

COLLIER GIN (MARBLE).—Bayou Bartholomew, not above Point Pleasant.

COLLUM'S LANDING, *Miss.*—152 miles up Big Deer Creek.

CLOUTIERVILLE, *La.*—On Cane river. (Red river.)

COAL BLUFF, *Ala.*—Alabama river, not above Selma.

COAL GROVE, *Ohio.*—Ohio river, 680 miles above its mouth, above Cincinnati.

COAL PORT, *Ohio.*—Ohio river, 750 miles above its mouth, above Cincinnati.

COBIN, *La.*—Red river, above Grand Ecore, not above Shreveport.

COCKERILL'S LANDING, *Ark.*—Arkansas river, 169 miles above Napoleon, above Arkansas Post, not above Pine Bluff.

COCKERILL'S UPPER PLACE, *Ark.*—Arkansas river, 199 miles above Napoleon, above Pine Bluff, not abov Little Rock.

COFFEEVILLE, *Miss.*—Jackson railroad, 310 miles from New Orleans.

COLD WATER RIVER (Mouth of), *Miss.*—Tallahatchie river.

COLD WATER RIVER, *Miss.*

COL. PLEASANT'S LANDING, *Ark.*—Arkansas river, 129 miles above Napoleon, above Arkansas Post, not above Pine Bluff.

COFFEEVILLE, *Ala.*—Tombigbee river, not above Demopolis.

COFEEE LANDING, *Tenn.*—Tennessee river, not above Eastport.

COLUMBIA, *Miss.*—Pearl river.

COLUMBIA, *Ark.*—Mississippi river, 610 miles above New Orleans, above Greenville, not above Memphis.

COLUMBIA SPRINGS, *Miss.*—Pearl river, above Columbia.

COLUMBIANA, *Ills.*—Illinois river, not above Beardstown.

COLEMAN'S FERRY, *Miss.*—Chickasaha river.

COLEMAN'S LANDING, *Miss.*—Tombigbee river, not above Demopolis.

COLEMAN'S LANDING, *Ala.*—Alabama river, not above Selma.

COLE'S MILLS, *Mo.*—Mississippi river, above the mouth of the Ohio, not above Alton.

COLE'S LANDING, *Ala.*—Tombigbee river, above Demopolis, not above Gainesville.

COLLINS, CHAS., LANDING, *La.*—Atchafalaya river, above Simmsport.

COLD SPRINGS, *Texas.*—Trinity river, above Smithville, not above Magnolia Landing.

COLBERT LANDING, *Miss.*—Tombigbee river, above Columbus, not above Cotton Gin Port.

COLGIN'S LANDING, *Ala.*—Tombigbee river, above Demopolis, not above Gainesville.

COLUMBIA, *Ark.*—Mississippi river, 557 miles above New Orleans, above Grand Gulf, not above Greenville.

COLUMBIA, *Ga.*—Chattahootchee river.

COLUMBIA, *Ohio.*—Ohio river, 537 miles above its mouth, above Cincinnati.

COLUMBIA, *La.*—Ouachita river, 210 miles above the mouth of Old river, above Harrisonburg, not above Trenton.

COLUMBUS, *Ky.*—Mississippi river, 1057 miles above New Orleans, above Memphis, not above mouth of the Ohio.

COLUMBUS, *Ala.*—Chattahootchee river, not above Eufala.

COLUMBUS, *Ala.*—Tombigbee river.

COL. WATKINS' LANDING, *Ark.*—Arkansas river, 216 miles above Napoleon, above Pine Bluff, not above Little Rock.

COL. HAWKIN'S LANDING, *Texas.*—Red river, 520 miles above Shreveport. above Mound City.

COL. WILLIAMS' LANDING, *Ark.*—Arkansas river, 139 miles above Napoleon, above Arkansas Post, not above Pine Bluff.

COLE'S LANDING, *Ark.*—White river, 293 miles above its mouth, below the junction of Black river.

COLE'S CREEK LANDING.—Mississippi river, above Grand Gulf, not above Greenville.

COMMERCE, *Mo.*—Mississippi river, 780 miles above New Orleans, above Memphis, not above mouth of the Ohio river.

COMMERCE, *Mo.*—Mississippi river, 1112 miles above New Orleans, above the mouth of the Ohio river, not above St. Louis.

COMO LANDING, *Ark.*—Below Arkansas Post, on Arkansas river.

COMMERCE, *Texas.*—Trinity river, above Smithville, not above Magnolia Landing.

COMPTON'S, SAM'L, LANDING, *La.*—Red river, not above Alexandria.

COMPTON'S, P., LANDING, *La.*—Red river, not above Alexandria.

COMPROMISE, *Ky.*—Mississippi river, above Memphis, not above mouth of the Ohio river.

CONVENT, *La.*—Mississippi river, 62 miles above New Orleans, below Bayou Sara.

CONCORD, *Ky.*—Ohio river, 613 miles above its mouth, above Cincinnati.

CONCORDIA, *Miss.*—Mississippi river, above Greenville, not above Memphis.

COLONY PLANTATION (or DR. CASTLE).—Red river, above Alexandria, not above Cane river.

COMPTON'S, W. J. LANDING.—Red river, not above Alexandria.

CONCORD.—Neches river, Texas.

CONCORDIA.—Red river, not above Alexandria.

COUSHATTA BLUFFS.—Red river, above foot of Raft, not above Fulton.

CONGO'S WOODYARD.—Yazoo river, above Yazoo City, not above Leflore.

CONGO.—Mississippi river, above Grand Gulf, not above Greenville.

CONWAY (or HEADLONG PRAIRIE.—Red river, above foot of Raft, not above Fulton.

CONN'S LANDING—Mississippi river, above Grand Gulf, not above Greenville.

CONVENT,—Red river, not above Alexandria.

COOK'S, *Ark.*.—Old river, above Carolina Bluffs, not above Fulton.

COOK'S LANDING (or FORD'S).—173 miles up Sunflower river.

COOK'S LANDING, *La.*—Mississippi river, not above Bayou Sara.

COOK'S POINT—Yazoo river, not above Yazoo City.

COOPER'S.—Yazoo river, above Yazoo City, not above Leflore.

COOPER'S LANDING.—Arkansas river, above Arkansas Post, not above Pine Bluff.

COPELAND, MAYER.—106 miles up Bœuf river, above Thomas' Landing.

CONSCHATTA CHUTE, *La.*—Red river, 560 miles from New Orleans, above Grand Ecore, not above Shreveport.

CONCORDIA, *La.*—Mississippi river, 277 miles above New Orleans, above Bayou Sara, not above Grand Gulf.

CONSTITUTION, *Ark.*—Arkansas river, above Norristown, not above Fort Smith.

CONNER'S LANDING, *La.*—Mississippi river, 282 miles above New Orleans, above Bayou Sara, not above Grand Gulf.

CONWAY, *Ark.*—Red river, 134 miles above Shreveport, above Carolina Bluff, not above Fulton.

CONCORD, *Ind.*—Wabash river, above Terre Haute.

CONCORDIA, *La.*—Black river, La.

CONSORT POINT, *Miss.*—Mississippi river, 220 miles above New Orleans, above Bayou Sara, not above Grand Gulf.

CONGO, *Miss.*—Mississippi river, 355 miles above New Orleans, above Grand Gulf, not above Greenville.

CONCHAGE LANDING, *Ark.*—Arkansas river, above Pine Bluff, not above Little Rock.

CONWAY'S LANDING, *Ala.*—Tombigbee river, above Gainesville, not above Columbus.

CONTENT LANDING, *Miss.*—Mississippi river, above Greenville, not above Memphis.

COOK'S, JNO. LANDING, *Ark.*—Little Red river, 35 miles from its mouth, below the junction of White and Black rivers.

COOK'S, DANL. LANDING, *Ark.*—Little Red river, below junction of White and Black rivers.

COOK'S, MAJ. LANDING, *Ala.*—Tombigbee river, above Gainesville, not above Columbus.

COOK'S LANDING, *Ala.*—Tombigbee river, above Demopolis, not above Gainesville.

COOSE'S LANDING, *Ark.*—Arkansas river, 36 miles above Napoleon, not above Arkansas Post.

COOKE'S LANDING, *Texas.*—Red river, 517 miles above Shreveport, above Mound City.

COOK'S LANDING, *Miss.*—Mississippi river, above Greenville, not above Memphis.

COOK'S LANDING, *Ark.*—Mississippi river, above Greenville, not above Memphis.

COOL SPRINGS, *La.*—Ouachita river, above Harrisonburg, not above Trenton.

COOSAWDA, *Ala*—Alabama river, above Selma, not above Wetumpka.

COPE'S FERRY, *Tex.*—Neches river, above junction Angelina river.

COPPERAS CREEK, *Ills.*—Illinois river, above Beardstown, not above mouth of Fox river.

COPENHAGEN, *La.*—Ouachita river, above Harrisonburg, not above Trenton.

CORE'S, E. R. LANDING, *Ark.*—Arkansas river, 240 miles above Napoleon, above Pine Bluff, not above Little Rock.

CORDOVA, *Ills.*—Mississippi river, 1543 miles above New Orleans, above the foot of the second Rapids, not above Galena.

CORNISH LANDING, *La.*—Red river, above Grand Ecore, not above Shreveport.

CORKFIELD'S LANDING, *La.*—Red river, above Cotile, not above Grand Ecore.

CORDELL'S LANDING, *Miss.*—Mississippi river, above Grand Gulf, not above Greenville.

COSLEY'S LANDING, *La.*—Red river, above Grand Ecore, not above Shreveport.

COSLEY'S LANDING, *La.*—Red river, above Alexandria, not above Cotile.

COTTON WOOD, *Ark.*—Arkansas river, 155 miles above Napoleon, above Arkansas Post, not above Pine Bluff.

COTTON WOOD, *Mo.*—Mississippi river, 935 miles above New Orleans, above Memphis, not above mouth of the Ohio river.

COTTON POINT, *La.*—Ouachita river, above Harrisonburg, not above Trenton.

COTTON PLANTATION, *La.*—Red river, above Grand Ecore, not above Shreveport.

COTTON WOOD PLANTATION, *Ark.*—Mississippi river, above Memphis, not above the mouth of the Ohio river.

COTTAGE BLUFF, *Ala.*—Alabama river, above Selma, not above Wetumpka.

COTTON PLANTATION, *Ark.*—White river, below the junction of Black river.

COTILE LANDING, *La.*—Red river, 380 miles above New Orleans, above Alexandria.

COTTON GIN PORT, *Miss.*—Tombigbee river.

COTE JOYEUSE, *La.*—Cane river (Red river).

COTE SANS DESSIN, *Mo.*—Missouri river, 135 miles above its mouth, not above Jefferson City.

COUNCIL POINT, *Ia.*—Missouri river, 670 miles above its mouth, above Iatan.

CORA'S BLUFF.—Bayon Bartholomew, above Point Pleasant, not above Arkansas line.

CORNEY'S BLUFF.—Bayou Darbonne, above Farmersville.
CORDELL'S LANDING.—Bayou Macon, not above Monticello.
COTHRAU'S.—Tallahatchie river, not above Cassidy Bayou.
COTILE (BOYCE PLACE).—Red river, above Alexandria, not above mouth of Cane river.
COTTONWOOD.—Mississippi river, above Grand Gulf, not above Greenville.
COTTON POINT (G W. ROBINSON).—Red river, above Grand Ecore, not above Shreveport.
COTTON PORT.—Ouachita river, above Harrisonburg, not above Trenton.
COTTINGHAM'S.—Ouachita river, above Harrisonburg, not above Trenton.
COURTRIGHT LANDING.—118 miles up Big Deer Creek, Miss.
COUNCIL BEND, *Miss.*—Mississippi river, 775 miles above New Orleans, above Greenville, not above Memphis.
COVINGTON, *Ky.*—Ohio river, 541 miles above the mouth of the Ohio, above Paducah, opposite Cincinnati.
COVINGTON, *La.*—Tchefuncta river.
COVINGTON, *Ind.*—Wabash river, above the Rapids, not above Terre Haute.
COVE CREEK, *Ark.*—Arkansas river, 430 miles above Napoleon, above Norristown, not above Fort Smith.
COWN'S LANDING, *Miss.*—Mississippi river, 472 miles above New Orleans, above Grand Gulf, not above Greenville.
COWEN'S LANDING, *La.*—Ouachita river, above Harrisonburg, not above Trenton.
COWEN'S LANDING, *Ala.*—Tombigbee river, not above Demopolis.
COWAN'S LANDING, *Ala*—Warrior river, not above Tuscaloosa.
COX'S POINT, *Miss.*—Mississippi river, 497 miles above New Orleans, above Grand Gulf, not above Greenville.
COX'S GIN, *Miss.*—Tombigbee river, above Gainesville, not above Columbus.
COX'S WOODYARD, *Miss.*—Tombigbee river, above Gainesville, not above Columbus.

COX'S, MRS., LANDING, *Miss.*—Mississippi river, above Grand Gulf, not above Greenville.

COX'S, W. A., LANDING, *La.*—Bayou Macon, 43 miles above its mouth, not above Monticello.

COX'S, JAS., LANDING, *Ala.*—Tombigbee river, not above Demopolis.

COX'S LANDING, *Miss.*—Tombigbee river, above Columbus, not above Cotton Gin Port.

CRAIG'S.—Arkansas river, above Pine Bluff, not above Little Rock.

CRAIG HOPE.—Ouachita river, above Harrisonburg, not above Trenton.

CRANE'S, W. (SUNNY POINT).—Red river, above Grand Ecore, not above Shreveport.

CRANE'S, WALTER GIN.—Red river, above Grand Ecore, not above Shreveport.

CRAWSER (L. C. NELSON).—Red river, above Grand Ecore, not above Shreveport.

CRAWFORD'S.—Bayou Bartholomew, above Arkansas line, not above Portland.

CRAWLEY.—Bayou Bartholomew, above Arkansas line, not above Portland.

CRENSHAW'S.—Red river, above foot of Raft, not above Fulton,

CRESSWELL, (or JETT PLANTATION).—Red river, above Fulton, not above Lanesport.

CRAIG'S FERRY, *Ala.*—Alabama river, above Gainesville, not above Columbus.

CRAIGHEAD'S LANDING, *Ark.*—Mississippi river, above Greenville, not above the mouth of the Ohio.

CRAWFORD'S LANDING, *Mo.*—Mississippi river, above the mouth of the Ohio river, not above Alton.

CRAWLEY'S LANDING, *Ark.*—Arkansas river, 186 miles above Napoleon, above Pine Bluff, not above Little Rock.

CRAVEN'S LANDING, *Ark.*—Arkansas river, 434 miles above Napoleon, above Norristown, not above Fort Smith.

CRAWFORD'S, C. H., *Ark.*—Arkansas river, 500 miles above Napoleon, above Norristown, not above Fort Smith.

CRAWFORD'S LANDING, *Ark.*—Little Red river, 37 miles above its mouth.

CRANE'S LANDING, *Mo.*—Mississippi river, above the mouth of the Ohio, not above Alton.

CREESLBURG, *Ky.*—Cumberland river, above Gainesboro.

CREEK AGENCY, *Ark.*—Arkansas river, 680 miles above Napoleon, above Fort Smith, not above Fort Gibson.

CRISIS, PHILIP, *Ark.*—Little Red river, 10 miles above its mouth, below the junction of White and Black rivers.

CRIN'S LANDING, *Ala.*—Tombigbee river, above Gainesville, not above Columbus.

CROCKETT'S POINT, *La.*—Bayou Macon, not above Monticello.

CROCKETT'S BLUFF, *Ark.*—White river, below the junction of Black river.

CROSS SARA LANDING, *Ark.*—White river, 34 miles from its mouth, below the junction of Black river.

CROW'S LANDING, *Miss.*—Mississippi river, 475 miles above New Orleans, above Grand Gulf, not above Greenville.

CROOK'S LANDING, *La.*—Bayou Macon, 29 miles from its mouth, not above Monticello.

CROOKED RIVER, *Mo.*—Missouri river, 32 miles above its mouth above Jefferson City, not above Lexington.

CROOKED POINT CUT-OFF, *Ark.*—White river, 150 miles above its mouth, below the junction of Black river.

CROOKSHANKS' LANDING, *La.*—Red river, above Alexandria, not above Cane river.

CROOM'S LANDING, *Ala.*—Tombigbee river, not above Demopolis.

CROTHER'S LANDING, *Tenn.*—Cumberland river, not above Nashville.

CROFT'S LANDING, *Ala.*—Tombigbee river, above Demopolis, not above Gainesville.

CROWELL'S LANDING, *Ark.*—Red river, 168 miles above Shreveport, above Carolina Bluff, not above Fulton.

CRYSTAL SPRINGS, *Miss.*—Jackson railroad, 158 miles from New Orleans.

CRYER'S, T. W., LANDING, *Ark.*—Red river, 278 miles above Shreveport, above Fulton, not above Lanesport.

CRESCENT (or J. BOND), *La.*—Red river, above Grand Ecore, not above Shreveport.

CRESCENT.—Yazoo river, above Yazoo City, not above Leflore.

CRESCENT—Bayou Bartholomew, above Point Pleasant, not above Arkansas line.

CRESCENT LANDING.—Red river, above Alexandria, not above Cane river.

CRISTIES, E.—Red river, above Cotile, not above Grand Ecore.

CROSBY'S LANDING.—Red river, above Alexandria, not above Cane river.

CROSS LANDING (P. C. RICHARDSON).—Bayou Bartholomew, above Point Pleasant, not above Arkansas line.

CROSSEAU PLACE.—Red river, above Grand Ecore, not above Shreveport.

CROSLEY.—Ouachita river, above Harrisonburg, not above Trenton.

CROTON GROVE.—Ouachita river, above Harrisonburg, not above Trenton.

CROWELL'S STORE.—Red river, above Grand Ecore, not above Shreveport.

CRUMP'S (UPPER AND LOWER).—Yazoo river above Yazoo City, not above Leflore

CROXTON (STAR LANDING).—Bayou Bartholomew, above Point Pleasant, not above Arkansas line.

CRYER, MORGAN.—Red river, above foot of Raft, not above Fulton.

CUBA, *Ala.*—Tombigbee river, above Gainesville, not above Columbus.

CUMBERLAND IRON WORKS, *Tenn.*—Cumberland river, not above Nashville.

CUMBERLAND RIVER, *Tenn.*—Above Gainesboro.

CUMMINS' PLACE, *Ark.*—Arkansas river, 105 miles above Napoleon, above Arkansas Post, not above Pine Bluff.

CUNNINGHAM'S LANDING, *Ala.*—Tombigbee river, not above Demopolis.

CUNNINGHAM'S, J. S., LANDING, *Ala.*—Tombigbee river, above Gainesvile, not above Columbus.

COURT (G. L. HALL (DR. MAGRUDER).—Red river, above Alexandria, not above mouth of Cane river.

CUNNINGHAM'S LANDING, *Ala.*—Alabama river, above Selma, not above Wetumpka.

CUT-OFF LANDING, *La.*—Bayou Macon, 20 miles from its mouth, not above Monticello.

CUNNINGHAM'S LANDING, *Ala.*—Warrior river, not above Tuscaloosa.

CUBA.—Ouachita river, above Harrisonburg, not above Trenton.

CUBA PLANTATION.—Ouachita river, above Trenton, not above Alabama Landing.

CUMMING'S GIN.—Red river, above Grand Ecore, not above Shreveport.

CUMMING'S (DEVIL'S ELBOW.—Red river, above Grand Ecore, not above Shreveport.

CUMMINGS, R. C.—Red river, above Grand Ecore, not above Shreveport.

CUNNEY.—Ouachita river, above Harrisonburg, not above Trenton.

CUNNINGHAM TOE HEAD.—97 miles up Bœuf river, above Thomas' Landing.

CUT OFF (MARCY'S ISLAND.—Red river, above Grand Ecore, not above Shreveport.

CUT OFF.—Red river, above foot of Raft, not above Fulton.

CURLEY'S.—Red river, above Alexandria, not above mouth of Cane river.

CURETON.—Yazoo river, above Yazoo City, not above Leflore.

CURU'S, JOE.—Arkansas river, above Arkansas Post, not above Pine Bluff.

CURTIS, C. R. C.—Bartholomew Bayou, above Portland.

CURRIE'S.—Red river, above Cane river, not above Grand Ecore.

CURRY, I. T. LANDING, *Miss.*—180 miles up Big Deer Creek.

CYPRESS BEND, *Ala.*—Tennessee river, above Eastport, not above Florence.

CYPRESS BAYOU, *Ark.*—Mississippi river, above Greenville, not above Memphis.

CYPRESS CREEK, *Ala.*—Alabama river, above Selma, not above Wetumpka.

CYPRESS POINT, *La.*—Atchafalaya river, below Simmsport.

CYNTHIANA LANDING, *Miss.*—118 miles up Big Deer Creek.

CYPRESS BEND, *Miss.*—100 miles up Sunflower river.

CYPRESS BAYOU.—Ouachita river, above Harrisonburg, not above Trenton.

D

DAILY W. Y. LANDING.—Ouachita river, above Trenton, not above Alabama Landing.

DAMEWOOD —257 miles up Sunflower river.

DANFORTH, W. E.—Red river, above Grand Ecore, not above Shreveport.

DANE MOORE.—100 miles ·p Bœuf river, above Thomas' Landing.

DANIELS, GEN.—Red river, above Grand Ecore, not above Shreveport.

DANVILLE.—Ouachita river, above Harrisonburg, not above Trenton

DA BAQUE'S LANDING, *Ark.*—White river, above Batesville.

DALIN'S LANDING, *Ark.*—Arkansas river, 83 miles from Napoleon, above Arkansas Post, not above Pine Bluff.

DALEY'S LANDING, *Tenn.*—Cumberland river, not above Nashville.

DALE'S FERRY, *Ala.*—Alabama river, not above Selma.

DALE'S LANDING, *La.*—Black river, La

DALLAS, *Texas.*—Trinity river, above Magnolia Landing.

DALLY'S, W. Y., LANDING.—Ouachita river, above Trenton, not above Alabama Landing.

DANDRIDGE LANDING, *Texas.*—Red river, 339 miles above Shreveport, above White Oak Shoals.

DANELL'S LANDING, *Tenn.*—Mississippi river, above Memphis, not above the mouth of the Ohio river.

DANVILLE BRIDGE, *Tenn.*—Tennessee river, not above Eastport.

DANIEL'S POINT, *Ark.*—Mississippi river, above Greenville, not above the mouth of the Ohio river.

D'ARCVILLE, *Ark.*—Arkansas river, above Norristown, not above Fort Smith.

DARDANELLES, *Ark.*—Arkansas river, 392 miles above Napoleon, above Little Rock, not above Norristown.

DARWIN'S LANDING, *Ills.*—Wabash river, above Terre Haute.

D'ARBONNE LANDING, *La.*—Ouachita river, above Trenton, not above Alabama Landing.

DARDEN'S FERRY, *Ala.*—Tombigbee river, not above Demopolis.

DARNEL'S POINT, *Tenn.*—Mississippi river, above Memphis, not above the mouth of the Ohio.

DARK CORNER, *Miss.*—Mississippi river, above Greenville, not above Memphis.

DART, *Ark.*—Arkansas river, above Little Rock, not above Norristown.

DAVID, MRS., LANDING, *La.*—Red river, not above Alexandria.

DAVE LEWIS' LANDING, *Ark.*—Arkansas river, 236 miles above Napoleon, above Pine Bluff, not above Little Rock.

DAVIS' SHOALS, *Texas.*—Red river, 358 miles above Shreveport, above Fulton, not above Lanesport.

DAVENPORT, *Ind.*—Mississippi river, 1518 miles above New Orleans, above the foot of second Rapids, not above Galena.

DAVIS' LANDING, *Miss.*—Mississippi river, above Grand Gulf, not above Greenville.

DAVIS', M. L. LANDING, *Ark.*—Arkansas river, 181 miles above Napoleon, above Pine Bluff, not above Little Rock.

DAVIS, W. T., LANDING, *La.*—Atchafalaya river, below Simmsport.

DAVIS, R. D., LANDING, *Ala.*—Alabama river, not above Selma.

DAVIS, BERY, LANDING, *Ala.*--Alabama river, not above Selma.

DAVIS' WOODYARD, *Ala.*—Alabama river, not above Selma.

DAVIS, GEO., LANDING, *Ala.*—Alabama river, not above Selma.

DAWSON, W. H. R., *Ala.*—Alabama river, not above Selma.

DARLEYS.—Bœuf river, not above Thomas' Landing.

DARRE LANDING.—Red river, above Alexandria, not above Cane river.

DAVITT, MRS (or DELOS).—Red river, not above Alexandria.

DAVIS, J. N.—Ouachita river, above Harrisonburg, not above Trenton.

DAVIS, MRS. I. N.—Ouachita river, above Harrisonburg, not above Trenton.

DAVIS, JOE (COL.)—Bayou Bartholomew, not above Pt. Pleasant.

DAVIS PLACE.—Bayou Bartholomew, above Point Pleasant, not above Arkansas line.

DAVIS' LANDING.—317 miles up Sunflower river.

DAWSON BAYOU.—165 miles up Sunflower river.

DAY'S.—Ouachita river, above Harrisonburg, not above Trenton.

DA JARNETT'S, J. S. LANDING, *Ala.*—Alabama river, above Selma, not above Wetumpka.

DEAS,' COL. JOE LANDING, *Ala.*—Alabama river, not above Selma.

DEAR'S, C., LANDING, *Ala.*—Alabama river, not above Selma.

DEADRICH'S LANDING, *Ark.*—Mississippi river, above Greenville, not above Memphis.

DEAN HENRY.—Bayou Bartholomew, above Arkansas line, not above Portland.

DEARMEM.—Mississippi river, above Grand Gulf, not above Greenville.

DEER CREEK LANDING.—Mississippi river, above Grand Gulf, not above Greenville.

DE GLAIZE.—Bayou Bartholomew, above Point Pleasant, not above Arkansas line.

DELOCHES, L.—Red river, above Cane river, not above Grand Ecore.

DELOCHES ROCKS.—Red river, above Alexandria, not above mouth of Cane river.

DELHOST, H.—Red river, not above Alexandria.

DELTA.—Yazoo river, above Yazoo City, not above Leflore.

DEASON'S LANDING, *La.*—Mississippi river, above Grand Gulf, not above Greenville.

DEAVIL'S ISLAND, *Mo. and Ills.*—Mississippi river, 1110 miles above New Orleans, above the mouth of the Ohio river, not above Alton.

DEAVIL'S TEA TABLE and CORNER ROCK, *Mo.*—Mississippi river, 1056 miles above New Orleans, above the mouth of the Ohio, not above Alton.

DEAVIL'S BAKE OVEN, *Ills*—Mississippi river, 1070 miles above New Orleans, above the mouth of the Ohio, not above Alton.

DEAVIL'S RACE GROUND, *Ark.*—Mississippi river, 857 miles above New Orleans, above Memphis, not above the mouth of the Ohio.

DECATURVILLE, *Tenn.*—Tennessee river, above Florence.

DECLOUET'S LANDING, *La.*—Bayou Teche.

DEER PRAIRIE, *Mo.*—Mississippi river, 1226 miles above New Orleans, above Alton, not above the foot of first Rapids.

DEER PLAIN, *Ills.*—Illinois river, not above Beardstown.

DEERFIELD LANDING, *La.*—Bayou Macon, not above Monticello.

DEER PARK LANDING, *La.*—Mississippi river, 247 miles above New Orleans, above Bayou Sara, not above Grand Gulf.

DEER RANGE, *La.*—Atchafalaya river, below Simmsport.

DEGIN'S LANDING, *Ark.*—Arkansas river, above Norristown, not above Fort Smith.

DELAWARE LANDING, *Ark.*—Arkansas river, above Norristown, not above Fort Smith.

DELHI, *La* (Interior.)—Shipping Point, Travis' Landing on Bayou Macon, not above Monticello.

DE LOST LANDING, *La*—Black river, La.

DELOCHE'S LANDING, *La.*—Red river, above Cane river, not above Grand Ecore.

DELPHI LANDING, *Ind.*—Wabash river, above the Rapids, not above Terre Haute.

DELTA LANDING, *Miss.*—Mississippi river, above Greenville, not above Memphis.

DELTA, *Miss.*—Mississippi river, 716 miles above New Orleans, above Greenville, not above Memphis.

DELAWARE LANDING, *Ark.*—Arkansas river, 405 miles above Napoleon, above Norristown, not above Fort Smith.

DE MUMBRY'S LANDING, *Miss.*—Mississippi river, above Greenville, not above Memphis.

DEMOPOLIS, *Ala.*—Tombigbee river.

DENMARK, *La.*—Tensas river, 25 miles from Trinity, not above the mouth of Bayou Macon.

DENT'S, GEN. T. LANDING, *Ala.*—Warrior river, not above Tuscaloosa.

DEN'S FORD LANDING, *Tenn.*—Mississippi river, above Memphis, not above the mouth of the Ohio river.

DERBY, *Ind.*—Ohio river, above Paducah, not above Cincinnati.

DES-ARKS, *Ark.*—White river, 210 miles from the Mississippi river, below Batesville.

DESKER'S LANDING, *La.*—Red river, not above Alexandria.

DE SOTO FRONT, *Miss.*—Mississippi river, above Greenville, not above Memphis.

DE SOTO, *Neb.*—Missouri river, 710 miles above its mouth, above Iatan.

DE SOTO, *Miss.*—Mississippi river, 405 miles above New Orleans, above Grand Gulf, not above Greenville.

DES MOINES CITY, *Mo.*—Mississippi river, 1363 miles above New Orleans, above the foot of the first, not above the foot of the second Rapids.

DES MOINES RIVER, *Iowa.*—Mississippi river, 1371 miles above New Orleans, above the foot of the first, not above the foot of the second Rapids.

DETROIT, *Ills.*—Illinois river, 181 miles above its mouth, above Beardstown, not above mouth of Fox river.

DEWITT, *Mo.*—Missouri river, 275 miles above its mouth, above Jefferson City, not above Lexington.

DESMOINE, JOHN B.—Red river, above Cane river, not above Grand Ecore.

DENNISON'S —Red river, above Grand Ecore, not above Shreveport.

DENT MILLS.—Yazoo river, not above Yazoo City.

DENMAN'S, Z. H., LANDING, *Miss.*—131 miles up Big Deer Creek.

DERRYBERRY.—Yazoo river, above Yazoo City, not above Leflore.

DEVIL'S ELBOW.—Mississippi river, above Memphis, not above the mouth of the Ohio.

DEVINEY'S LANDING.—112 miles up Sunflower river.

DEVIL'S ELBOW (CUMMINGS).—Red river, above Grand Ecore, not above Shreveport.

DEW DROP.—Yazoo river, above Yazoo City, not above Leflore.

DE YAMPERT, J. L.—Bayou Bartholomew, above Arkansas line, not above Portland.

DIAMOND'S PLACE, *Miss.*—Mississippi river, above Grand Gulf, not above Greenville.

DIAMOND'S LANDING, *Ark.*—Mississippi river, above Greenville, not above Memphis.

DICKSON'S LANDING, *La.*—Red river, above Grand Ecore, not above Shreveport.

DICK FLETCHER'S LANDING, *Ark.*—Arkansas river, 276 miles above Pine Bluff, not above Little Rock.

DICKSON'S (D. H.) LANDING, *Ark.*—Red river, 282 miles above Shreveport, above Fulton, not above Lanes port.

DIGG'S BLUFF, *Ark.*—Red river, 108 miles above Shreveport, above Carolina Bluff, not above Fulton.

DILLARD'S LANDING, *Ark.*—Red river, 172 miles above Shreveport, above Carolina Bluff, not above Fulton

DICKSON, B. S., MAJOR.—Red river, above Grand Ecore, not above Shreveport.

DICKSON'S, SARAH (UPPER PLACE).—Red river, above Fulton, not above Lanesport.

DICKSON, SARAH J. (FOSTER PLANTATION).—Red river, above foot of Raft, not above Fulton.

DICKSON, ANN, MRS. (WILLOW BEND).—Red river, above Shreveport, not above foot of Raft.

DICKSON, D. E.—Red river, above foot of Raft, not above Fulton.

DILLARD'S (BIG EDDY BEND).—Red river, above Lanesport, not above Mound City.

DIOZART'S, *La.*—Red river, not above Alexandria.

DIXIE PLACE (S. L. CALHOUN).—Red river, above Grand Ecore, not above Shreveport.

DIXIE REACH.—Red river, above Grand Ecore, not above Shreveport.

DIXIE.—Red river, above foot of Raft, not above Fulton.

DIXIE LANDING.—Mississippi river, near Helena.

DIXON'S, WM., LANDING.—Ouachita river, above Harrisonburg, not above Trenton.

DIXON'S, JIM.—Yazoo river, above Yazoo City, not above Leflore.

DIXON'S ISLAND.—Ouachita river, above Harrisonburg, not above Trenton.

DIZOART'S LANDING.—Red river, not above Alexandria.

DOCTOR FORT, *Ark.*—Old river, above Carolina Bluff, not above Fulton.

DOHERTY.—Ouachita river, not above Harrisonburg.

DOLES, W.—Red river, above Carolina Bluff, not above Fulton.

DILLARD'S POINT, *Ala.*—Alabama river, not above Selma.

DINGRAVE'S LANDING, *La*,—Ouachita river, above Harrisonburg, not above Trenton.

DOCK KING'S, *Ala.*—Alabama river, not above Selma.

DR. RAWLINGS' LANDING, *Ark.*—Arkansas river, 27 miles above Napoleon, below Arkansas Post.

DR. ROBB'S LANDING, *Ark.*—Arkansas river, 122 miles above Napoleon, above Arkansas Post, not above Pine Bluff.

DR. CENTER'S LANDING, *Ark*—Arkansas river, 466 miles above Napoleon, above Norristown, not above Fort Smith.

DR. STEWART'S LANDING, *La.*—Red river, 35 miles above Shreveport, not above Carolina Bluff.

DR. O. S. JONES' LANDING, *Ark.*—Red river, 271 miles above Shreveport, above Fulton, not above Lanesport.

DR. FOOT'S LANDING, *Texas.*—Red river, 313 miles above Shreveport, above Fulton, not above Lanesport.

DR. MURRAY'S, *Texas.*—Red river, 383 miles above Shreveport, above Lanesport, not above Mound City.

DR. BOYD'S, *Texas.*—Red river, 386 miles above Shreveport, above Lanesport, not above Mound City.

DR. GORDON'S, *Texas.*—Red river, 453 miles above Shreveport, above Lanesport, not above Mound City.

DODSON, *Ala.*—Tennessee river, above Florence, not below Eastport.

DODD'S, ELISHA, *La.*—Ouachita river, above Trenton, not above Alabama Landing.

DODSON'S LANDING, *Ala.*—Tombigbee river, above Gainesville, not above Columbus.

DODSON'S LANDING, *Mo.*—Mississippi river, above Greenville, not above Memphis.

DOLARD'S LANDING, *Mo.*—Mississippi river, 315 miles above New Orleans, above Bayou Sara, not above Grand Gulf.

DOLLY HYDE'S LANDING, *Ark.*—Arkansas river, 33 miles above Napoleon, above Arkansas Post, not above Pine Bluff.

DOMINIQUE'S LANDING, *La.*—Mississippi river, not above Bayou Sara.

DONALDSON'S LANDING, *Miss.*—Mississippi river, above Greenville, not above Memphis.

DONALDSON, MAJ., LANDING, *Ark.*—Arkansas river, 152 miles above Napoleon, above Arkansas Post, not above Pine Bluff.

DONALDSON, WM., LANDING, *Ky.*—Mississippi river, above Memphis, not above the mouth of the Ohio.

DONOHE'S FERRY, *Texas.*—Sabine river, above Sabine City, not above Belgrade.

DONIPHAN'S LANDING, *Ark.*—Currant river, a tributary of White and Black rivers.

DONIPHAN'S LANDING, *La.*—Tensas river, 42 miles from Trinity, not above the mouth of Bayou Macon.

DOOLEY'S' FERRY, *Ark.*—Red river, 217 miles above Shreveport, above Carolina Bluff, not above Fulton.

DOREMUS' LANDING, *Ala.*—Alabama river, above Selma, not above Wetumpka.

DOUGLAS' LANDING, *Ark.*—Arkansas river, 94 miles above Napoleon, above Arkansas Post, not above Pine Bluff

DOVER, *Tenn.*—Cumberland river, 103 miles above its mouth, not above Nashville.

DOVER, *Mo.*—Missouri river, above Jefferson City, not above Lexington.

DOVER, *Ky.*—Ohio river, 583 miles above its mouth, above Cincinnati.

DOWDY'S LANDING, *La.*—Ouachita river, above Harrisonburg, not above Trenton.

DOWN'S LANDING, *La.*—Ouachita river, above Harrisonburg, not above Trenton.

DONALDSONVILLE, *La.*—Mississippi river, not above Bayou Sara.

DORSEY, E.—Ouachita river, not above Harrisonburg.

DOUBS' OLD PLANTATION (or DR. FISHER).—Red river, above Grand Ecore, not above Shreveport.

DOUBLE OAK.—Yazoo river, above Yazoo City, not above Leflore.

DOUBLE EDDIES.—Red river, not above Alexandria.

DOUGLASS BROS.—Bayou Bartholomew, above Point Pleasant, not above Arkansas line.

DOUGLASS.—Red river, above Shreveport, not above foot of Raft.

DRAKE'S LANDING, *Ala.*—Warrior river, not above Tuscaloosa.

DRAKE'S LANDING, *Ala.*—Tombigbee river, above Gainesville, not above Columbus.

DRESDEN, *Mo.*—Mississippi river, above the mouth of the Ohio river, not above Alton.

DREW'S LANDING, *La.*—Ouachita river, above Harrisonburg, not above Trenton.

DRIESBACH'S LANDING, *Ala.*—Alabama river, not above Selma.

DOUGHERTY FERRY.—260 miles up Sunflower river.

DOWS, A (WOOD YARD).—Red river, above Alexandria, not above mouth Cane river.

DOWN'S PLACE, *Miss.*—162 miles up Big Deer Creek.

DOYALS.—48 miles up Bœuf river, not above Thomas' Landing.

DOYLE'S LANDING.—Bœuf river, not above Thomas' Landing.

DRUERISS, THOMAS (OLD POINT).—Red river, above foot of Raft, not above Fulton.

DRY BAYOU.—Tallahatchie river, not above Cassidy Bayou.

DRIGGIN'S LANDING, *Texas.*—Red river, above Lanesport, not above Mound City.

DRUMGOOD'S BLUFF, *Miss.*—Yazoo river, 31 miles from Vicksburg, below Yazoo City.

DRY BAYOU, *Mo*—Mississippi river, above Memphis, not above the mouth of the Ohio.

DUNN'S LANDING.—Bayou Bartholomew, above Arkansas line, not above Portland.

DUNN'S.—Yazoo river, above Yazoo City, not above Leflore.

DUNCANSBY LANDING.—Mississippi river, above Vicksburg, not above Greenville.

DUNCAN'S WOOD YARD.—76 miles up Bœuf river, above Thomas' Landing.

DUBUQUE, *Ia.*—Mississippi river, 1622 miles above New Orleans, above Galena.

DUBROCA LANDING, *Ala.*—Alabama river, not above Selma.

DUBOSE'S LANDING, *Ala.*—Tombigbee river, not above Demopolis.

DUCRO'S LANDING, *La.*—Mississippi river, 12 miles below New Orleans.

DUCKPORT, *La.*—Mississippi river, above Grand Gulf, not above Greenville.

DUDLEY DREAD, *Ark.*—White river, 306 miles above its mouth, below the junction of Black river.

DUGGIN'S LANDING, *Miss.*—Yallabusha river, not above Granada.

DUKE'S LANDING, *Ark.*—Mississippi river, above Greenville, not above Memphis.

DUNN'S LANDING, *Ark.*—Arkansas river, 113 miles above Napoleon, above Arkansas Post, not above Pine Bluff.

DUMBARTON'S LANDING, *La.*—Tensas river, 20 miles from Trinity, not above the mouth of Bayou Macon.

DUNN'S LANDING, *Ark.*—Mississippi river, above Greenville, not above Memphis.

DUNBAR'S LANDING, *La.*—Atchafalaya river, below Simmsport.

DUNCAN'S POINT, *La.*—Mississippi river, 120 miles above New Orleans, not above Bayou Sara.

DUNCAN'S LANDING, *La.*—Mississippi river, above Bayou Sara not above Grand Gulf.

DUFRAINE, J. A.—Red river, above Grand Ecore, not above Shreveport.

DUBUISON, P. J.—Yazoo river, not above Yazoo City.

DUBOIS, DR. & GOLDMAN.—Red river, above Grand Ecore, not above Shreveport.

DUCHEM.—82 miles up Bœuf river, above Thomas' Landing.

DUCOURNEAU'S LANDING.—Red river, above Cane river, not above Grand Ecore.

DUBLEUX, E. V.—Red river, above Cane river, not above Grand Ecore.

DULIU'S.—Arkansas river, above Arkansas Post, not above Pine Bluff.

DUKE'S BEND.—Red river, above foot of Raft, not above Fulton (or E. & B. Jacobs).

DUKE'S, T. J. LANDING.—Ouachita river, above Harrisonburg, not above Trenton.

DUKE, H.—Ouachita river, above Harrisonburg, not above Trenton.

DUKE'S.—Red river, above foot of Raft, not above Fulton.

DUKE, T. W.—Ouachita river, above Harrisonburg, not above Trenton.

DUNBARTON.—Mississippi river, above Grand Gulf, not above Greenville.

DUNCAN'S LANDING, *Mo.*—Mississippi river, above the mouth of the Ohio, not above Alton.

DUNLEITH, *Ill.*—Mississippi river, 1622 miles above New Orleans, above Galena.

DUNBARTON, *Miss.*—Mississippi river, 452 miles above New Orleans, above Grand Gulf, not above Greenville.

DUNDEE LANDING, *Ala.*—Alabama river, above Selma, not above Wetumpka.

DUNLAP'S LANDING, *Ala.*—Warrior river, not above Tuscaloosa.

DUPREE LANDING, *Ala.*—Alabama river, not above Selma.

DURANT'S BEND, *Ala.*—Alabama river, above Selma, not above Wetumpka.

DURAND'S, CHAS., LANDING, *La.*—Bayou Teche.

DURAND, CHAS , Jr., LANDING.—Bayou Teche.

DURANT'S LANDING, *La* —Red river, 431 miles from New Orleans, above Cane river, not above Grand Ecore.

DUTCH BEND, Ala.—Alabama river, above Selma, not above Wetumpka.

DUTY'S, P. LANDING, *La* —Red river, 486 miles above Shreveport, above White Oak Shoals.

DUVALL'S BLUFF, *Ark.*—White river, 176 miles above its mouth, below the junction of Black river.

DWIGHT, *Ark.*—Arkansas river, above Norristown, not above Fort Smith.

DYCUSBURG, *Ky.*—Cumberland river, not above Nashville.

DYDER'S LANDING, *Tenn*—Cumberland river, not above Nashville.

DYESBURG, *Tenn.*—Mississippi river, above Memphis, not above the mouth of the Ohio.

DUPREE, MAD.—Red river, above Grand Ecore, not above Shreveport.

DUREN LANDING.—156 miles up Sunflower river.

DUTCH BAYOU.—164 miles up Sunflower river.

DUTCHMEN.—Red river, above Shreveport, not above Carolina Bluff.

DYER'S LANDING.—267 miles up Sunflower river.

DYSAR, A. T.—121 miles up Bœuf river, above Thomas' Landing.

E

EADES FERRY, *Ala.*—Alabama river, not above Selma.

EADS' PORT.—South Pass, mouth of Mississippi river, below New Orleans.

EAGLE BEND, *La.*—Red river, above Grand Ecore, not above Shreveport.

EARLE'S, JAS. LANDING, *Ala.*—Alabama river, not above Selma.

EARLE'S, FRANK, LANDING.—Alabama river, not above Selma.

EASTPORT, *Ala.*—Warrior river, not above Tuscaloosa.

EASTPORT, *Tenn.*—Tennessee river.

ECONOMY, *Tenn.*—Ohio river, 986 miles above its mouth, above Cincinnati.

EAGLE CREEK.—Missouri river, 2598 miles from its mouth, above Iatan.

EAGLE BANK.—Yazoo river, above Yazoo City, not above Leflore.

EAGLE BEND.—Yazoo river, not above Yazoo City.

EAGLE ISLAND.—Bœuf river, not above Thomas' Landing.

EAGLE LAKE.—Yazoo river, above Yazoo City, not above Leflore.

EAGLE NEST BAYOU.—Red river, above Cane river, not above Grand Ecore.

EARL'S.—Tallahatchie river, not above Cassidy Bayou.

EAST AND WEST LANDING.—Red river, above Grand Ecore, not above Shreveport.

EAST POINT.—Red river, above Grand Ecore, not above Shreveport

EAST'S, SAM.—Tallahatchie river, not above Cassidy Bayou.

EATON'S, GEN'L, LANDING.—Arkansas river, above Pine Bluff, not above Little Rock.

ECHO LANDING, *La.*—Red river, below Alexandria.

EDEN.—Yazoo river, above Yazoo City, not above Leflore.

EDINGTON, W. H. (EAGLE BEND).—Mississippi river, above Grand Gulf, not above Greenville.

EDWARDS, CAPT.—Red river, above Fulton, not above Lanesport.

EDWINGS (or ANNA DALE).—Yazoo river, not above Yazoo City.

EDDYVILLE, *Ky.*—Cumberland river, 50 miles above its mouth, not above Nashville.

EDGEFIELD, *Tenn.*—Cumberland river, not above Nashville.

EDGEWOOD LANDING, *La.*—Mississippi river, above Grand Gulf, not above Greenville.

EDWARDS' LANDING, *La.*—Red river, not above Alexandria.

EDWARDS', J. P. LANDING, *Ala.*—Alabama river, above Selma, not above Wetumpka.

EDWARDS' LANDING, *Ala.*—Alabama river, above Selma, not above Wetumka.

EDDYVILLE, *Ind.*—Ohio river, 195 miles from its mouth, above Paducah, not above Cincinnati.

EGGS POINT, *Miss.*—Mississippi river, 524 miles above New Orleans, above Grand Gulf, not above Greenville.

EGYPT LANDING, *La.*—Bayou Macon, 55 miles from its mouth, not above Mohticello.

EGYPT.—Yazoo river, above Yazoo City, not above Leflore.

EGYPT (or R. Y. GRAVES).—Red river, above foot of Raft, not above Fulton.

ELDER GROVE (A. W. BEARD).—Red river, above Grand Ecore, not above Shreveport.

ELDORADO (VALENTINE'S).—Yazoo river, above Yazoo City.

ELLIOTT FERRY.—Red river, above Fulton, not above Lanesport.

ELLIS, *Miss.*—68 miles up Sunflower river.

ELLIS PLANTATION.—Red river, above Fulton, not above Lanesport.

EL DORADO LANDING, *Ark.*—Ouachita river, above Alabama Landing, not above Camden.

ELIZABETH, *Ark.*—White river, 220 miles from the Mississippi river, below Batesville.

ELIZABETHTOWN, *Ills.*—Ohio river, 90 miles above its mouth, above Paducah, not above Cincinnati.

ELIZABETHTOWN, *Va.*—Ohio river, 898 miles above its mouth, above Cincinnati.

ELLAWORA'S LANDING, *La.*—Mississippi river, above Grand Gulf, not above Greenville.

ELLIOTT'S, WIDOW, LANDING, *La.*—Mississippi river, above Bayou Sara, not above Grand Gulf.

ELLIOTT'S, CAPT., LANDING, *La.*—Mississippi river, above Bayou Sara, not above Grand Gulf.

ELLIS' LANDING, *Ala.*—Tombigbee river, not above Demopolis.

ELLIS', MRS., LANDING, *Ala.*—Alabama river, not above Selma.

ELM GROVE (DR. J. HUNTER).—Red river, above Grand Ecore, not above Shreveport.

ELMWOOD PLACE.—Red river, above Grand Ecore, not above Shreveport.

ELMWOOD PLANTATION.—Red river, above Grand Ecore, not above Shreveport.

ELMWOOD, *La.*—Atchafalaya river, not below Simmsport.

ELMWOOD, *Miss.*—Yazoo river, above Yazoo City, not above Leflore.

ELSER LAFAUCHE.—70 miles up Bœuf river, above Thomas' Landing.

ELTON.—Bayou Bartholomew, not above Point Pleasant.

ELLIS CLIFF, *Miss.*—Mississippi river, 250 miles above New Orleans, above Bayou Sara, not above Grand Gulf.

ELLIOTT'S, *Texas.*—Red river, 304 miles above Shreveport, above Fulton, not above Lanesport.

ELLIOTTSVILLE, *Ohio.*—Ohio river, 145 miles above its mouth, above Cincinnati.

ELM BLUFF, *Ala.*—Alabama river, 251 miles above Mobile, not above Selma.

EMPORIUM, *Ill.*—Ohio river, 6 miles above its mouth, not above Paducah.

ELTON'S LANDING, *La.*—Mississippi river, above Grand Gulf, not above Greenville.

EMLEY LANDING, *La.*—Black river, not above Harrisonburg.

EMERSON'S LANDING.—Black river, La.

EMPIRE, *Tenn.*—Cumberland river, not above Nashville.

EMLY'S LANDING, *La.*—Black river, La.

ENTERPRISE (JOHN WILLIAMS).—Red river, not above Alexandria.

ENGLISH TURN, *La.*—Mississippi river, 19 miles below New Orleans.

ENTERPRISE, *Ind.*—Ohio river, 215 miles above its mouth, above Paducah, not above Cincinnati.

EPPERNAL, W. C.—97 miles up Bœuf river, above Thomas' Landing.

EPPERSON PLANTATION (or JENE BOYCE PLACE.—Red river, above Lanesport, not above Mound City.

EPPS, CHAS. LANDING, *Miss.*—120 miles up Big Deer Creek.

ERIE'S LANDING, *Ala.*—Warrior river, not above Tuscaloosa.

ERWIN'S BLUFF, *Ark.*—Red river, 59 miles above Shreveport, above Carolina Bluff, not above Fulton.

ERWIN'S, MRS., LANDING, *Ala.*—Alabama river, not above Selma.

ERWIN'S, DR., LANDING, *Ala.*—Alabama river, not above Selma.

ERWIN'S UPPER LANDING, *Ala.*—Alabama river, not above Selma.

ERWIN'S LANDING, *Ala.*—Tombigbee river, above Gainesville, not above Columbus.

ERWIN, JAMES, *Ark.*—Red river, 275 miles above Shreveport, above Fulton, not above Lanesport.

ERNEST'S, B (WOOD YARD).—Red river, not above Alexandria.

ESLY (J. E. FRAZOU).—Red river, above Grand Ecore, not above Shreveport.

ESTATE OF R. FINN, *Ark.*—Red river, 266 miles above Shreveport, above Fulton, not above Lanesport.

ESTATE OF JANES, *Texas.*—Red river, 294 miles above Shreveport, above Fulton, not above Lanesport.

ESQUIRE LINTSE'S LANDING, *Ark.*—Little Red river, 1 mile from its mouth.

ESPERANCE LANDING, *La.*—Ouachita river, above Harrisonburg, not above Trenton.

ESTATE OF COPLEY, *La.*—Ouachita river, above Harrisonburg, not above Trenton.

ESTATE OF HENDRICK, *Ala.*—Warrior river, not above Tuscaloosa.

ESTATE OF JOS. BOOTH, *Ala.*—Alabama river, not above Selma.

ESTATE OF OLIVER, *Ala.*—Alabama river, not above Selma.

ESMERALDA.—Yazoo river, above Yazoo City, not above Leflore.

ESTELLE, ATTERBURY & CO. LANDING, *Miss.*—158 miles up Big Deer Creek.

ESTATE OF W. O. NIXON, *Ala.*—Alabama river, above Selma, not above Wetumpka.

ETHRIDGE LANDING, *Ala.*—Alabama river, not above Selma.

EUBANKS, *La.*—Ouachita river, not above Harrisonburg.

EUREKA.—Yazoo river, above Yazoo City, not above Leflore.

EUREKA, *La.*—Black river, not above Harrisonburg.

EUREKA PLANTATION.—Bayou Teche, near Morgan City.

EUREKA.—181 miles up Sunflower river.

EUTAW.—Tallahatchie river, not above Cassady Bayou.
EUFAULA, *Ala.*—Chatahootchie river.
EUNICE, *Ark.*—Mississippi river, 573 miles above New Orleans, above Greenville, not above the mouth of the Ohio river.
EUREKA LANDING, *La.*—Red river, above Grand Ecore, not above Shreveport.
EUREKA LANDING, *Ala.*—Alabama river, not above Selma.
EUTAW LANDING, *La.*—Black river, not above Harrisonburg.
EUTAW LANDING, *Miss.*—Mississippi river, above Greenville, not above Memphis.
EUTAW LANDING, *La.*—Bayou Macon, 4 miles from its mouth, not above Monticello.
EUTAW LANDING, *Ala.*—Warrior river, not above Tuscaloosa.
EVANSVILLE, *Ind.*—Ohio river, 187 miles above its mouth, above Paducah, not above Cincinnati.
EVANS' LANDING, *Mo.*—Mississippi river, above the mouth of the Ohio, not above Alton.
EVERGREEN, *La.*—Bayou Rouge.
EVENING SHADE.—Strawberry river, above Batesville.
EWINGS, DR.—Tallahatchie river, not above Cassady Bayou.
EWING'S LANDING.—Angelina river, Texas.
EXCELSIOR.—Yazoo river, above Yazoo City, not above Leflore.
EXCELSIOR.—Red river, above Alexandria, not above Cane river.
EXCELSIOR LANDING, *Ark.*—Mississippi river, above Greenville, not above Memphis.
EXTRA LANDING, *La.*—Ouachita river, above Harrisonburg, not above Trenton.

F

FAIR VIEW (P. HICKMAN'S).—Red river, above Alexandria, not above mouth of Cane river.
FAIRVIEW, *Miss.*—74 miles up Sunflower river.
FABEN'S RIVER, *Mo.*—Mississippi river, 1333 miles above New Orleans, above Alton, not above foot of first Rapids.
FAIRVIEW LANDING, *La.*—Mississippi river, above Bayou Sara, not above Grand Gulf.

FAIR DALE LANDING, *Ark.*—Arkansas river, 86 miles above Napoleon, above Arkansas Post, above Pine Bluff.

FAIRPORT, *Iowa.*—Mississippi river, 1493 miles above New Orleans, above second Rapids, not above Galena.

FAIRVIEW, *Miss.*—Mississippi river, 603 miles above New Orleans, above Greenville, not above Memphis.

FAIRMOUNT, *La.*—Red river, above Alexandria, not above mouth of Cane river.

FAIRFIELD LANDING, *Ala.*—Tombigbee river, above Gainesville, not above Columbus.

FAIR'S LANDING, *Ala.*—Alabama river, above Selma, not above Wetumpka.

FALLS OF ST. ANTHONY, *Minn.*—Mississippi river, 1869 miles above New Orleans, above Galena.

FALL'S LANDING, *Ga.*—Flint river, above Newton, not above Albany.

FALL'S LANDING, *Ind.*—Wabash river, above the Rapids, not above Terre Haute.

FALK'S, D., LANDING, *La.*—Ouachita river, above Harrisonburg, not above Trenton.

FALK'S, ROBERT, LANDING, *La.*—Ouachita river, above Harrisburg, not above Trenton.

FAUSSE POINT, *La.*—Near Bayou Teche.

FAVRON'S LANDING, *La.*—Red river, 443 miles above New Orleans, above Cane river, not above Grand Ecore.

FARLEIGH'S LANDING, *Ark.*—Arkansas river, above Arkansas Post, not above Pine Bluff.

FARRAR'S DR., LANDING, *La.*—Black river, La.

FARMERSVILLE, *La.*—Bayou D'Arbonne, not above.

FAUST, J. M., LANDING, *La.*—Ouachita river, above Harrisonburg, not above Trenton.

FAZZARD'S LANDING, *La.*—Red river, above Cotile, not above Grand Ecore.

FAISONIA.—Sunflower county, Sunflower river, Miss.

FAISONIA.—206 miles up Sunflower river.

FAIR PLAY.—Yazoo river, above Yazoo City, not above Leflore.

FALL'S PLACE, *Miss.*—166 miles up Big Deer Creek.

FAULK, D.—Ouachita river, above Harrisonburg, not above Trenton.
FAULK, L.—Ouachita river, above Harrisonburg, not above Trenton.
FAULK, R.—Ouachita river, above Harrisonburg, not above Trenton.
FAULKER.—Mississippi river, above Grand Gulf, not above Greenville.
FARRES.—Ouachita river, above Alabama Landing, not above Camden.
FARNESS, S. M.—Red river, above Grand Ecore, not above Shreveport.
FARMER PLACE, *Miss.*—151 miles up Big Deer Creek.
FARMER, W. W.—Bayou Bartholomew, not above Point Pleasant.
FARRELL'S BURT.—Arkansas river, not above Arkansas Post.
FEVER RIVER, *Ills.*—Mississippi river, 1607 miles above New Orleans, above second Rapids, not above Galena.
FELANAS LANDING, *Ala.*—Tombigbee river, not above Demopolis.
FERRAND'S LANDING.—Ouachita river, above Alabama Landing, not above Camden.
FERRAND'S LANDING, *La.*—Ouachita river, above Harrisonburg, not above Trenton.
FERRAND'S, J., LANDING, *La.*—Ouachita river, above Harrisonburg, not above Trenton.
FERRELL'S LANDING, *Ala.*—Tombigbee river, not above Demopolis.
FEAUGUIER EST.—Red river, not above Alexandria.
FELLERS, J. T.—Red river, not above Alexandria.
FERGUSON, A. LANDING, *Miss.*—151 miles up Big Deer Creek.
FELTUS LANDING, *Miss.*—182 miles up Big Deer Creek.
FIELD, HARRIS, LANDING, *Miss.*—Big Deer Creek.
FILHIOL'S, J. B., LANDING, *La.*—Ouachita river, above Harrissonburg, not above Trenton.
FILHIOL'S, GEO., LANDING, *La.*—Ouachita river, above Harrissonburg, not above Trenton.
FILE'S LANDING, *Ala.*—Tombigbee river, not above Demopolis.
FINCH'S FERRY, *Ala.*—Warrior river, not above Tuscaloosa.
FINNER'S, WM., LANDING, *Texas.*—Red river, 548 miles above Shreveport, above Mound City.
FIRST RAPIDS, *Mo.*—Mississippi river.
FIRST CHICKASAW BLUFF, *Tenn.*—Mississippi river, above Memphis, not above the mouth of the Ohio.

FISHER'S LANDING, *La.*—Mississippi river, above Bayou Sara, not above Grand Gulf.

FISHER & SIMM'S, *La.*—Red river, above Grand Ecore, not above Shreveport.

FIELD, SWANSON, LANDING, *Miss.*—Big Deer Creek.

FIFE.—Ouachita river, above Harrisonburg, not above Trenton.

FILE'S, JESSEE.—Bayou Bartholomew, above Arkansas line, not above Portland.

FINLAY (or LEWIS).—Red river, above foot of Raft, not above Fulton.

FIRE POINT, *La.*—Red river, above Shreveport, not above Carolina Bluff.

FISHER'S.—Red river, above Shreveport, not above foot of Raft.

FISHER'S, DR. (or DOUB'S OLD PLANTATION.—Red river, above Grand Ecore, not above Shreveport.

FISHER'S LANDING, *La.*—Black river, La.

FISHER'S LANDING, *La.*—Mississippi river, not above Bayou Sara.

FITZPATRICK'S LANDING, *Ala.*—Alabama river, above Selma, not above Wetumpka.

FLAGLAND.—Red river, above Alexandria, not above mouth of Cane river.

FLAT BAYOU.—Red river, above Grand Ecore, not above Shreveport.

FLEMMING, CHAS. B.—Rèd river, above foot of Raft, not above Fulton.

FLETA'S LANDING.—Mississippi river, above Bayou Sara, not above Grand Gulf.

FLETA'S LANDING.—Mississippi river, below New Orleans.

FLETCHER'S, JUDGE.—Arkansas river, not above Arkansas Post.

FLETCHER'S.—Ouachita river, above Alabama Landing, not above Camden.

FLINT'S, MRS.—Red river, above Alexandria, not above Cane river.

FLORENCE, *Ga.*—Challahoochie river, above Eufaula, not above Columbus.

FLORENCE.—Red river, above Grand Ecore, not above Shreveport.

FLORIDA, *Miss.*—158 miles up Big Deer Creek.

FLORNEAU.—Red river, not above Alexandria.

FLOURNLY.—Mississippi river, above Grand Gulf, not above Greenville.

FLAG'S LANDING, *La.*—Red river, above Cotile, not above Grand Ecore.

FLAT ROCK, *Ark.*—Arkansas river, 531 miles above Napoleon, above Norristown, not above Fort Smith.

FLEMING'S LANDING, *Ala.*—Tombigbee river, above Demopolis, not above Gainesville.

FLEMING'S BLUFF, *La.*—Red river, above Grand Ecore, not above Shreveport.

FLETCHER LAKE, *La.*—Tensas river, not above mouth Bayou Macon.

FLETCHER'S LANDING, *Ark.*—Mississippi river, above Greenville, not above Memphis.

FLINN'S, J. P. LANDING, *Ala.*—Alabama river, not above Selma.

FLINT RIVER, *Ga.*—Not above Newtown.

FLINT ISLAND.—Ohio river, above Paducah, not above Cincinnati.

FLORENCE, *Tenn.*—Tennessee river, 280 miles above its mouth, above Eastport.

FLORANCE, *Neb.*—Missouri river, 695 miles above its mouth, above Iatan.

FLORANCE, *Ills.*—Illinois river, 55 miles above its mouth, not above Beardstown.

FLORAE PLANTATION, *La.*—Bayou Lafourche.

FLOYD'S LANDING, *Ark.*—Bayou Macon, 201 miles from its mouth, above Monticello.

FLOYD SMITH'S LANDING, *Ark.*—Arkansas river, 64 miles above Napoleon, above Arkansas Post, not above Pine Bluff.

FLORIDA, *Ark.*—Mississippi river, above Greenville, not above the mouth of the Ohio.

FLOWER McGREGOR'S LANDING, *Ark.*—Arkansas river, 185 miles above Napoleon, above Pine Bluff, not above Little Rock.

FLOWER MOUND, *La.*—Black river.

FLOWERY MOUND, *La.*—Black river, La., not above Harrisonburg.

FLOT'S LANDING.—Alabama river, not above Selma.

FLYNN'S LANDING, *La.*—Tensas river, 35 miles from Trinity, not above the mouth of Bayou Macon.

FLUCKER'S LANDING.—Bayou Bartholomew, not above Point Pleasant.

FLUCKER WAREHOUSE.—Bayou Bartholomew, not above Point Pleasant.

FLUITT'S.—Ouachita river, above Harrisonburg, not above Trenton.

FLUITT'S, JNO.—Ouachita river, above Harrisonburg, not above Trenton.

FOGLEMAN'S WOODYARD, *Ark.*—Mississippi river, above Greenville, not above Memphis.

FOIVELER'S LANDING, *Tenn.*—Tennessee river, not above Eastport.

FONTAINE LANDING, *La.*—Mississippi river, not above Bayou Sara.

FOOT OF LITTLE ISLAND, *Ark.*—White river, 44 miles above its mouth, below the junction of Black river.

FOOT OF BIG ISLAND, *Ark.*—White river, 54 miles above its month, below the junction of Black river.

FOOT OF TREMBLE ISLAND, *Ark.*—White river, 193 miles above its mouth, below the junction of Black river.

FOOT OF GRAND ISLAND, *Ills.*—Illinois river, above Beardstown, not above the mouth of Fox river.

FOOT OF ISLAND No. 14.—Mississippi river, above Greenville, not above Memphis.

FOOTE'S, L. B. LANDING, *Ark.*—Red river, 176 miles above Shreveport, above Carolina Bluff, not above Fulton.

FOOTE'S, J. B. LANDING, *Texas.*—Red river, 309 miles above Shreveport, above Fulton, not above Lanesport.

FOOL RIVER.—Bœuf river, not above Thomas' Landing.

FORDSVILLE, *Miss.*—Pearl river, above Gainesville, not above Columbia.

FORD'S, or COOK'S LANDING.—172 miles up Sunflower river.

FORD'S LANDING.—Mississippi river, above Grand Gulf, not above Greenville.

FORDA DEER.—Big Deer Creek, 109 miles from Vicksburg.

FORD'S LAKE.—Big Deer Creek, 120 miles up.

FORMOSA.—Ouachita river, above Harrisonburg, not above Trenton.

FORMOSA, *Mo.*—Missouri river, 140 miles above its mouth, not above Jefferson City.

FOREST HOME.—Ouachita river, above Harrisonburg, not above Trenton.

FORSYTH'S LANDING, *Ark.*—White river, above Batesville.

FOREST HOME, *Miss.*—Mississippi river, 421 miles above New Orleans, above Grand Gulf, not above Greenville.

FORDVILLE, *Miss.*—Pearl river, above Gainesville, not above Columbia.

FORT ADAMS, *La.*—Mississippi river, 258 miles above New Orleans, above Bayou Sara, not above Grand Gulf.

FORT ST. PHILIP, *La.*—Mississippi river, 73 miles below New Orleans.

FORT ST. PHILIP, *Ala.*—Alabama river, 222 miles above Mobile, not above Selma.

FORT SMITH, *Ark.*—Arkansas river, 548 miles above Napoleon, above Norristown.

FORT JACKSON, *La.*—Mississippi river, 73 miles below New Orleans.

FORT PILLOW, *Tenn.*—Mississippi river, 885 miles above New Orleans, above Memphis, not above the mouth of the Ohio.

FORT BYRON.—Ouachita river, above Alabama Landing, not above Camden.

FORT COFFEE.--Arkansas river, above Fort Smith.

FORT COPELINE.—Missouri river, 2212 miles from its mouth, above Iatan.

FORT CLAGGETT.—Missouri river, 2561 miles from its mouth, above Iatan.

FORT STEVENSON.—Missouri river, 1724 miles from its mouth, above Iatan.

FORT PLACE.—Yazoo river, above Yazoo City, not above Leflore.

FORT PEMBERTON.—Yazoo river, above Yazoo City, not above Leflore.

FORT BENTON.—Missouri river, 2663 miles from its mouth, above Iatan.

FORT BERTHOLD.—Missouri river, 1749 miles from its mouth, above Iatan.

FORT BUFORT.—Missouri river, 1994 miles from its mouth, above Iatan.

FORT HAWLEY.—Missouri river, 2434 miles from its mouth, above Iatan.

FORT LINCOLN.—Missouri river, 1609 miles from its mouth, above Iatan.

FORT LORING.—Yazoo river, above Yazoo City, not above Leflore.

FORT RICE.—Missouri river, 1569 miles above its mouth, above Iatan.

FORT THOMPSON.—Missouri river, 1230 miles above its mouth, above Iatan.

FORT PECK.—Missouri river, 2227 miles from its mouth above Iatan.

FORT RANDALL.—Missouri river, 1102 miles from its mouth, above Iatan.

FORT SULLY.—Missouri river, 1359 miles from its mouth, above Iatan.

FORT JACKSON, *Ala.*—Alabama river, above Selma.

FORT GIBSON, *Ark.*—Arkansas river, 683 miles above Napoleon, above Fort Smith.

FORT CHESTER, *Ill.*—Mississippi river, 1178 miles above New Orleans, above the mouth of the Ohio, not above Alton.

FORT COFFEE, *Ark.*—Arkansas river, 569 miles above Napoleon, above Fort Smith, not above Fort Gibson.

FORT CALHOUN, *Neb.*—Missouri river, 695 miles above its mouth, above Iatan.

FORT LEAVENWORTH, *Kan.*—Missouri river, 439 miles above its mouth, above Lexington, not above Iatan.

FORT MITCHELL, *Ga.*—Chattahoochee river, not above Columbus.

FORT GAINES, *Ga.*—Chattahoochee river, not above Columbus.

FORT MADISON, *Iowa.*—Mississippi river, 1397 miles above New Orleans, above second Rapids, not above Galena.

FORT CRAWFORD, *Wis.*—Mississippi river, 1675 miles above New Orleans, above Galena.

FORT SNELLING, *Minn.*—Mississippi river, 1861 miles above New Orleans, above Galena.

FORT RIPLEY, *Minn.*—Mississippi river, 1993 miles above New Orleans, above Galena.

FORT MASSACRE, *Ills.*—Ohio river, 46 miles above its mouth, not above Paducah.

FORT TOWNSEND, *Tex.*—Red river, 516 miles above Shreveport, above Mound City.

FORT HENRY, *Tenn.*—Tennessee river, 65 miles above its mouth, not above Eastport.

FORT DONELSON, *Tenn.*—Tennessee river, 65 miles above its mouth, not above Eastport.

FORT PINCKNEY, *Miss.*—Mississippi river, above New Orleans, above Greenville, not above Memphis.

FORT HARRIS, *Miss.*—Mississippi river, 907 miles above New Orleans, above Greenville, not above Memphis.

FORT RANDOLPH, *Tenn.*—Mississippi river, 965 miles above New Orleans, above Memphis, not above mouth of the Ohio.

FORT WRIGHT, *Tenn.*—Mississippi river, 975 miles above New Orleans, above Memphis, not above mouth of the Ohio.

FORT HOLT, *Ky.*—Mississippi river, 1145 miles above New Orleans, above Memphis, not above mouth of Ohio.

FORT JEFFERSON, *Ky.*—Mississippi river, 1135 miles above New Orleans, above Memphis, not above mouth of the Ohio.

FORT CHARTRES, *Mo.*—Mississippi river, 1280 miles above New Orleans, above the mouth of the Ohio river, not above Alton.

FORT DE RUSSY, *La.*—Red river, 200 miles from New Orleans, not above Alexandria.

FORT SCOTT, *Ga.*—Flint river, not above Newton.

FORT FARRAR, *Texas.*—Neches river, above the junction of the Angelina river.

FORT WORTH, *Texas.*—Trinity river, above Magnolia Landing.

FORT JACKSON, *La.*—Ouachita river, above Harrisonburg, not above Trenton.

FORT STODDARD, *Ala.*—Tombigbee river, not above Demopolis.

FORT PINEY, *Ark.*—Mississippi river, above Greenville, not above Memphis.

FOSTER'S, HARDY, LANDING, *Ala.*—Warrior river, not above Tuscaloosa.

FOSTER'S LANDING, *Ala.*—Warrior river, not above Tuscaloosa.

FOSTER'S, MRS. ANN, LANDING, *Ala.*—Warrior river, not above Tuscaloosa.

FOSTER'S, J. COLLIER, LANDING, *Ala.*—Warrior river, not above Tuscaloosa.

FOSTER'S, J. H., LANDING, *Ala.*—Warrior river, not above Tuscaloosa.

FOSTER'S FERRY, *Ala*—Warrior river, not above Tuscaloosa.

FOSTER'S, GEO., LANDING, *Ala.*—Alabama river, not above Selma.

FOSTER'S, ARTHUR, LANDING, *Ala*—Alabama river, not above Selma.

FOX'S LANDING, *Miss.*—Tombigbee river, above Columbus, not above Cotton Gin Port.

FORTSON'S LANDING, *La.*—Red river, above Grand Ecore, not above Shreveport.

FORT, J. P., DR.—Red river, above Fulton, not above Lanesport.

FORTS, DR.—Red river, above foot of Raft, not above Fulton.

FOSTER PLANTATION (SARAH J. DICKSON).—Red river, above foot of Raft, not above Fulton.

FOSTER (or LOCKS).—Red river, above Fulton, not above Lanesport.

FOUCHE PLACE.—Arkansas river, above Pine Bluff, not above Little Rock.

FRANKLIN, *La.*—Bayou Teche.

FRANKLIN, *Mo.*—Missouri river, above Jefferson City, not above Lexington.

FRANKLIN, *Ga.*—Chattahootchee river, not above Columbus.

FRANKLIN FUR, *Ohio*—Ohio river, above Cincinnati.

FRANKLINTON, *La.*—Bogue Chitto river.

FRANKFORD, *Ind.*—Mississippi river, 1645 miles above New Orleans, above Galena.

FRAZIER'S LANDING, *La.*—Red river, above Cotile, not above Grand Ecore.

FRANKLIN (or GRANVILLE).—Red river, above Grand Ecore, not above Shreveport.

FRANZON'S, J. E. (EELY).—Red river, above Grand Ecore, not above Shreveport.

FRAVUKELAN (RED HILL).—Red river, above Grand Ecore, not above Shreveport.

FRAOUKELAL, *La.*—Red river, above Grand Ecore, not above Shreveport.

FRAZIER'S.—Red river, not above Alexandria.

FRAZIER'S, JOHN.—Red river, above Cane river, not above Grand Ecore.

FREILY, DAVID, LANDING, *Miss.*—155 miles up Big Deer Creek.

FREMONT, NOAH.—Bayou Bartholomew, above Point Pleasant, not above Arkansas line.

FRENCH BEND.—Yazoo river, above Yazoo City, not above Leflore.

FRENCHMAN.—Ouachita river, above Alabama Landing, not above Camden.

FREEDMAN.—108 miles up Bœuf river, above Thomas' Landing.

FREEDMAN.—112 miles up Bœuf river, above Thomas' Landing.

FREEDMEN'S BUREAU.—Yazoo river, above Yazoo City, not above Leflore.

FREE NIGGER LANDING.—137 miles up Sunflower river.

FRELLSEN PLANTATION.—Mississippi river, not above Bayou Sara.

FROLTER & COCK'S.—Red river, above foot of Raft, not above Fulton.

FROLSON, COL.—2 miles up Kiomittia river, Ind. Terr., Red river, above Mound City.

FRANKLIN, *La.*—Red river, above Grand Ecore, not above Shreveport.

FRANK'S, COL., LANDING, *Miss.*—Tombigbee river, above Columbus, not above Cotton Gin Port.

FRENCH'S LANDING, *Tenn.*—Cumberland river, not above Nashville.

FREDVILLE, *Miss.*—Pearl river, above Gainesville, not above Columbia.

FREDERICK'S LANDING, *Ala.*—Alabama river, above Selma, not above Wetumpka.

FRENCH PORT.—Ouachita river, 483 miles from the mouth of Old river, above Alabama Landing, not above Camden.

FRENCH JACK'S LANDING, *Ark.*—Arkansas river, 585 miles above Napoleon, above Fort Smith, not above Fort Gibson.

FRENCH'S LANDING, *Ala.*—Alabama river, 90 miles above Mobile, not above Selma.

FRENCHMEN'S LANDING, *Mo.*—Mississippi river, 1275 miles above New Orleans, above the mouth of the Ohio river, not above Alton.

FREEDOM, *Penn.*—Ohio river, 980 miles above its mouth, above Cincinnati.

FREDONIA, *Ind.*—Ohio river, 315 miles above its mouth, above Paducah, not above Cincinnati.

FREDERICKSVILLE, *Ills.*—Illinois river, 93 miles above its mouth, above Beardstown, not above the mouth of Fox river.

FRENIER'S POINT, *La.*—Jackson railroad, 24 miles from New Orleans.

FRIAR'S POINT, *Miss.*—Mississippi river, 715 miles above New Orleans, above Greenville, not above Memphis.

FROG BAYOU, *Ark.*—Arkansas river, 506 miles above Napoleon, above Norristown, not above Fort Smith.

FULLER'S.—Ouachita river, above Harrisonburg, not above Trenton.

FULSOM'S, *La.*—Red river, above Grand Ecore, not above Shreveport.

FROZEN ROCK, *Ark.*—Arkansas river, 676 miles above Napoleon, above Fort Smith, not above Fort Gibson.

FULLITT'S, D. LANDING, *La.*—Ouachita river, above Harrisonburg, not above Trenton.

FULTON PORT, *Tenn.*—Mississippii river, above Memphis, not above the mouth of the Ohio.

FULTON, *Tenn.*—Mississippi river, 884 above New Orleans, above Memphis, not above the mouth of the Ohio.

FULTON, *Ark.*—Red river, 247 miles above Shreveport.

FULTON CITY, *Ind.*—Mississippi river, 1561 miles above New Orleans, above second Rapids, not above Galena.

FULTON PLACE, *Texas.*—Red river, 566 miles above Shreveport, above Mound City.

FURGUSON'S, WIDOW, LANDING.—Red river, not above Alexandria.

FUR POINT (or LE ARNICK'S).—Red river, above Shreveport, not above foot of Raft.

FUQUA (or LONGWOOD).—Yazoo river, not above Yazoo City.

G

GAFFIN, MRS., LANDING, *Texas.*—Red river, 468 miles above Shreveport, above Lanesport, not above Mound City.

GAGER'S POINT, *Ark.*—White river, below the junction of Black river.

GAINESVILLE, *Miss.*—Pearl river.

GAINESVILLE, *Ala.*—Tombigbee river.

GAINESVILLE, *Tenn.*—Cumberland river, above Nashville, not above Gainesboro.

GAINESTOWN, *Ala.*—Alabama river, 98 miles above Mobile, not above Selma.

GAINESBORO, *Tenn.*—Cumberland river, above Nashville.

GAINES' LANDING, *Ark.*—Mississippi river, 538 miles above New Orleans, above Greenville, not above Memphis.

GAINES' & GUNTER'S LANDING, *Ark.*—Mississippi river, 575 miles above New Orleans, above Greenville, not above Memphis.

GAINES' LANDING, *La.*—Red river, not above Alexandria.

GAINES' FERRY, *Texas.*—Sabine river, above Belgrade, not above Hamilton.

GAINESTOWN, *Ala.*—Alabama river, not above Selma.

GAINES', GEO. LANDING, *Ala.*—Tombigbee river, not above Demopolis.

GALLOWAY'SLANDING, *Tenn.*—Tennessee river, not above Eastport.

GALENA, *Ills.*—Mississippi river, above the foot of second Rapids.

GALLA ROCK, *Ark.*—Arkansas river, 370 miles above Napoleon, above Little Rock, not above Norristown.

GALLATIN, *Tenn.*—Cumberland river, 25 miles north-east of Nashville.

GALLIPOLIS, *Ohio.*—Ohio river, 734 miles above its mouth, above Cincinnati.

GARRETSON'S LANDING, *Ark.*—Arkansas river, 127 miles above Napoleon, above Arkansas Post, not above Pine Bluff.

GARRETT'S MILL, *Ala.*—Tombigbee river, above Demopolis, not above Gainesville.

GADDIS LANDING, *Miss.*—177 miles up Big Deer Creek.

GAFFNEY'S, MRS.—Red river, above Rowland and Mound City.

GAHAGAN'S, MRS.—Ouachita river, above Alabama Landing, not above Camden.

GAINO LANDING.—272 miles up Sunflower river.

GALVEZ PORT, *La.*—Amite river.

GAINS, MRS.—Red river, above Shreveport, not above Carolina Bluff (opposite Shreveport).

GALE'S, JIM.—Yazoo river, not above Yazoo City.

GALTNEY'S.—Yazoo river, not above Yazoo City.

GANDERSBURG.—Yazoo river, not above Yazoo City.

GANDERCLEUGH.—Yazoo river, not above Yazoo City.

GANNIER, VALERY.—Red river, above Grand Ecore, not above Shreveport.

GARLAND, GEN.—Red river, above Lanesport, not above Mound City.

GARLAND & LEE (or FISHER'S PRAIRIE).—Red river, above foot of Raft, not above Fulton.

GARLAND'S NEW PLACE.—Red river, above foot of Raft, not above Fulton.

GARNETT'S.—Tallahatchie river, above Cassidy Bayou, not above Cold Water.

GARRETT'S, GEN.—Arkansas river, above Arkansas Post, not above Pine Bluff.

GARVIN FERRY.—197 miles up Sunflower river.

GASCONADE.—Missouri river, not above Jefferson City.

GASPARD LANDING.—Red river, not above Alexandria.

GASPAN'S MILL.—Ouachita river, above Trenton, not above Alabama Landing.

GASSEWAY.—Yazoo river, above Yazoo City, not above Leflore.

GASTER'S (or SMITH'S).—80 miles up Bœuf river, above Thomas' Landing.

GASPARD, *La.*—Red river, not above Alexandria.

GARRETT'S LANDING, *La.*—Ouachita river, above Harrisonburg, not above Trenton.

GARDNER'S, V. H. LANDING, *Ala.*—Alabama river, above Selma, not above Wetumpka.

GASCONDA RIVER, *Mo.*—Missouri river, above its mouth, not above Jefferson City.

GATLIN'S LANDING, *La.*—Red river, above Grand Ecore, not above Shreveport.

GATLIN'S GIN, *La.*—Red river, above Grand Ecore, not above Shreveport.

GAUSSE'S LANDING, *Ala.*—Alabama river, above Selma, not above Wetumpka.

GAYOSO, *Mo.*—Mississippi river, above Memphis, not above the mouth of the Ohio.

GAY'S LANDING, *Ark.*—Arkansas river, 341 miles above Napoleon, above Little Rock, not above Norristown.

GAY'S PLANTATION, *La.*—Mississippi river, not above Bayou Sara.

GAY'S LANDING, *Ala.*—Tombigbee river, not above Demopolis.

GEM PLANTATION, *La.*—Ouachita river, above Harrisonburg, not above Trenton.

GENEVA, *Texas.*—Trinity river, above Smithville, not above Magnolia landing.

GEN. WILLIAM'S LANDING, *Ark.*—Arkansas river, 112 miles above Napoleon, above Arkansas Post, not above Pine Bluff.

GEN. GARRETT'S LANDING, *Ark.*—Arkansas river, 126 miles above Napoleon, above Arkansas Post, not above Pine Bluff.

GEN. YELL'S LANDING, *Ark*—Arkansas river, 175 miles above Napoleon, above Pine Bluff, not above Little Rock.

GEN. WARREN'S LANDING, *Ark.*—Arkansas river, 184 miles above Napoleon, above Pine Bluff, not above Little Rock.

GEN. EATON'S LANDING, *Ark.*—Arkansas river, 196 miles above Napoleon, above Pine Bluff, not above Little Rock.

GEN. CLAYTON'S (OAKLAND), *Ark.*—Arkansas river, 131 miles above Arkansas Post, not above Pine Bluff.

GEORGETOWN, *Penn.*—Ohio river, 961 miles above its mouth, above Cincinnati.

GENEVA, *Ala.*—Choctawatchee river.

GEORGETOWN, *Ga.*—Chattahoochee river, not above Columbus.

GEORGETOWN, *Miss.*—Pearl river, above Columbia.

GEORGE'S, B. W. LANDING, *La.*—Red river, 20 miles above Shreveport, not above Black Bayou.

GENEVA PLANTATION, *La.*—Mississippi river, above Bayou Sara, not above Grand Gulf.

GENEVA.—191 miles up Sunflower river.

GEORGE'S, MAD.—Red river, not above Alexandria.

GERALD, FRANK.—88 miles up Bœuf river, above Thomas' Landing.

GERSON.—Yazoo river, above Yazoo City, not above Leflore.

GERMAN BEND.—Yazoo river, above Yazoo City, not above Leflore.

GHENT, *Ky.*—Ohio river, 474 miles above its mouth, above Paducah, not above Cincinnati.

GIBB'S FERRY, *Tenn.*—Tennessee river, not above Eastport.

GIBSON'S LANDING, *La.*—Mississippi river, above Bayou Sara, not above Grand Gulf.

GIBSON'S LANDING, *Miss.*—Mississippi river, above Grand Gulf, not above Greenville.

GIBBON'S, JUDGE LANDING. *Ala.*—Alabama river, not above Selma.

GIFFORD'S LANDING, *Ark.*—Arkansas river, 35 miles above Napoleon, below Arkansas Post.

GILL'S LANDING, *Texas.*—Red river, 508 miles above Shreveport, above Mound City.

GILLAD, *Ill.*—Mississippi river, 1253 miles above New Orleans, above Alton, not above first Rapids.

GILLESPIES' LANDING, *La.*—Black river, La.

GILLOWS', P. O. *Ark.*—Mississippi river, above Greenville, not above Memphis.

GILMORE'S LANDING, *La.*—Red river, above Grand Ecore, not above Shreveport.

GIRARD'S LANDING, *Ala.*—Chattahootchee river, not above Columbus.

GISHAM'S LANDING, *Ala.*—Alabama river, above Selma, not above Wetumpka.

GIB BARNES.—Yazoo river, above Yazoo City, not above Leflore.

GIBSON'S (or BOUTROE'S).—Red river, above Cane river, not above Grand Ecore.

GIBSON'S.—Ouachita river, above Harrisonburg, not above Trenton.

GIBSON'S, MRS.—Ouachita river, above Harrisonburg, not above Trenton.

GILL'S LANDING.—120 miles up Sunflower river.

GILLAM'S (or M. LISSO.—Red river, above Grand Ecore, not above Shreveport.

GILLESPIE (or STARLIGHT).—Red river, above Grand Ecore, not above Shreveport.

GILMER.—Up Shurlety, Texas.

GILMER.—Red river, above foot of Raft, not above Fulton.

GILMER'S.—Red river, above Shreveport, not above foot of Raft.

GIROD, MRS.—93 miles up Bœuf river, above Thomas' Landing.

GLASSGOW, *Mo.*—Missouri river, above Jefferson, not above Lexington.

GLASGOW, *Ill.*—Illinois river, not above Beardstown.

GLASSGOW, *Penn.*—Ohio river, 961 miles above its mouth, above Cincinnati.

GLASS', J. B. LANDING, *Ark*—Red river, 273 miles above Shreveport, above Fulton, not above Lanesport.

GLASS', J. M. LANDING, *Texas.*—Red river, 357 miles above Shreveport, above Fulton, not above Lanesport.

GLENCER'S LANDING, *Ark.*—Mississippi river, above Greenville, not above Memphis.

GLOVER'S LANDING, *Ala.*—Tombigbee river, not above Demopolis.

GLADE, ANNY.—Red river, above Shreveport, not above Carolina Bluff.

GLANVILLE.—193 miles up Sunflower river.

GLASS, JOE, ESTATE OF.—Red river, above Fulton, not above Lanesport.

GLENCOE.—Tallahatchie river, above Cassidy Bayou, not above Cold Water.

GLEN BURR.—Tallahatchie river, not above Cassidy Bayou.

GLEN, MARY.—Yazoo river, above Yazoo City, not above Leflore.

GLENDORA.—Tallahatchie river, above Cassidy Bayou, not above Cold Water.

GLEN OAK.—Yazoo river, above Yazoo City, not above Leflore.

GLENDALE.—193 miles up Sunflower river.

GILMER, DICK.—Red river, above Grand Ecore, not above Shreveport.

GLENDORA.—Ouachita river, above Trenton, not above Alabama Landing.

GLOVER'S BAR (L. J. SMITH).—Red river, not above Alexandria.

GLOVER (COL'D).—Bayou Bartholomew, not above Point Pleasant.

GLOVER'S, M., LANDING, *Texas.*—Red river, 359 miles above Shreveport, above Fulton, not above Lanesport.

GLOVERY'S LANDING, *La.*—Red river, not above Alexandria.

GOASEY'S, PETER C.—Yazoo river, not above Yazoo City.

GOLDEN'S, ELI.—Yazoo river, above Yazoo City, not above Leflore.

GOLDEN'S, I.—Yazoo river, above Yazoo City, not above Leflore.

GOLD POINT.—Red river, above Shreveport, not above foot of Raft.

GOOSE CREEK.—Bœuf river, not above Thomas' Landing.

GOOD HOPE.—Yazoo river, above Yazoo City, not above Leflore.

GOODLOE, W. W. *Miss.*—123 miles up Big Deer Creek.

GORDON'S BLUFF.—Bayou Bartholomew, above Point Pleasant, not above Arkansas line.

GORDON'S LANDING (or BARBIN'S(.—Red river, not above Alexandria.

GOSKINS' (B. BLAKE.—Yazoo river, not above Yazoo City.

GOBEAU'S LANDING, *La.*—Tensas river, 10 miles from Trinity, not above mouth of Bayou Macon.

GODFREY'S LANDING, *La.*—Ouachita river, above Harrisonburg, not above Trenton.

GODBOLD'S, JR., LANDING, *Ala.*—Alabama river, not above Selma.

GOLCONDA, *Ills.*—Ohio river, 70 miles from its mouth, above Paducah, not above Cincinnati.

GOLDEN LAKE, *Ark.*—Mississippi river, above Greenville, not above Memphis.

GOLDEN GROVE, *La.*—Mississippi river, 50 miles New Orleans, not above Bayou Sara.

GOLNE'S LANDING, *Ark.*—Mississippi river, 655 miles above New Orleans, above Greenville, not above Memphis.

GOLD BUTTON LANDING, *Miss.*—Mississippi river, above Bayou Sara, not above Grand Gulf.

GOLDEN GROVE LANDING, *La.*—Mississippi river, not above Bayou Sara.

GOOSE ISLAND, *Mo.*—Mississippi river, above the mouth of the Ohio river, not above Alton.

GOODMAN, *Miss.*—Jackson railroad, 234 miles from New Orleans.

GOODRICH'S LANDING, *La.*—Mississippi river, above Grand Gulf, not above Greenville.

GOOD HOPE, *La.*—Mississippi river, 28 miles above New Orleans, not above Bayou Sara.

GOODWIN'S LANDING (or ULSTER PLACE), *La.*--Red river, above Grand Ecore, not above Shreveport.

GOODWIN'S LANDING, *La.*—Black river, La.

GOODRICH'S LANDING, *La.*—Mississippi river, above Grand Gulf, not above Greenville.

GORDON'S, S. J. C., LANDING, *La.*—Atchafalaya river, below Simmsport.

GORDON'S, T. D., LANDING, *La.*—Atchafalaya river, below Simmsport.

GORDON'S, W. C. LANDING, *La.*—Atchafalaya river, below Simmsport.

GORDON'S, T. H., LANDING, *La.*—Atchafalaya river, below Simmsport.

GORDON'S, MRS. M. S., LANDING, *La.*—Atchafalaya river, below Simmsport.

GORE'S, J. W., LANDING, *Miss.*—Tombigbee river, above Columbus, not above Cotton Gin Port.

GOSPORT, *Ala.*—Alabama river, 107 miles above Mobile, below Selma.

GOSLIN'S LANDING, *Ark.*—Little Red river, 12 miles above its mouth, below the junction of Black and White rivers.

GOSTER'S LANDING, *Ark.*—Mississippi river, 655 miles above its mouth, above Greenville, not above Memphis.

GOUGE'S, DR. LANDING, *La.*—Black river, not above Harrisonburgh.

GOZA'S LANDING, *La.*—Mississippii river, above Grand Gulf, not above Greenville.

GRAND CLAIRE, *Ark.*—White river, 332 miles above its mouth, below the junction of Black river.

GRAND ECORE, *La.*—Red river, 480 miles above New Orleans, above mouth of Cane river, not above Grand Ecore.

GRAND BAYOU, *La.*—Red river, 575 miles from New Orleans, above Grand Ecore, not above Shreveport.

GRAND GULF, *Miss.*—Mississippi river, 340 miles above New Orleans.

GRAND LAKE, *Ark.*—Mississippi river, 500 miles above New Orleans, above Grand Gulf, not above Greenville.

GRAND JUNCTION, *Tenn.*—Jackson railroad, 395 miles from New Orleans.

GRAND GEAZE, *Ark.*—White river, below the junction of Black river.

GRAND RIVER, *Mo.*—Missouri river, 271 miles above its mouth, above Jefferson City, not above Lexington.

GRAND TOWER, *Mo.*—Mississippi river, 1069 miles above New Orleans, above the mouth of the Ohio, not above Alton.

GRAND PASS, *Ills.*—Illinois river, not above Beardstown.

GRAND BEND, *La.*—Red river, above Grand Ecore, not above Shreveport.

GRAND GULF, *Miss.*—Big Black river.

GRAND CANE, *Texas.*—Sabine river, above Hamilton.

GRAND CANE, *Texas.*—Trinity river, above Liberty, not above Smithville.

GOUGE EYES.—Bayou Bartholomew, above Arkansas line, not above Portland.

GRABALL.—Tallahatchie river, not above Cassidy Bayou.

GRABTREES.—Red river, above foot of Raft, not above Fulton.

GRACY, D (E. K. HALL).—Red river, above Grand Ecore, not above Shreveport.

GRAHAM THOMAS.—Red river, above foot of Raft, not above Fulton.

GRAHAMS.—Red river, above Rowland and Mound City.

GRAIGS.—Tallahatchie river, not above Cassidy Bayou.

GRAND BLUFF.—Sabine river, Texas.

GRAND LAKE LANDING, *La.*—Red river, above Grand Ecore, not above Shreveport.

GRAND MARY.—Ouachita river, above Alabama Landing, not above Camden.

GRAND RIVER AGENCY.—Missouri river, 1479 miles from its mouth, above Iatan.

GRAPP, J. P (ON THE HILL).—Red river, above Grand Ecore, not above Shreveport.

GRAPP, B (or F. LATTICK).—Red river, above Grand Ecore, not above Shreveport.

GRAND VIEW.—Ouachita river, above Yazoo City, not above Leflore

GRAND VIEW.—Ouachita river, above Harrisonburg, not above Trenton.

GRAND VIEW (or SHEARER'S).—125 miles up Sunflower river.

GRANVILLE (or FRANKLIN).—Red river, above Grand Ecore, not above Shreveport.

GRANT'S POINT —Red river, above Cane river, not above Grand Ecore.

GRANT, D. M.—Bayou Bartholomew, above Arkansas line, not above Portland.

GRANT'S, R (WOODYARD).—Red river, above Cane river, not above Grand Ecore.

GRAPP'S BLUFF.—Red river, above Grand Ecore, not above Shreveport.

GRASSY MOUND, *Miss.*—92 miles up Sunflower river.

GRAVES, TOM.—Yazoo river, above Yazoo City, not above Leflore.

GRAVES, R. Y (or EGYPT).—Red river, above foot of Raft, not above Fulton.

GRAVES (or JOHN P. HALEYS).—Red river, above foot of Raft, not above Fulton.

GRAY, B. W.—Red river, above Grand Ecore, not above Shreveport.

GRAY, G. Y.—Red river, above Shreveport, not above foot of Raft.

GRAND VIEW.—Ohio river, 353 miles from its mouth, above Paducah, not above Cincinnati.

GRAYSON, *Ark.*—Mississippi river, 807 miles above New Orleans, above Greenville, not above Memphis.

GRAFTON, *Ills.*—Mississippi river, 1220 miles above New Orleans, above Alton, not above first Rapids.

GRANT'S LANDING, *Miss.*—Mississippi river, above Greenville, not above Memphis.

GRAVES' LANDING, *Ala.*—Alabama river, above Selma, not above Wetumpka.

GRASSY LAKE, *La.*—Black river, not above Harrisonburg.

GRADLY'S LANDING, *Ark.*—Mississippi river, above Greenville, not above Memphis.

GRAY'S LANDING, *La.*—Red river, above Grand Ecore, not above Shreveport.

GRAY'S LANDING, *La.*—Black river, La., not above Harrisonburg.

GRAY'S PORT, *Miss.*—Yallabusha river, above Grenada.

GRAY'S WALLOW, *Ind.*—Wabash river, above Terre Haute.

GRAY'S BEND, *Ark.*—White river, 273 miles above its mouth, below the junction of Black river.

GRAY'S, MRS,, LANDING.—Red river, 340 miles above Shreveport, above Fulton, not above Lanesport.

GRAHAM'S LANDING, *Ark.*—Arkansas river, 116 miles above Napoleon, above Arkansas Post, not above Pine Bluff.

GRAPP'S BLUFF, *La.*—Red river, 520 miles from New Orleans, above Grand Ecore, not above Shreveport.

GREENBACK, *Ark.*—Not above Pine Bluff.

GREEN BRIAR —164 miles up Sunflower river.

GREENS.—Red river, above foot of Raft, not above Fulton.

GREENING, J. J. & BRO (STORE).—Red river, above Grand Ecore, not above Shreveport.

GREENING, J. J (HOUSE).—Red river, above Grand Ecore, not above Shreveport.

GREEN RIVER.—Ohio river, 196 miles above the mouth of the Ohio, above Paducah, not above Cincinnati.

GREENSBURG, *La.*—Tickfaw river, 10 miles from the line of the Jackson railroad, station at Tangipahoa.

GREENUPSBURG, *Ky.*—Ohio river, 667 miles above its mouth, above Cincinnati.

GREEN GROVE, *Ark.*—Arkansas river, 310 miles above Napoleon, above Little Rock, not above Norristown.

GREENEY'S LANDING, *La.*—Red river, above Grand Ecore, not above Shreveport.

GREENBORO, *Miss.*—Big Black river.

GREENO'S LANDING, *Miss.*—Pearl river, above Columbia.

GREEN'S LANDING, *Ala.*—Tombigbee river, above Demopolis, not above Gainesville.

GREENWOOD, *Miss.*—Yazoo river, 654 miles from Vicksburg, above Yazoo City, not above Leflore.

GREENVILLE, *Miss.*—Mississippi river, 247 miles above New Orleans.

GREENVILLE (HUNT CITY),—Texas.

GREENLEAF, *Ark.*—Arkansas river, 655 miles above Napoleon, above Fort Smith, not above Fort Gibson.

GREENING'S LANDING, *La.*—Red river, above Grand Ecore, not above Shreveport.

GREENOCK, *Ark.*—Mississippi river, 842 miles above New Orleans, above Greenville, not above Memphis.

GREGORO'S LANDING, *Ark.*—White river, 263 miles above its mouth, below the junction of Black river.

GREAT MIAMI RIVER, *Ohio.*—Ohio river, 520 miles above its mouth, above Paducah, not above Cincinnati.

GREAT KANAWHA RIVER, *Va.*—Ohio river, 738 miles above its mouth, above Cincinnati.

GRENADA, *Miss.*—Jackson railroad, 293 miles from New Orleans.

GRENADA, *Miss.*—Yallabusha river.

GREGG'S LANDING, *La.* (or CHINA GROVE.—Red river, above Grand Ecore, not above Shreveport.

GREGG'S LANDING, *La.*—Lake Bistenau.

GREGGSVILLE, *Ills.*—Illinois river, not above Beardstown.

GREGORY'S LANDING, *Ala.*—Tombigbee river, above Gainesville, not above Columbus.

GRESHAM'S LANDING, *Ala* —Tombigbee river, above Gainesville, not above Columbus.

GREENOUGH (or PROTHROE.)—Red river, above Cane river, not above Grand Ecore.

GREGSBY PLACE.—Red river, above Grand Ecore, not above Shreveport.

GRISLY'S LANDING, *La.*—Red river, above Grand Ecore, not above Shreveport.

GRIFFIN'S, GEO. W. LANDING, *La.*—Bayou Macon, 40 miles from its mouth, not above Monticello.

GRIFFIN'S, JOHN, LANDING, *La.*—Bayou Macon, 42 miles from its mouth, not above Monticello.

GRIFFIN'S (WOODYARD).—Yazoo river, above Yazoo City, not above Leflore.

GRIFFIN'S, T. R.—Yazoo river, above Yazoo City, not above Leflore.

GRIFFIN'S, TOM, LANDING, *La.*—Bayou Macon, 75 miles from its mouth, not above Monticello.

GRIFFIN'S LANDING, *Ala.*—Alabama river, above Selma, not above Wetumpka.

GRIFFIN'S LANDING, *Ala.*—Tombigbee river, not above Demopolis.

GRIMSHAW'S LANDING, *Ark*—Red river, 219 miles above Shreveport, above Carolina Bluff, not above Fulton.

GRISWOLD, *Mo.*—Missouri river, 85 miles above its mouth, not above Jefferson City.

GRIFFITH (J. J. SPEARS).—Red river, above Alexandria, not above mouth of Cane river.

GRIMES, W.—Red river, not above Alexandria.

GRIGSBY PLACE.—Red river, above Grand Gulf, not above Shreveport.

GRISWOLD, C. R. (or SILVER POINT).—Red river, above Shreveport, not above foot of Raft.

GROVE LAKE, *Miss.*—Mississippi river, 746 miles above New Orleans, above Greenville, not above Memphis.

GROVER'S LANDING, *Ala.*—Warrior river, not above Tuscaloosa.

GROSSE TETE RAILROAD DEPOT, *La*—Mississippi river, not above Bayou Sara.

GRUIKSHAUK, D.—Red river, above Alexandria, not above Cane river.

GRYER'S, DR.—Red river, above Fulton, not above Lanesport.

GUM BAYOU.—Yazoo river, above Yazoo City, not above Leflore.

GULLETT'S, GEN. LANDING, *Ala.*—Alabama Landing, not above Selma,

GUILFORD, *Ills.*—Illinois river, 17 miles above its mouth, not above Beardstown.

GULLETT'S GIN, *Ala.*—Alabama river, not above Selma.

GUNN'S LANDING, *Miss.*—Yazoo river, above Yazoo City, not above Leflore.

GUM GROVE.—Yazoo river, above Yazoo City, not above Leflore.

GUM POINT.—Bœuf river, above Thomas' Landing.

GUTHRIE (LOWER QUARTERS).—Bayou Bartholomew, not above Point Pleasant.

GUTHRIE, J. L.—Bayou Bartholomew, not above Point Pleasant.

GUNTER'S, C. A. LANDING, *Ala.*—Alabama river, above Selma, not above Wetumpka.

GURNEY'S, LANDING, *La.*—Red river, 470 miles above New Orleans, above Cane river, not above Grand Ecore.

GURLAND'S LANDING, *Ark.*—Red river, 177 miles above Shreveport, above Carolina Bluff, not above Fulton.

GUTTENBERG, *Ind.*—Mississippi river, 1651 miles above New Orleans, above Galena.

GUTWRIGHT'S LANDING, *La.*—Ouachita river, above Trenton, not above Alabama Landing.

GUYNDOTTE RIVER, *Va.*—Ohio river, 698 miles above its mouth, above Cincinnati.

GUYDEN'S LANDING.—Mississippi river, 720 miles above New Orleans, above Greenville, not above Memphis.

H

HACKLEROD'S LANDING, *Ark.*—Mississippi river, above Greenville, not above Memphis.

HADDOCK'S LANDING, *Tenn.*—Tennessee river, not above Eastport.

HAGGIN'S LANDING, *Tenn.*—Mississippi river, above Memphis, not above the mouth of the Ohio.

HAIR'S, J. D. LANDING, *La.*—Bayou Macon, 35 miles from its mouth, not above Monticello.

HAIRSTON'S LANDING, *Miss.*—Tombigbee river, above Gainesville, not above Columbus.

HALE'S FERRY, *Texas.*—Sabine river, above Hamilton.

HALE'S GIN, *Ala.*—Tombigbee river, above Demopolis, not above Gainesville.

HALE'S LANDING, *Ala.*—Tombigbee river, not above Demopolis.

HALL'S LANDING, *Ala.*—Warrior river, not above Tuscaloosa.

HALL'S, W. B LANDING, *Ala.*—Alabama river, not above Selma.

HAES, J. G. LANDING.—Red river, above Alexandria not above mouth of Cane river.

HADLEY'S, JOHN.—Bayou Bartholomew, above Arkansas line, not above Portland.

HAGGERTY (or HUMPHREYS).—Bayou Bartholomew, above Point Pleasant, not above Arkansas line.

HAGAN'S.—Yazoo river, above Yazoo City, not above Leflore.

HAGGMON.—Mississippi river, above Grand Gulf, not above Greenville.

HAILEY'S.—Red river, above Rowland and Mound City.

HAINES' LANDING.—132 miles up Bœuf river, above Thomas' Landing.

HAILEYS, JNO. T (or GRAVES).—Red river, above foot of Raft, not above Fulton.

HALL'S, W. B. LANDING, *Ala.*—Alabama river, above Selma, not above Wetumpka.

HALES'S POINT, *Tenn.*—Mississippi river, 938 miles above New Orleans, above Memphis, not above mouth of the Ohio.

HALSEY'S LANDING, *Ala.*—Tombigbee river, above Gainesville, not above Columbus.

HALF WAY, *La.*—Red river, above Grand Ecore, not above Shreveport.

HALL'S, HENRY.—Yazoo river, above Yazoo City, not above Leflore.

HALL, E. K. (D. GRACY).—Red river, above Grand Ecore, not above Shreveport.

HALL PLANTATION (KOUNS).—Red river, above Shreveport, not above foot of Raft.

HALL'S, DR. (or DR. MAGRUDER).—Red river, above Alexandria, not above Cane river.

HALSEY.—Mississippi river, above Greenville, not above Memphis.

HAMBRIE'S LANDING, *Ark.*—Mississippi river, above Greenville, not above Memphis.

HAMILTON, *Texas.*—Sabine river.

HAMILTON'S LANDING, *Ark.*—Arkansas river, above Little Rock, not above Norristown.

HAMILTON, *Ky.*—Ohio river, 486 miles from its mouth, above Paducah, not above Cincinnati.

HAMILTON CITY, *Ills.*—Mississippi river, 1375 miles above New Orleans, above the first, not above the second Rapids.

HAMILTON'S LANDING, *La.*—Ouachita river, above Trenton, not above Alabama Landing.

HAMILTON'S LANDING, *Ala.*—Alabama river, not above Selma.

HAMILTON'S LANDING, *Miss.*—Tombigbee river, above Columbus, not above Cotton Gin Port.

HAMBURG, *Ills.*—Mississippi river, 1262 miles above New Orleans, above Alton, not above first Rapids.

HAMBURG, *Tenn.*—Tennessee river, above Eastport, not above Florence.

HAMBURG LANDING, *Ky.*—Mississippi river, 1112 miles above New Orleans, above the mouth of the Ohio river, not above Alton.

HAMBURG LANDING (J. S. SANFORD).—Bayou Bartholomew, above Arkansas line, not above Portland.

HANNA'S LANDING.—264 miles up Sunflower river.

HAMITER'S LANDING, *Ark.*—Red river, 363 miles above Shreveport, above Fulton, not above Lanesport.

HAMPTON, *Ill.*—Mississippi river, 1530 miles above New Orleans, above second Rapids, not above Galena.

HAMBURG, *Tenn.*—Tennessee river, not above Eastport.

HANNA'S LANDING, *Ala.*—Tombigbee river, above Demopolis, not above Gainesville.

HANCOCK'S LANDING, *Ala.*—Tombigbee river, above Demopolis, not above Gainesville.

HANNIBAL, *Mo.*—Mississippi river, 1316 miles above New Orleans, above Alton, not above foot of first Rapids.

HANOVER LANDING, *Ind.*—Ohio river, 436 miles above its mouth, above Paducah, not above Cincinnati.

HANGING ROCK, *Ohio.*—Ohio river, 673 miles from its mouth, above Cincinnati.

HANLEY'S, JUDGE, LANDING, *Texas.*—Red river, 310 miles above Shreveport, above Fulton, not above Lanesport.

HAURONET'S (W. O. BRAZILLE).—Red river, above Cane river, not above Grand Ecore.

HARBINS.—Yazoo river, not above Yazoo City.

HARBINSON LANDING.—153 miles up Sunflower river.

HARD TIMES.—Yazoo river, not above Yazoo City.

HARD TIMES LANDING.—Red river, not above Alexandria.

HARDIE'S.—Red river, above Cane river, not above Grand Ecore.

HARDIN SCALES.—Tallahatchie river, not above Cassidy Bayou.

HARGES, W. C.—Red river, above Grand Ecore, not above Shreveport.

HARLAND'S FIELD.—122 miles up Bœuf river, above Thomas' Landing.

HARINER, *Ohio.*—Ohio river, 836 miles from its mouth, above Cincinnati.

HARTSVILLE, *Tenn.*—Cumberland river, above Nashville, not above Gainesboro.

HARBERT'S WOODYARD, *La.*—Ouachita river, above Harrisonburg, not above Trenton.

HARD TIMES, *La.*—Mississippi river, 354 miles above New Orleans, above Grand Gulf, not above Greenville.

HARPER'S LANDING, *Ark.*—Arkansas river, 362 miles above Napoleon, above Little Rock, not above Norristown.

HARDIN, *Ills.*—Illinois river, 21 miles above its mouth, not above Beardstown.

HARDY'S, B. LANDING, *La.*—Red river, above Grand Ecore, not above Shreveport.

HARDY'S LANDING, *La.*—Ouachita river, above Harrisonburg not above Trenton.

HARDIN'S LANDING, *Ark.*—White river, not above Batesville.

HARDIN'S LANDING, *La.*—Red river, above Cane river, not above Grand Ecore.

HARDWICK'S LANDING, *Ala.*—Warrior river, not above Tuscaloosa.

HARMINSON'S LANDING, *La.*—Atchafalaya river, below Simmsport.

HARTFORD, *Ind.*—Wabash river, not above the Rapids.

HARPETH RIVER, *Tenn.*—Cumberland river, not above Nashville.

HARBECK'S LANDING, *Miss.*—Mississippi river, above Greenville, not above Memphis.

HAROLD & WHIK'S LANDING, *La.*—Red river, above Grand Ecore, not above Shreveport.

HARD SCRABBLE LANDING, *La.*—Red river, above Grand Ecore, not above Shreveport.

HARD SCRABBLE LANDING, *La.*—Mississippi river, above Bayou Sara, not above Grand Gulf.

HARD SCRABBLE LANDING, *Ills.*—Mississippi river, above the mouth of the Ohio, not above Alton.

HARWELL'S, MRS. LANDING, *Ala.*—Tombigbee river, not above Demopolis.

HARVEY'S LANDING, *Miss.*--Tombigbee river, above Gainesville, not above Columbus.

HART'S LANDING, *Miss.*—Mississippi river, above Bayou Sara, not above Grand Gulf.

HART'S LANDING, *Ala.*—Tombigbee river, not above Demopolis.

HARCOUS' LANDING, *Ill.*—Mississippi river, above the mouth of the Ohio, not above Alton.

HARLOW'S LANDING, *Ills.*—Mississippi river, above the mouth of the Ohio, not above Alton.

HARDIN'S POINT, *Ark.*—Mississippi river, above Greenville, not above Memphis.

HARDIN'S LANDING, *Tenn.*—Mississippi river, above Memphis, not above the mouth of the Ohio.

HARDIN'S, DR. LANDING, *Ark.*—Mississippi river, above Greenville, not above Memphis.

HARDING'S LANDING, *Mo.*—Mississippi river, above Memphis, not above the mouth of the Ohio.

HARRISON'S LANDING, *Miss.*—Yazoo river, above Yazoo City, not above Leflore.

HARRISONVILLE, *Ky.*—Mississippi river, 1191 miles above New Orleans, above the mouth of the Ohio river, not above Alton.

HARRISONBURG, *La.*—Ouachita river, 135 miles above the mouth of Old river.

HARRIS CROSS, *Ark*—Arkansas river, 89 miles from Napoleon, above Arkansas Post, not above Pine Bluff.

HARRIMAN'S LANDING, *La.*—Black river, La., not above Harrisonburg.

HARRIS' KIM LANDING, *Ark.*—Little Red river, 35 miles from its mouth, below the junction of White and Black rivers.

HARRIS' LANDING, *La.*—Ouachita river, above Harrisonburg, not above Trenton.

HARRIS' LANDING, *Ill.*—Illinois river, not above Beardstown.

HARRIS' LANDING, *La.*—Mississippi river, above Grand Gulf, not above Greenville.

HARRIS', J. LANDING, *Ala.*—Alabama river, not above Selma.

HARRIS', MRS. LANDING, *Ala.*—Alabama river, not above Selma.

HARTMAN & SIMMONS' LANDING, *Miss.*—180 miles up Big Deer Creek.

HART'S (or MURRAY'S).—Red river, above Grand Ecore, not above Shreveport.

HARLAND'S LANDING.—268 miles up Sunflower river.

HARRELL & WHITE.—Red river, above Grand Ecore, not above Shreveport.

HARRINGTON LANDING.—Yazoo river, above Yazoo City, not above Leflore.

HARRIS' FIELDS LANDING.—Big Deer Creek, Miss.

HARRIS, H. (VILLA VISTA), *La.*—Mississippi river, above Grand Gulf, not above Greenville.

HARRIS, MRS.—Red river, above Lanesport, not above Mound City.

HARRISON'S, DR. T. O.—Red river, above Cane river, not above Grand Ecore.

HARRISON'S LANDING, *Ind.*—Ouachita river, above the Rapids, not above Terre Haute.

HARRISON'S LANDING, *La.*—Bayou Macon, two miles from its mouth, not above Monticello.

HARRISON'S LANDING, *La.*—Red river, above Cotile, not above Grand Ecore.

HARRISON'S, DICK LANDING, *Ala.*—Alabama river, above Selma, not above Wetumpka.

HARRISON'S BLUFF, *Texas.*—Trinity river, above Smithville, not above Magnolia Landing.

HARRELL'S LANDING, *Ala.*—Tombigbee river, not above Demopolis.

HASKELLVILLE, *Ohio.*—Ohio river, 707 miles from its mouth, above Cincinnati.

HASLEY'S LANDING, *La.*—Ouachita river, above Trenton, not above Alabama Landing.

HASKELL'S LANDING, *Ark.*—Arkansas river, 189 miles above Napoleon, above Pine Bluff, not above Little Rock.

HASKIN'S LANDING, *Mo.*—Yallabusha river, above Grenada.

HASTING'S, *Minn.*—Mississippi river, 1838 miles above New Orleans, above Galena.

HATCH, R. W.—111 miles up Bœuf river, above Thomas' Landing.

HATCH'S LANDING.—163 miles up Sunflower river.

HATHAWAY.—Bayou Bartholomew, above Portland.

HATCHEE TOWN, *Miss.*—Hatchee river, not above Bolivar.

HATCHE'S LANDING, *Ala.*—Warrior river, not above Tuscaloosa.

HATCHER'S BLUFF, *Ala.*—Alabama river, not above Selma.

HATTON & BRYANT'S LANDING, *La.*—Mississippi river, 170 miles above New Orleans, above Bayou Sara, not above Grand Gulf.

HATCHEE RIVER, *Tenn.*—Mississippi river, 860 miles above New Orleans, above Memphis, not above the Ohio river.

HATCHES, MRS. LANDING, *Ark.*—White river, 127 miles above its mouth, below the junction of Black river.

HAUSE BACK.—Red river, above Cane river, not above Grand Ecore.

HAUSE BACK.—Red river, above Grand Ecore, not above Shreveport.

HAVANA, *Ill.*—Illinois river, 127 miles above its mouth, above Beardstown, not above the mouth of Fox river.

HAW BLUFF.—Yazoo river, not above Yazoo City.

HAWKINS, BEN.—Bayou Bartholomew, above Point Pleasant, not above Arkansas line.

HAWKINS, HY. A.—Red river, above Fulton, not above Lanesport.

HAWESVILLE, *Ky.*—Ohio river, 261 miles above its mouth, above Paducah, not above Cincinnati.

HAWKINS' LANDING, *Ark.*—Red river, above Carolina Bluff, not above Fulton.

HAWKIN'S LANDING, *Ark.*—Bayou Bartholomew, above Arkansas line, not above Portland.

HAWKIN'S, W. A. LANDING, *Ark.*—Red river, 360 miles above Shreveport, above Fulton, not above Lanesport.

HAWLEYVILLE.—Ohio river, 262 miles above its mouth, above Paducah, not above Cincinnati.

HAWESVILLE, *Ky.*—Ohio river, 275 miles from its mouth, above Paducah, not above Cincinnati.

HAYDEN'S LANDING.—Mississippi river, 605 miles above its mouth, above Grand Gulf, not above Greenville.

HAYDEN'S LANDING, *Ark.*—Mississippi river, above Greenville, not above Memphis.

HAYSBORO, *Tenn.*—Cumberland river, above Nashville, not above Gainesboro.

HAYES' FERRY, *Mo.*—Mississippi river, above the Ohio river, not above Alton.

HAYES' FERRY, *Ala.*—Tombigbee river, above Demopolis, not above Gainesville.

HAYNES' LANDING, *Ala.*—Tombigbee river, above Gainesville, not above Columbus.

HAZZARD'S LANDING, *Ala.*—Tombigbee river, not above Demopolis.

HAZLEHURST, *Miss.*—Jackson railroad, 149 miles from New Orleans.

HAYS.—Mississippi river, above Grand Gulf, not above Greenville.

HAYDEN, EDWARDS.—Red river, not above Alexandria.

HAYGOOD, PHILIPS.—Yazoo river, above Yazoo City, not above Leflore.

HAYMES' BLUFF.—Yazoo river, not above Yazoo City.

HAYNES' BLUFF.—Ouachita river, above Alabama Landing, not above Camden.

HAZEL DELL.—Yazoo river, above Yazoo City, not above Leflore.

HEAD OF LITTLE ISLAND, *Ark.*—White river, 53 miles above its mouth, below junction of Black river.

HEAD OF BIG ISLAND, *Ark.*—White river, 73 miles above its mouth, below the junction of Black river.

HEAD OF TREMBLE ISLAND, *Ark.*—White river, 196 miles above its mouth, below the junction of Black river.

HEAD OF GREAT RAFT.—Red river, 77 miles above Shreveport, above Carolina Bluff, not above Fulton.

HEARING'S LANDING, *Ala.*—Tombigbee river, not above Demopolis.

HEAD OF THE ISLAND, *Miss.*—Yazoo river, 214 miles from Vicksburg, above Yazoo City, not above Leflore.

HECKATOO LANDING, *Ark.*—Arkansas river, 108 miles above Napoleon, above Arkansas Post, not above Pine Bluff.

HELENA, *Ark.*—Mississippi river, 728 miles from New Orleans, above Greenville, not above Memphis.

HEMP HILLS, *Ark.*—Red river, 318 miles above Shreveport, above White Oak Shoals.

HENDERSON, *Ky.*—Ohio river, 180 miles above its mouth, above Paducah, not above Cincinnati.

HEAD OF BIG BEND.—Missouri river, 1270 miles from its mouth, above Iatan.

HEAD OF HONEY ISLAND.—Yazoo river, above Yazoo City, not above Leflore.

HEBERT'S.—73 miles up Bœuf river, above Thomas' Landing.

HEBREW.—Ouachita river, above Harrisonburg, not above Trenton.

HECK POINT.—Yazoo river, not above Yazoo City.

HELLEN PLACE.—114 miles up Big Deer Creek, Miss.

HENAIRE, S. A.—Red river, not above Alexandria.

HENDERSON, RUSK CITY.—Texas.

HENDERSON, *La.*—Mississippi river, above foot of Raft, not above Fulton.

HEISON'S.—Ouachita river, above Harrisonburg, nòt above Trenton.

HENDRICKS, JOHN.—Yazoo river, above Yazoo City, not above Leflore.

HENRY, DR.—Yazoo river, above Yazoo City, not above Leflore.

HERRICAN BLUFF (JOHN PICKETT'S).—Red river, above Shreveport, not above foot of Raft.

HERMITAGE.—Mississippi river, above Bayou Sara, not above Greenville.

HENDERSONVILLE, *Ky.*—Ohio river, 177 miles above its mouth, above Paducah, not above Cincinnati.

HENDERSONVILLE, *Tenn.*—Cumberland river, above Nashville, not above Gainesboro.

HENRY SIMPSON, or TOM SMITH'S LANDING, *Ark.*—Arkansas river, 115 miles above Napoleon, above Arkansas Post, not above Pine Bluff.

HENRY KEAT'S LANDING, *Ark.*—Arkansas river, 270 miles above Napoleon, above Pine Bluff, not above Little Rock.

HENRY, *Ill.*—Illinois river, 215 miles above its mouth, above Beardstown, not above the mouth of Fox river.

HENNEPIN, *Ill.*—Illinois river, 228 miles above its mouth, above Beardstown, not above the mouth of Fox river.

HENDERSON'S LANDING, *Texas.*—Angelina river, above Bevilport.

HENDERSON'S, WM. LANDING, *Ala.*—Alabama river, not above Selma.

HENRY'S FERRY, *La.*—Tensas river, 31 miles from Trinity, not above the mouth of Bayou Macon.

HENRY'S, SAML. LANDING, *La.*—Red river, not above Alexandria.

HENRY'S LANDING, JOS., *La.*—Red river, above Grand Ecore, not above Shreveport.

HERRIN'S, W. Y. LANDING, *Ala.*—Alabama river, not above Selma.

HERMITAGE, *Mo.*—On the Railroad to Iron Works, near the Mississippi river, 1215 miles above New Orleans.

HERCULANEUM, *Mo.*—Mississippi river, 1180 miles above New Orleans, above the mouth of the Ohio river, not above Alton.

HERMANN, *Mo.*—Missouri river, 120 miles above its mouth, not above Jefferson City.

HERVEY'S LANDING, *Texas.*—Red river, 428 miles above Shreveport, above Lanesport, not above Mound City.

HIBERNIA.—Tallahatchie river, not above Cassidy Bayou.

HIBBARD'S, MRS.—Yazoo river, above Yazoo City, not above Leflore.

HIBERNIA, *Mo.*—Missouri river, not above Jefferson City.

HIBLAR'S LANDING, *Ala.*—Tombigbee river, above Gainesville, not above Columbus.

HICK'S LANDING, *Ala.*—Tombigbee river, above Gainesville, not above Columbus.

HICKMAN'S FERRY, *Texas.*—Sabine river, above Belgrade, not above Hamilton.

HICKMAN'S, MRS. WM. LANDING, *La.*—Red river, not above Alexandria.

HICKMAN, *Ky.*—Mississippi river, 1020 miles above New Orleans, above Greenville, not above the mouth of the Ohio river.

HICKMAN'S BEND, *Ark.*—Mississippi river, above Greenville, not above Memphis.

HICKORY FLATS, *La.*—Attakapas.

HIDDEN BLUFF, *Ark.*—White river, 185 miles above its mouth, below the junction of Black river.

HIGGINSPORT, *Ohio.*—Ohio river, 579 miles from its mouth, above Cincinnati.

HIGG'S LANDING, *Ark.*—Red river, 152 miles above Shreveport, above Carolina Bluff, not above Fulton.

HIGGINBOTHAM'S WOODYARD, *Ala.*—Alabama river, not above Selma.

HIGH BLUFF, *Ga.*—Flint river, not above Newton.

HIGH TOWER, *La.*—Ouachita river, above Trenton, not above Alabama Landing.

HIGH'S LANDING, *Ala.*—Tombigbee river, above Demopolis, not above Gainesville.

HILDRETH'S, D. H, LANDING, *Ala*—Tombigbee river, not above Demopolis.

HILL'S LANDING, *La.*—Black river, La., not above Harrisonburg.

HILL'S LANDING, *Ala.*—Tombigbee river, not above Demopolis.

HILLAMON, *Ill.*—Ohio river, 29 miles from its mouth, not above Paducah.

HILL'S LANDING, *Mo.*—Missouri river, 301 miles above its mouth, above Jefferson City, not above Lexington.

HILL'S LANDING, *Ala.*—Tombigbee river, above Gainesville, not above Columbus.

HILL'S, T. J., LANDING, *Ala.*—Warrior river, not above Tuscaloosa.

HILL'S, GEO., LANDING, *Ala.*—Tombigbee river, above Gainesville, not above Columbus.

HINE'S LANDING, *Ala.*—Tombigbee river, above Gainesville, not above Columbus.

HISHERINCK'S LANDING, *La.*—Atchafalaya river, below Simmsport.

HINE'S LANDING, *Ala.*—Warrior river, not above Tuscaloosa.

HICKMAN'S, PETER, MRS.—Red river, above Alexandria, not above Cane river.

HICKMAN'S, M. A., MRS.—Red river, above Alexandria, not above Cane river.

HICKORY BLUFF.—168 miles up Sunflower river.

HIGH DIE (D. PIPES).—Red river, above Cane river, not above Grand Ecore.

HIGH TOWER.—Yazoo river, above Yazoo City, not above Leflore.

HILL'S PLACE.—Tallahatchie river, above mouth of Cold Water.

HILL, BOB.—Bayou Bartholomew, above Arkansas line, not above Portland.

HILLMAN.—Yazoo river, above Yazoo City, not above Leflore.

HILLARD.—Mississippi river, above Grand Gulf, not above Greenville.

HINCKSTON'S, DAVE.—Bayou Bartholomew, above Arkansas line, not above Portland.

HINDMAN'S.—195 miles up Sunflower river.

HOBOLOCHITTO LANDING, *Miss.*—Pearl river, above Gainesville, not above Columbia.

HOCK HOOKING RIVER, *Ohio.*—Ohio river, 809 miles from its mouth, above Cincinnati.

HOBSON, DR., LANDING.—337 miles up Sunflower river.

HODGES (or PEACE POINT).—Red river, above Grand Ecore, not above Shreveport.

HODGES, J. S. (HOPEWELL).—Red river, above Grand Ecore, not above Shreveport.

HODGE'S LANDING, for WHEELOCK, *Ind. Terr.*—Red river, above Rowland and Mound City.

HOGDES (STATEN PLACE).—Red river, above Grand Ecore, not above Shreveport.

HODGDON.—Yazoo river, not above Yazoo City.

HOLMES, WILLIS (WOOD YARD).—Red river, not above Alexandria.

HOGAN'S, MRS.—Ouachita river, above Harrisonburg, not above Trenton.

HOLE IN THE WOODS.—Yazoo river, above Yazoo City, not above Leflore.

HOLLAND, R. P.—Black river, La.

HOLLAND'S LANDING.—118 miles up Sunflower river.

HOLLAND'S, DR. LANDING, *Miss.*—150 miles up Big Deer Creek.

HOLLEY, P. B. LANDING, *Miss.*—156 miles up Big Deer Creek.

HOLLINGSWORTH.—Red river, above Shreveport, not above foot of Raft.

HOLLY BLUFF.—Ouachita river, above Alabama Landing, not above Camden.

HOLLOWAY.—Bayou Bartholomew, above Portland.

HOLLY BEND.—Yazoo river, not above Yazoo City.

HOLLY BANK.—Yazoo river, above Yazoo City, not above Leflore.

HOLLY GROVE.—Tallahatchie river, not above Cassidy Bayou.

HOLLY GROVE.—111 miles up Bœuf river, above Thomas' Landing.

HOLLY MOUND.—Yazoo river, above Yazoo City, not above Leflore.

HOLLY PLACE.—Bayou Bartholomew, not above Point Pleasant.

HOLLY RIDGE.—Bœuf river, above Thomas' Landing.

HOLMES, *La.*—Black river, not above Harrisonburg.

HOLSTEIN, G. BEND (WOOD YARD).—Red river, not above Alexandria.

HOLT, D. M.—Bayou Bartholomew, above Point Pleasant, not above Arkansas line.

HOLTZ.—Yazoo river, not above Yazoo City.

HOME PARK.—Yazoo river, above Yazoo City, not above Leflore.

HOG'S POINT, *La.*—Mississippi river, above Grand Gulf, not above Greenville.

HOGIN'S LANDING, *Ark.*—Arkansas river, 441 miles above Napoleon, above Norristown, not above Fort Smith.

HOKAH RIVER, *Mo.*—Mississippi river, 1727 miles above New Orleans, above Galena.

HOLLY'S POINT, *Ark.*—Bayou Bartholomew, above Arkansas line, not above Portland.

HOLLY SPRINGS, *Miss.*—Jackson railroad, 370 miles from New Orleans.

HOLE IN THE WALL, *La.*—Mississippi river, 292 miles above New Orleans, above Bayou Sara, not above Grand Gulf.

HOLLAND'S LANDING, *La.*—Black river, La.

HOLLIDAY'S LANDING, *La.*—Ouachita river, above Harrironburg, not above Trenton.

HOLLINGER'S LANDING, *Ala.*—Tombigbee river, not above Demopolis.

HOLCOMBO SLOUGH, *Ala.*—Warrior river, not above Tuscaloosa.

HOLLINGER'S LANDING, *Ala.*—Alabama river, not above Selma.

HOLT'S LANDING, *Ala.*—Tombigbee river, above Gainesville, not above Columbus.

HOLLEY'S LANDING, *Ala.*—Alabama river, not above Selma.

HOLMES, DR. LANDING, *Alà.*—Alabama river, not above Selma.

HOLME'S FERRY, *Texas.*—Neches river, above Wyse's Bluff, not above the junction of Angelina river.

HOLLIWOOD'S PLANTATION, *La.*—Mississippi rivei, not above Bayou Sara.

HOMOCHITTO LANDING, *Miss.*—Mississippi river, above Grand Gulf, not above Greenville.

HOME CITY, *Ohio.*—Ohio river, 517 miles from its mouth, above Paducah, not above Cincinnati.

HOMESTEAD, *Ark.*—Arkansas river, 61 miles above Napoleon, above Arkansas Post, not above Pine Bluff.

HOMOCHITTO RIVER, *Miss.*—Mississippi river, 269 miles above New Orleans, above Bayou Sara, not above Grand Gulf.

HOOPER'S LANDING, *Ala.*—Alabama river, above Selma, not above Wetumpka.

HOOK GALLAN'S LANDING, *Texas.*—Red river, 376 miles above Shreveport, above Lanesport, not above Mound City.

HOPEWELL'S LANDING, *La.*—Ouachita river, above Harrisonburg, not above Trenton.

HOPEWELL'S (or T. S. HODGES) LANDING, *La.*—Red river, above Grand Ecore, not above Shreveport.

HOPE FIELD, *Ark.*—Mississippi river, 905 miles above New Orleans, above Greenville, not above Memphis.

HOPKINSVILLE, *Tenn.*—Tennessee river, above Eastport, not above Florance.

HOPKIN'S, B. M. LANDING, *Texas.*—Red river, 505 miles above Shreveport, above White Oak Shoals.

HORNE'S BLUFF, *Texas.*—Trinity river, above Smithville, not above Magnolia Landing.

HORN LAKE, *Tenn.*—Mississippi river, above Memphis, not above the mouth of the Ohio.

HOOKS, DR.—Red river, above Fulton, not above Lanesport.

HORSE SHOE BEND, *Miss.*—Mississippi river, above Greenville, not above Memphis.

HORSE HEAD, *Ark.*—Arkansas river, above Dardenelle, not above Roseville.

HORSE PRAIRIE, *Texas.*—Red river, 560 miles above Shreveport, above Mound City.

HORN LAKE, *Miss.*—Mississippi river, 887 miles above New Orleans, above Greenville, not above Memphis.

HOUMAS, *La.*—Mississippi river, 72 miles above New Orleans, not above Bayou Sara.

HOUMA PLACE, *La.*—Mississippi river, not above Bayou Sara.

HOUSER'S, L. LANDING, *Ala.*—Alabama river, above Selma, not above Wetumpka.

HOUSTON'S LANDING, *Ala.*—Tombigbee river, above Demopolis, not above Gainesville.

HOOD'S LANDING.—Little river, not above White Oak Shoals (Red river).

HOOPER, TOM, *La.*—Black river, not above Harrisonburg.

HOOKS, WARREN.—Red river, above Lanesport, not above Mound City.

HOOKS.—Red river, above Mound City.

HOOKS, D. S. (MERRIWETHER).—Red river, above Grand Ecore, not above Shreveport.

HOOTERS.—Yazoo river, not above Yazoo City.

HOPAKA, *La.*—Tensas river, mouth of Bayou Macon.

HOPE PLANTATION.—Ouachita river, above Harrisonburg, not above Trenton.

HOPEWELL.—Yazoo river, not above Yazoo City.

HOPE WHETSONE.—Bayou Bartholomew, above Point Pleasant, not above Arkansas line.

HOPE WOODYARD (LEBARGE).—Ouachita river, not above Harrisonburg.

HORSE HEAD.—Ouachita river, above Alabama Landing, not above Camden.

HOUGH, JNO.—Ouachita river, above Harrisonburg, not above Trenton.

HOUGH, W. H.—Ouachita river, above Harrisonburg, not above Trenton.

HOUSE BLUFF, *Ala.*—Alabama river, above Selma, not above Wetumpka.

HOWARD'S (or DR. CANDLER'S).—Red river, above foot of Raft, not above Fulton.

HOWELL'S LANDING.—Red river, above foot of Raft, not above Fulton.

HOWELL, WASH (Lower and Upper).—Bayou Bartholomew, above Arkansas line, not above Portland.

HOWARD'S LANDING, *Ark.*—Arkansas river, 336 miles above Napoleon, above Little Rock, not above Norristown.

HOWARD'S LANDING, *Ark.*—Red river, 166 miles above Shreveport, above Carolina Bluff, not above Fulton.

HOWARD'S, TOM., LANDING, *Ala.*—Alabama river, not above Selma.

HOWELL'S, MRS., LANDING, *Ark.*—Arkansas river, 388 miles above Napoleon, above Little Rock, not above Norristown.

HUBBARD, H. H. (PLUNKETT).—Red river, above Grand Ecore, not above Shreveport.

HUBERTSVILLE, *La.*—Attakapas.

HUDSONVILLE, *Miss.*—Jackson railroad, 377 miles above New Orleans.

HUDSONVILLE, *Ills.*—Wabash river, above Terre Haute.

HUFFPOWER.—Atchafalaya river, below Simmsport.

HUGHES, MRS. (ELISEE PLANTATION).—Bayou Bartholomew, not above Point Pleasant.

HUGHES, JNO. (WILLOW GROVE), *La.*—Red river, above Grand Gulf, not above Shreveport.

HUGHEY'S POINT.—132 miles up Sunflower river.

HUMPHRIES' GIN.—Bayou Bartholomew, above Point Pleasant, not above Arkansas line.

HUMPHRIES (or HAGGERTY).—Bayou Bartholomew, above Point Pleasant, not above Arkansas line.

HUNTER, J. A.—Red river, above Grand Ecore, not above Shreveport.

HUNTER, TOM.—Red river, above Grand Ecore, not above Shreveport.

HURD'S, STEVE.—281 miles up Sunflower river.

HUNTER'S (or W. WILLIAMS').—Red river, above Grand Ecore, not above Shreveport.

HUNTER, M. S.—Bayou Bartholomew, above Point Pleasant, not above Arkansas line.

HUNTONIA, *Miss.*—118 miles up Sunflower river.

HURD'S, SAM.—276 miles up Sunflower river.

HUNT'S LANDING, *Miss.*—Mississippi river, above Greenville, not above Memphis.

HUNT'S LANDING, *Mo.*—Mississippi river, above the mouth of the Ohio, not above Alton.

HUNTER'S, BENJ. LANDING, *La.*—Tensas river, 27 miles from Trinity, not above mouth of Bayou Macon.

HUNTER'S, DR. LANDING, *La.*—Red river, above Grand Ecore, not above Shreveport.

HUNT'S LANDING, *Mo.*—Mississippi river, 1044 miles above New Orleans, above the mouth of the Ohio, not above Alton.

HUNTER'S, SAML. LANDING, *Ala.*—Alabama river, not above Selma.

HUNTER'S, T. S. LANDING, *Ala.*—Alabama river, not above Selma.

HUNTER'S LANDING, *Ala.*—Tombigbee river, not above Demopolis.

HUNTER'S, J. LANDING, *Ala.*—Tombigbee river, not above Demopolis.

HUNTER'S LANDING, *Mo.*—Mississippi river, above Memphis, not above mouth of the Ohio.

HUNTINGTON, *Ind.*—Wabash river, not above the Rapids.

HURRICANE BLUFF, *Ala.*—Alabama river, not above Selma.

HURRICANE LANDING, *Miss.*—Mississippi river, 439 miles above New Orleans, above Grand Gulf, not above Greenville.

HURRICANE BLUFF, *Ark.*—Arkansas river, above Little Rock, not above Norristown.

HURON, *Iowa* —Mississippi river, 1475 miles above New Orleans, above second Rapids, not above Galena.

HUTCHING'S LANDING, *Miss.*—Mississippi river. 252 miles above New Orleans, above Bayou Sara, not above Grand Gulf.

HUTCHIN'S LANDING. *Ark.*—White river, 215 miles above its mouth, below the junction of Black river.

HUTTON'S OLD FERRY, *Ala.*—Tombigbee river, above Gainesville, not above Columbus.

HUT ISLAND, *Ill.*—Mississippi river, above the mouth of the Ohio, not above Alton.

HURTS.—Red river, above foot of Raft, not above Fulton.

HUTCHINSON, R. C (BOTTOM PLANTATION).—Red river, above Alexandria, not above mouth Cane river.

HUTCHINSON, W. J.—Red river, above Grand Ecore, not above Shreveport.

HUTCHINSON (MAGNOLIA).—Red river, above Grand Ecore, not above Shreveport.

HYAM, K. R (RAVEN CAMP).—Red river, above Alexandria, not above mouth Cane river.

HYAM, COL. S. M.—Red river, above Grand Ecore, not above Shreveport.

HYMES.—Upper Ouachita river, above Harrisonburg.

I

IATAN, *Mo.*—Missouri river.

IBERVILLE, *La.*—Mississippi river, 106 miles above New Orleans, not above Bayou Sara.

IDLE BRYANT'S (RIVER).—Red river, above Grand Ecore, not above Shreveport.

ILLAWARA.—Mississippi river, above Grand Gulf, not above Greenville.

ILLIWA, *La.*—Mississippi river, 455 miles above New Orleans, above Grand Gulf, not above Greenville.

ILLINOIS, *Ark.*—Arkansas river, 633 miles from Napoleon, above Fort Smith, not above Fort Gibson.

ILLINOIS RIVER, *Ills.*—Mississippi river, 1220 miles above New Orleans, above Alton, not above first Rapids.

ILLINOIS BAYOU, *Ark.*—Arkansas river, 400 miles from Napoleon, above Norristown, not above Fort Smith.

ILLINOISTOWN, *Ill.*—Mississippi river, 1278 miles above New Orleans, opposite St. Louis.

INDIAN BAY, *Ark.*—White river, 74 miles above its mouth, below the junction of Black river.

INDUSTRY, *Ohio.*—Ohio river, 519 miles above its mouth, above Paducah, not above Cincinnati.

INDEPENDENCE CREEK.—Missouri river, above Iatan.

INDIAN VILLAGE, *La.*—Tensas river, 31 miles from Trinity, below the mouth of Bayou Macon.

INGE'S, A. LANDING, *Ala.*—Tombigbee river, above Demopolis, not above Gainesville.

INDIAN BAYOU.—113 miles up Big Deer Creek, not above Yazoo City.

INDIAN BAYOU.—177 miles up Sunflower river.

INDIAN JOHN'S (WOOD YARD).—Red river, above Lanesport, not above Mound City.

INDEPENDENCE.—Red river, above Shreveport, not above foot of Raft.

INGERSOLLS.—Yazoo river, above Yazoo City, not above Leflore.

INNO ALBINO.—Yazoo river, above Yazoo City, not above Leflore.

INGOMAR.—Mississippi river, above Grand Gulf, not above Greenville.

INGLESIDE.—Yazoo river, above Yazoo City, not above Leflore.

IOWA, *Ia.*—Mississippi river, 1500 miles above New Orleans, above second Rapids, not above Galena.

IOWA RIVER, *Ia.*—Mississippi river, 1460 miles above New Orleans, above second Rapids, not above Galena.

IOWA POINT, *Mo.*—Missouri river, 562 miles above its mouth, not above Iatan.

IRBY'S, W. W. LANDING, *Ala.*—Alabama river, not above Selma.

IRISHMAN'S WOOD YARD.—Red river, above Grand Ecore, not above Shreveport.

IRWINS, MRS.—78 miles up Bœuf river, above Thomas' Landing.

IRBY'S, C., LANDING, *Ala.*—Alabama river, not above Selma.

IRON BANKS, *Ky.*—Mississippi river, above Memphis, not above the mouth of the Ohio.

IRON WOOD BLUFF, *Miss.*—Tombigbee river, above Smithville.

IRONTON, *Ohio.*—Ohio river, 677 miles from its mouth, above Cincinnati.

IRON WORKS, *Tenn.*—Cumberland river, not above Nashville.

IRWIN'S LANDING, *Ark.*—Arkansas river, 239 miles from Napoleon, above Pine Bluff, not above Liitle Rock.

ISCARD.—Tallahatchie river, not above Cassidy Bayou.

ISCARIA.—Tallahatchie river, above Cassidy Bayou, not above Cold Water.

ISLAND BAYOU.—Black river, Louisiana, not above Trinity.

ISLAND WOOD YARD.—Black river, Louisiana, not above Trinity.

ISHEE.—Ouachita river, above Harrisonburg, not above Trenton.

IUKA (DR. BUTLER'S).—Red river, above Cane river, not above Grand Ecore.

IXUDIN (or ANDREWS).—Yazoo river, above Yazoo City, not above Leflore.

ISLAND No. 1.—Mississippi river, 994 miles above New Orleans, above Memphis, not above the mouth of the Ohio river.

ISLAND No. 10.—Mississippi river, 978 miles above New Orleans, above Memphis, not above the mouth of the Ohio river.

ISLAND No. 18.—Mississippi river, above Memphis, not above the mouth of the Ohio river.

ISLAND No. 40.—Mississippi river, above Memphis, not above the mouth of the Ohio river.

ISLAND No. 60.—Mississippi river, above Greenville, not above Memphis.

ISLAND No. 63.—Mississippi river, above Greenville, not above Memphis.

ISLAND No. 66.—Mississippi river, above Greenville, not above Memphis.

ISLAND No. 74.—Mississippi river, above Greenville, not above Memphis.

ISLE BREVILLE, *La.*—Red river, above Cane river, not above Grand Ecore.

ISLE DERBAUNE, *La.*—Red river, above Cane river, not above Grand Ecore.

ITASKA, *Minn.*—Mississippi river, 1898 miles above New Orleans, above Galena.

J

JACK HILL'S LANDING, *Ark.*—Arkansas river, 140 miles above Napoleon, above Arkansas Post, not above Pine Bluff.

JACK'S ISLAND.—Ouachita river, above Alabama Landing, not above Camden.

JACKSON'S, C. M. LANDING, *Ala.*--Alabama river, above Selma, not above Wetumpka.

JACKSON'S FERRY.—Bayou Macon, above Monticello.

JACKSON'S, A. B., LANDING, *Ala* —Alabama river, above Selma, not above Wetumpka.

JACKSON, *Miss.*—Jackson railroad, 183 miles from New Orleans.

JACKSON, *La* —(Interior) shipping port Bayou Sara.

JACKSONPORT, *Ark.*—White river, 358 miles above its mouth, at the junction of Black river.

JACKSON, *Ala.*—Tombigbee river, not above Demopolis.

JACKSON, *Miss.*—Pearl river, above Columbia.

JACKSON'S FERRY, *La.*—Bayou Macon, 190 miles from its mouth, above Monticello.

JACKSON'S FERRY, *Ala.*—Tombigbee river, above Gainesville, not above Columbus.

JACKSON'S LANDING, *Ala.*—Tombigbee river, not above Demopolis.

JACKSON'S, BEN., LANDING, *Miss.*—Mississippi river, above Bayou Sara, not above Grand Gulf.

JACOBSBURG, *Penn.*—Ohio river, 975 miles above the mouth, above Cincinnati.

JACOB'S, E. LANDING, *La.*—Red river, above Grand Ecore, not above Shreveport.

JACOB'S, E. & B (or DUKE'S BEND).—Red river, above foot of Raft, not above Fulton.

JAKE JONES' LANDING, *Ark.*—Arkansas river, 275 miles above Napoleon, above Pine Bluff, not above Little Rock.

JAIVEY'S, REV.—Red river, above Alexandria, not above Cane river.

JAMES BLUFF.—Red river, 503 miles above Shreveport, above Mound City.

JAME'S LANDING, *Ala.*—Alabama river, 84 miles from Mobile, not below Selma.

JAMESTOWN, *Mo.* –Missouri river, 6 miles above its mouth, not above Jefferson.

JAMESTOWN, *Ky.*—Cumberland river, above Gainesboro.

JAMESTOWN, *Wis.*—Mississippi river, 1627 miles above New Orleans, above Galena.

JAMESTOWN, *Ky.*—Ohio river, 536 miles above its mouth, above Cincinnati.

JAMES' LANDING, *Mo.*—Mississippi river, above the mouth of the Ohio, not above Alton.

JAMES' F. LANDING, *Ala.*—Alabama river, not above Selma.

JAMES' BLUFF, *Ala.*—Tombigbee river, not above Demopolis.

JAMES' BAYOU, *Mo.*—Mississippi river, above Memphis, not above the mouth of the Ohio.

JANE'S, STEPHEN LANDING, *Ark.*—Red river, 275 miles above Shreveport, above Fulton, not above Lanesport.

JAMES & BRO.—Bayou Bartholomew, above Point Pleasant, not above Arkansas line.

JAMES VALLE.—

JANUARY PLANTATION, *La.*—Tensas river, 47 miles from Trinity, below the mouth of Bayou Macon.

JARVIS' POINT, *Miss.*—Mississippi river, above Bayou Sara, not above Grand Gulf.

JAYNES, IRWIN.—Red river, above Fulton, not above Lanesport.

JEANNERETTE, *La.*—Bayou Teche.

JEFFERSON, *Texas.*—Lake Caddo.

JEAN'S LANDING.—Big Deer Creek, 107 miles up.

JEANS, JOE LANDING.—Big Deer Creek, 117 miles up.

JEFFRIES, CAPT. (or CAPTS. MEAD & AVOCA).—Red river, above Alexandria, not above the mouth of Cane river.

JEFFERSON'S.—Red river, above Shreveport, not above Carolina Bluff.

JEFFRON'S, O.—Red river, not above Alexandria.

JENKINS'.—Yazoo river, above Yazoo City, not above Leflore.

JENKINS, DR.—Red river, above Grand Ecore, not above Shreveport.

JENKINS' CUT OFF.—Red river, above Grand Ecore, not above Shreveport.

JEFFERSON, *La.*—Morgan railroad, 18 miles above New Orleans.

JEFFERSON, *Ohio.*—Wabash river, not above the Rapids.

JEFFERSON, *Texas.*—Sabine river, above Sabine City, not above Belgrade.

JEFFERSON CITY, *Mo.*—Missouri river, 164 miles above its mouth.

JEFFERSONVILLE, *Ind.*—Ohio river, 384 miles above its mouth, above Paducah, not above Cincinnati, opposite Louisville, Ky.

JEFFERSON BARRACKS, *Mo.*—Mississippi river, 218 miles above the mouth of the Ohio river, not above Alton.

JEFFERSON COLLEGE, *La.*—Mississippi river, 66 miles above New Orleans, below Bayou Sara.

JEFFERSON'S LANDING, *La.*—Red river, not above Alexandria.

JENKINS' LANDING, *Ark.*—Arkansas river, 165 miles above Napoleon, above Arkansas Post, not above Pine Bluff.

JENKINS' LANDING, *La.*—Mississippi river, 204 miles above New Orleans, above Bayou Sara, not above Grand Gulf.

JENKINS', DR. LANDING, *Miss.*—Mississippi river, above Bayou Sara, not above Grand Gulf.

JENNING'S FERRY, *Ala.*—Warrior river, not above Tuscaloosa.

JERSEY LANDING.—Mississippi river, above Alton, not above the first Rapids.

JERSEY POINT, *Miss.*—Mississippi river, above Greenville, not above the mouth of the Ohio.

JESSIE'S LANDING, *La.*—Red river, above Cotile, not above Grand Ecore.

JEWETT'S, O. LANDING, *Ala.*—Alabama river, not above Selma.

JOE'S BAYOU.—49 miles up Bœuf river, not above Thomas' Landing.

JOE'S WALK.—Yazoo river, not above Yazoo City.

JOHNSON'S, BRADISH PLANTATION.—Below New Orleans, on Mississippi river.

JOHNSON'S, BOB.—Yazoo river, not above Yazoo City.

JOHNSON'S LANDING, *Miss.*—165 miles up Big Deer Creek.

JOHNSONS, E. M.—Bayou Bartholomew, above Point Pleasant, not above Arkansas line.

JOHNSONVILLE.—On Sunflower river, 189 miles up.

JOHNSON'S LANDING.—330 miles up Sunflower river.

JOHNSONS, DR.—337 miles up Sunflower river.

JOE CARY'S LANDING, *Ark.*—Arkansas river, 128 miles above Napoleon, above Arkansas Post, not above Pine Bluff.

JOHNSON'S FERRY, *Mo.*—Missouri river, 45 miles above its mouth, not above Jefferson City.

JOHNSON'S LANDING, *Ark.*—Arkansas river, 28 miles above Napoleon, not above Arkansas Post.

JOHNSON'S LANDING.—Mississippi river, above Grand Gulf, not above Greenville.

JOHNSON'S, R. H. LANDING, *Ark.*—Arkansas river, 262 miles above Napoleon, above Pine Bluff, not above Little Rock.

JOHNSON, *Ark.*—White river, 395 miles from Mississippi river, above Batesville.

JOHNSON'S LANDING, *La.*—Bayou Macon, one mile from its mouth, not above Monticello.

JOHNSON'S LANDING.—Mississippi river, above Alton, not above the foot of the first Rapids.

JOHNSON'S, SAMUEL LANDING, *La.*—Red river, not above Alexandria.

JOHNSON'S WOOD YARD, *Ala.*—Alabama river, not above Selma.

JOHNSONVILLE, *Tenn.*—Tennessee river, not above Eastport.

JOHNSON PORT.—Mississippi river, above Galena.

JONESBORO.—Red river, above Carolina Bluff, not above Fulton.

JONES & TURNER'S LANDING, *Ark.*—Arkansas river, 100 miles above Napoleon, above Arkansas Post, not above Pine Bluff.

JONES' LANDING, *Ky.*—Mississippi river, above Memphis, not above the mouth of the Ohio.

JONES', J. W. LANDING, *Ark.*—Arkansas river, 95 miles above Napoleon, above Arkansas Post, not above Pine Bluff.

JONES', DR. LANDING, *La.*—Ouachita river, above Harrisonburg, not above Trenton.

JONES', DR. LANDING, *La.*—Red river, above Grand Ecore, not above Shreveport.

JONES', R. LANDING, *Ala.*—Alabama river, not above Selma.

JONES' LANDING, *Ala.*—Alabama river, not above Selma

JONES', E. S. LANDING, Alabama river, not above Selma.

JONES' LANDING, *Mo.*—Mississippi rivet, above Memphis, not above the mouth of the Ohio river.

JONES' BLUFF, *Ala.*—Tombigbee river, not above Demopolis.

JONES' POINT, *Mo.*—Mississippi river, above the mouth of the Ohio river, not above Alton.

JONES' POINT, *Mo.*—Missouri river, 61 miles above its mouth, not above Jefferson City.

JORDAN'S, MRS. LANDING, *Ark.*—Arkansas river, 81 miles above Napoleon, above Arkansas Post, not above Pine Bluff.

JOUTY'S LANDING, *Miss.*—Mississippi river, above Bayou Sara. not above Grand Gulf.

JOHNSON, B.—Ouachita river, above Alabama Landing, not above Camden.

JOHNSON'S, S. K. (KAY PLACE).—Red river, not above Alexandria.

JOHNSON'S STORE (or MOORE LANDING).—Red river, above Rowland and Mound City.

JOINER, JUDGE.—Red river, above Fulton, not above Lanesport.

JONESBORO (or BAILEY'S).—Red river, above Rowland and Mound City.

JONES, CAL.—Red river, above Fulton, not above Lanesport.

JONES, R. M. (or SHAWNEETOWN).—Red river, above Rowland and Mound City.

JONES.—Tallahatchie river, not above Cassidy Bayou.

JONES, MAJOR, LANDING.—117 miles up Sunflower river.

JONES, S. J., LANDING.—268 miles up Sunflower river.

JONES, MRS.—Red river, above Grand Ecore, not above Shreveport.

JONES, Z.—Ouachita river, above Harrisonburg, not above Trenton.

JUDGE FLETCHER'S LANDING, *Ark.*—Arkansas river, 50 miles above Napoleon, below Arkansas Post.

JUMA POINT.—Missouri river, above Iatan.

K

KAGLE'S LANDING.—279 miles up Sunflower river.

KANSAS WOODYARD, *Tenn.*—Mississippi river, above Memphis, not above the mouth of the Ohio river.

KANSAS, *Wis.*—Mississippi river, 1757 miles above New Orleans, above Galena.

KANSAS, *Kan.*—Missouri river, 405 miles above its mouth, above Lexington, not above Iatan.

KANSAS RIVER, *Kan.*—Missouri river, 405 miles above its mouth, above Lexington, not above Iatan.

KAPOICE.—Mississippi river, above Galena.

KASKASKIA, *Ills.*—Mississippi river, 1163 miles above New Orleans, above the mouth of the Ohio river, not above Alton.

KAVOR'S CAMP, *La.*—Red river, above Cotile, not above Grand Ecore.

KAY'S LANDING, *La.*—Red river, not above Alexandria.

KEARNEY'S.—Yazoo river, above Yazoo City, not above Leflore.

KELLOGG'S.—Ouachita river, not above Harrisonburg.

KELLY'S GIN.—Bayou Bartholomew, above Point Pleasant, not above Arkansas line.

KEMP'S FERRY.—Ouachita river, above Alabama Landing, not above Camden.

KEMP.—Bayou Bartholomew, above Arkansas line, not above Portland.

KENNEDY, W. L., LANDING, *Miss.*—174 miles up Big Deer Creek.

KEATON'S LANDING, *Miss.*—Tombigbee river, above Columbus not above Cotton Gin Port.

KEE'S, DR., LANDING.—Mississippi river, above Greenville, not above Memphis.

KEENAN'S, M. J., LANDING, *Ala.*—Alabama river, not above Selma.

KEITHSBURG.—Mississippi river, above the first, not above the second Rapids.

KELLEY'S FERRY, *Tenn.*—Cumberland river, not above Nashville.

KELLEY'S LANDING, *Ark.*—Little Red river, 31 miles above its mouth, below the junction of White and Black rivers.

KELLEY'S, T. A., LANDING, *Ala.*—Tombigbee river, not above Demopolis.

KELLY'S BLUFF.—Red river, 114 miles above Shreveport, above Black Bayou, not above White Oak Shoals.

KELSOE'S LANDING, *Ark.*—Arkansas river, 153 miles above Napoleon, above Arkansas Post, not above Pine Bluff.

KEMP'S LANDING, *Miss.*—Mississippi river, above Bayou Sara, not above Grand Gulf.

KEMP'S, MRS., LANDING, *Ala.*—Tombigbee river, not above Demopolis.

KENNERVILLE, *La.*—Mississippi river, 16 miles above New Orleans, not above Bayou Sara.

KENNER, *La.*—Jackson railroad, 10 miles from New Orleans.

KENNEDY'S LANDING, *Ala.*—Alabama river, not above Selma.

KENO SHO, *Neb.*—Missouri river, 642 miles above its mouth, above Iatan.

KENTUCKY RIVER, *Ky.*—Ohio river, 452 miles above its mouth, above Paducah, not above Cincinnati.

KENTUCKY LANDING.—Mississippi river, above Memphis, not above the mouth of the Ohio.

KERNEGAY'S LANDING, *Ala.*—Alabama river, above Selma, not above Wetumpka.

KEOKUK, *Iowa.*—Mississippi river, 100 miles above St. Louis, above Alton, not above foot of first Rapids.

KEY'S LANDING, *Tenn.*—Mississippi river, above Memphis, not above the mouth of the Ohio.

KEYTESVILLE, *Mo.*—Missouri river, above Jefferson City, not above Lexington.

KIAMITIA RIVER.—Red river, 519 miles above Shreveport, above White Oak Shoals.

KICKAPOO VILLAGE, *Texas.*—Trinity river, above Smithville, not above Magnolia Landing.

KICKPATRICK'S LANDING, *Ala.*—Tombigbee river, above Demopolis, not above Gainesville.

KICKAPOO CITY, *Kan.*—Missouri river, 453 miles above its mouth, above Iatan.

KILROY, *Ia.*—Mississippi river, 1665 miles above New Orleans, above Galena.

KEPHART'S.—Red river, above Grand Ecore, not above Shreveport.

KILKENNY, *Texas.*—Sabine river, above Sabine City, not above Belgrade.

KIDD'S, A. J., LANDING, *Ala.*—Alabama river, not above Selma

KILLUM'S LANDING, *Ala.*—Alabama river, not above Selma.

KIMBALL'S BAYOU, *La.*—Tensas river, 30 miles from Trinity, not above mouth of Bayou Macon.

KIMMSVILLE, *Mo.*—Mississippi river, above New Orleans, above the mouth of the Ohio, not above Alton.

KIMBRO'S LANDING, *Ark.*—Arkansas river, 114 miles above Napoleon, above Arkansas Post, not above Pine Bluff.

KIERNON'S LANDING.—Black river, La.

KIGER, B. G (EAGLE BEND)—Mississippi river, above Grand Gulf, not above Greenville.

KINLOCH LANDING.—165 miles up Sunflower river.

KINLEY'S LANDING.—313 miles up Sunflower river.

KINCADE'S.—Yazoo river, not above Yazoo City.

KINCADE'S.—Tallahatchie river, not above Cassidy Bayou.

KINCADE'S BAYOU, *La.*—Black river, not above Harrisonburg.

KINGS.—Mississippi river, above Grand Gulf, not above Greenville.

KING'S GIN.—115 miles up Bœuf river, above Thomas' Landing.

KING'S LANDING.—115 miles up Bœuf river, above Thomas' Landing.

KINSEY'S LANDING.—270 miles up Sunflower river.

KINGSWORTHY, B. H.—Red river, above Fulton, not above Lanesport.

KINKADE, A.—Yazoo river, not above Yazoo City.

KIOMITTIA (MOUTH OF).—Red river, above Mound City.

KIRKPATRICKS.—Bayou Bartholomew, above Portland.

KITTRELL'S.—Bayou Bartholomew, above Portland.

KINDER & HUTCHIN'S LANDING, *Ark.*—Little Red river, 32 miles above its mouth, below the junction of White and Black rivers.

KINGSTON, *Ill.*—Illinois river, above Beardstown, not above the mouth of Fox river.

KING'S GIN, *Ala.*—Alabama river, not above Selma.

KING'S BEND, *Ala.*—Alabama river, not above Selma.

KING'S F. B. LANDING, *Ala.*—Alabama river, not above Selma.

KING'S LANDING, *Ala.*—Warrior river, not above Tuscaloosa.

KINYON, *Ark.*—Black river, above the junction of White river.

KIRKWOOD, *La.*—Atchafalaya river, below Simmsport.

KIRK'S FERRY, *La.*—Tensas river, 42 miles from Trinity, not above the mouth of Bayou Macon.

KIRKLAND'S LANDING, *Ala.*—Tombigbee river, above Gainesville, not above Columbus.

KITHSBURY, *Ill.*—Mississippi river, 1454 miles above New Orleans, above second Rapids, not above Galena.

KLADY PLACE (SCARBOROUGH)—Bayou Bartholomew, not above Point Pleasant.

KNIGHT'S LANDING, *Ark.*—Little Red river, 15 miles above its mouth, below the junction of White and Black rivers.

KNIGHT'S LANDING, *Ala.*—Tombigbee river, above Demopolis, not above Gainesville.

KNIGHT, MRS.—Ouachita river, above Harrisonburg, not above Trenton.

KNOX, J. S. PLACE.—Bayou Bartholomew, above Point Pleasant, not above Arkansas line.

KNOX, J. S. BLUFF.—Bayou Bartholomew, above Point Pleasant, not above Arkansas line.

KNOX, R. J (AND FERRY).—Bayou Bartholomew, above Point Pleasant, not above Arkansas line.

KNOWLTON'S, E. E. LANDING, *Ark.*—Mississippi river, above Greenville, not above Memphis.

KNOWLTON'S LANDING.—Mississippi river, above Greenville, not above Memphis.

KNOXVILLE, *Ala.*—Alabama river, above Selma, not above Wetumpka.

KNOX'S, MRS. LANDING, *Ark.*—Arkansas river, 526 miles above Napoleon, above Norristown, not above Fort Smith.

KOPELY, EST.—Ouachita river, above Harrisonburg, not above Trenton.

KOKO.—Ouachita river, above Harrisonburg, not above Trenton.

KOELUNSA.—Yazoo river, above Yazoo City, not above Leflore.

KOUNS CANAL.—Red river, above foot of Raft, not above Fulton.

KOUNS (or HALL PLANTATION).—Red river, above Shreveport, not above foot of Raft.

KUILWORTH.—Red river, above Grand Ecore, not above Shreveport.

L

LAC DES MEURS.—Red river, above Grand Ecore, not above Shreveport.

LACK MINACKS (or P. A. MORSE).—Red river, above Grand Ecore, not above Shreveport.

LABADIEVILLE, *La.*—Bayou Lafourche.

LABEY'S LANDING.—Mississippi river, above Grand Gulf, not above Greenville.

LACKEY'S LANDING, *Miss.*—Tombigbee river, above Columbus, not above Cotton Gin Port.

LACEY'S SPRING, *Ala.*—Tennessee river, above Florence, not below Eastport.

LACON, *Ill.*—Illinois river, 209 miles above its mouth, above Beardstown, not above the mouth of Fox river.

LACONIA, *Ark.*—Mississippi river, above Greenville, not above Memphis.

LACROSSE, *Miss.*—Mississippi river, 1730 miles above New Orleans, above Galena.

LAFAYETTE CITY, *La.*—Mississippi river, 5 miles above New Orleans.

LAFAYETTE, *Ind.*—Wabash river, above Rapids, not above Terre Haute.

LAFLORE'S LANDING, *Ark.*—Arkansas river, 560 miles above Napoleon, above Fort Smith, not above Fort Gibson.

LAFOURCHE, *La.*—Morgan railroad, 55 miles from New Orleans.

LAFOURCHE CROSSING, *La.*—Bayou Lafeurche.

LAFAYFTTE, *Tenn.*—Cumberland river, not above Nashville.

LAGRANGE, *Ill.*—Illinois river, 81 miles above its mouth, not above Beardstown.

LAGRANGE, *Miss.*—Mississippi river, 1345 miles above New Orleans, above first, not above second Rapids.

LA GREW, *Ark.*—White river, 29 miles above its mouth, below the junction of Black river.

LAKE LANDING, *Miss.*—Mississippi river, above Greenville, not above the mouth of the Ohio.

LAKE PORT, *Ark.*—Mississippi river, above Grand Gulf, not above Greenville.

LAKE CADDO, *La.*—Any point.

LAKE BISTENAU. *La.*—Any point.

LAKE PROVIDENCE, *La.*—Mississippi river, 477 miles above New Orleans, above Grand Gulf, not above Greenville.

LAKE WASHINGTON, *Miss*—Mississippi river, 490 miles above New Orleans, above Grand Gulf, not above Greenville.

LAKE PONTCHARTRAIN, *La.*

LAKE MAUREPAS, *La.*

LAKE BORGNE, *La.*

LAKE BLUFF, *Ark.*—White river, below junction of Black river.

LAKE PEPIN, *Miss.*—Mississippi river, 1812 miles above New Orleans, above Galena.

LAKE CHARLES, C. H. *Texas.*—Sabine river, above Sabine City, not above Belgrade.

LAKE CATHERINE STATION.—Mobile railroad, 24 miles from New Orleans.

LAKE LEE.—Mississippi river, above Grand Gulf, not above Greenville.

LAKE LANDING, or ROLAND'S RAFT.—Ouachita river, above Alabama Landing, not above Camden.

LAKE DICK.—Yazoo river, not above Yazoo City.

LAKE GEORGE (or McMASTER'S).—81 miles up Sunflower river.

LAKE HOME.—Red river, above foot of Raft, not above Fulton.

LAKE WILLIAM (CHICKASAW BAYOU).—Yazoo river, not above Yazoo City.

LAKE PLACE (or CAPT. THOMAS').—Red river, above Shreveport, not above foot of Raft.

LAKE POINT (or CAPT. SENTELL'S).—Red river, above foot of Raft, not above Fulton.

LAKE PAUL.—Red river, above Grand Ecore, not above Shreveport.

LA MINE RIVER, *Mo.*—Missouri river, 208 miles above its mouth above Jefferson City, not above Lexington.

LAMAR, *Miss.*—Jackson railroad, 381 miles from New Orleans.

LANCASTER, *Ind.*—Wabash river, not above the Rapids.

LANESPORT, *Ark.*—Red river, 364 miles above Shreveport.

LAFITTA.--Ouachita river, above Harrisonburg, not above Trenton.

LAHAGAN, DR. W.—Red river, above Grand Ecore, not above Shreveport.

LAMNAY, MAD.—Red river, above Grand Ecore, not above Shreveport.

LAMKIN.—Tallahatchie river, not above Cassidy Bayou.

LANDANAN'S.—95 miles up Bœuf river, above Thomas' Landing.

LANDRY, BALLIE, LANDING.—Red river, not above Alexandria.

LANDRY, ST. ANDRY.—Red river, above Cane river, not above Grand Ecore.

LANTANNEA BAYOU.—Red river, not above Alexandria.

LANGSLEY'S.—Mississippi river, above Grand Gulf, not above Greenville.

LANGSTON, *Ala.*—Tennessee river, above Florence, not below Eastport.

LANGSLEY'S, S. LANDING, *La.*—Black river, La., not above Harrisonburg.

LANSING, *Iowa.*—Mississippi river, 1694 miles above New Orleans. above Galena.

LANE'S LANDING, *La.*—Lake Caddo.

LANE'S LANDING, *Mo.*—Mississippi river, above the mouth of the Ohio, not above Alton.

LANCASTER, *Ill.*—Illinois river, above Beardstown, not above the mouth of Fox river.

LANCERS WOODYARD, *Ark.*—Mississippi river, above Greenville, not above Memphis.

LANCERS' LANDING, *Ark.*—Mississippi river, above Greenville, not above Memphis.

LANGO, W. W., *Ala.*—Tombigbee river, not above Demopolis.

LARGO, *Ind.*—Wabash river, above the Rapids, not above Terre Haute.

LARIO.—Red river, above Alexandria, not above mouth of Cane river.

LARKEY SPRING.—Ouachita river, above Alabama Landing, not above Camden.

LASALLE, *Ill.*—Illinois river, 247 miles above its mouth, above Beardstown, not above the mouth of Fox river.

LAST RETREAT, *La.*—Bayou Macon, 59 miles from its mouth, not above Monticello.

LAST ALBAN CANAL (or Wreck of Cuba No. 2.)—Red river, above foot of Raft, not above Fulton.

LAST LANDING.—Yazoo river, not above Yazoo City.

LAST RESORT.—Tallahatchie river, not above Cassidy Bayou.

LAST CHANCE (J. A. PICKETT).—Red river, above Grand Ecore, not above Shreveport.

LATENACHE LANDING, *La.*—Atchafalaya river, below Simmsport.

LATTIER, F. (or B. GRAFF).—Red river, above Grand Ecore, not above Shreveport.

LATTIER, ADOLPH.—Red river, above Grand Ecore, not above Shreveport.

LATTIER'S, M. (MUD HOUSE).—Red river, above Grand Ecore, not above Shreveport.

LATTIER'S, M. (RUSH ISLAND).—Red river, above Grand Ecore, not above Shreveport.

LATOAKA.—Red river, above Grand Ecore, not above Shreveport.

LATROBE LANDING.—Mississippi river, above Greenville, not above Memphis.

LAUREL HILL.—Mississippi river, 1115 miles above New Orleans, above the mouth of the Ohio, not above Alton.

LAUREL HILL, *La.*—(Interior.) Shipping point at Bayou Sara.

LAVONA, *Ky.*—Ohio river, 583 miles above its mouth, above Cincinnati.

LAVONIA, *Ark.*—Mississippi river, above Greenville, not above Memphis.

LAVELLERS, JUDGE LANDING, *Mo.*—Mississippi river, above Memphis, not above the mouth of the Ohio.

LAWRY'S, WM. LANDING, *Ark.*—Little Red river, 38 miles from its mouth, below the junction of White and Black rivers.

LAWRENCEVILLE, *Ark.*—White river, below the junction of Black river.

LAWDEN'S (D. F.) LANDING, *Texas.*—Red river, 424 miles above Shreveport, above Lanesport, not above Mound City.

LAWRENCEBURG, *Ind.*—Ohio river, 519 miles above its mouth, above Paducah, not above Cincinnati.

LAW'S LANDING, *Miss.*—Tombigbee river, above Gainesville, not above Columbus.

LAYSARD, MALIFORD.—Red river, above Alexandria, not above mouth of Cane river.

LAYSARD, F. E. (Store).—Red river, above Alexandria, not above mouth of Cane river.

LAYTON'S LANDING, *La.*—Ouachita river, above Harrisonburg, not above Trenton.

LAZARE'S LANDING, *La.*—Ouachita river, above Harrisonburg, not above Trenton.

LE ARNICK'S (or FUR POINT).—Red river, above Shreveport, not above foot of Raft.

LEAST, SAM.—Yazoo river, not above Yazoo City.

LEBANON.—Ouachita river, not above Harrisonburg.

LEBARGE (HOPE WOODYARD).—Ouachita river, not above Harrisonburg.

LEBAUM, H.—Ouachita river, above Harrisonburg, not above Trenton.

LEACHMAN, *Mo.*—Missouri river, 482 miles above its mouth, above Iatan.

LEAKESVILLE, *Miss.*—Chicasaha river.

LEES' LANDING, *Ill.*—Mississippi river, above the mouth of the Ohio, not above Alton.

LEAVENWORTH, *Ind.*—Ohio river, 319 miles above its mouth, above Paducah, not above Cincinnati.

LEE'S LANDING, *Ala.*—Alabama river, not above Selma.

LEE'S, BENJ. LANDING.—Red river, above Cotile, not above Grand Ecore.

LEE'S LANDING, *La.*—Red river, 4 miles above Shreveport, not above Carolina Bluff.

LECLAIRE, *Ia.*—Mississippi river, 1535 miles above New Orleans, above second Rapids, not above Galena.

LEFLORE, *Miss.*—Yazoo river, 257 miles from Vicksburg, above Yazoo City, not above Leflore.

LEE, F. D. & WESLEY LEE.—Red river, above Carolina Bluff, not above Fulton.

LEE'S, MRS.—Red river, above Carolina Bluff, not above Fulton.

LEE, MAJOR.—Red river, above Fulton, not above Lanesport.

LEE'S LANDING.—Sunflower river.

LEE, JOHN, LANDING, *Miss.*—180 miles up Big Deer Creek.

LEE, BEN. S.—Red river, above Grand Ecore, not above Shreveport.

LECOMPTE, F.—Red river, above Grand Ecore, not above Shreveport.

LEGGETTS, J.—Ouachita river, above Harrisonburg, not above Trenton.

LEGGETT'S LANDING, *Ala.*—Alabama river, not above Selma.

LEMAY'S LANDING, *Ark.*—Red river, 156 miles above Shreveport, above Carolina Bluff, not above Fulton.

LEMANDER, *La.*—(Interior) Shipping port Bayou Sara.

LEMOYNE'S LANDING, *Ark.*—Arkansas river, 403 miles above Napoleon, above Norristown, not above Fort Smith.

LENOIR'S LANDING, *Ala.*—Alabama river, not above Selma.

LEOTA, *La.*—Black river, not above Harrisonburg.

LEOTA LANDING, *Miss.*—Lake Washington, Mississippi river, above Grand Gulf, not above Greenville.

LEONA LANDING, *Miss.*—Mississippi river, above Grand Gulf, not above Greenville.

LESLER'S FERRY, *La.*—Bayou Macon, 180 miles from its month not above Monticello.

LESLIE'S LANDING. Alabama river, not above Selma.

LETARTSVILLE, *Ohio.*—Ohio river, 765 miles above its mouth, above Cincinnati.

LEVASSIEUR, E. B.—Red river, above Grand Ecore, not above Shreveport.

LEVEL'S LANDING.—339 miles up Sunflower river.

LEAVENWORTH.—Missouri river, 438 miles from its mouth, above Lexington, not above Iatan.

LEVETT'S BLUFF.—Bayou Bartholomew, not above Point Pleasant, above Arkansas line.

LEVY, J. L.—Red river, above Grand Ecore, not above Shreveport.

LEVEE CHALK.—Red river, above Grand Ecore, not above Shreveport.

LEVY & HAAS.—Ouachita river, above Harrisonburg, not above Trenton.

LEWIS, E. (or MRS. BUTLER'S).—Red river, above foot of Raft, not above Fulton.

LEWIS, DR. LANDING.—135 miles up Bœuf river, above Thomas' Landing.

LEWIS (WOODYARD).—Red river, not above Alexandria.

LEWIS (or FINLAY).—Red river, above foot of Raft, not above Fulton.

LETARD, X. (J. A. TURNER).—Red river, above Grand Ecore, not above Shreveport.

LEWISBURG, *Ind.*—Wabash river, above the Rapids, not above Terre Haute.

LEWIS' LANDING, *Ark.*—Arkansas river, 383 miles above Napoleon, above Little Rock, not above Norristown.

LEWIS,' M. W., LANDING, *Ark.*—Arkansas river, 125 miles above Napoleon, above Arkansas Post, not above Pine Bluff.

LEWISPORT, *Ky.*—Ohio river, 249 miles above its mouth, above Paducah, not above Cincinnati.

LEWISVILLE, *Ark*—Red river, above Black Bayou, not above White Oak Shoals.

LEWIS' FERRY, *Texas.*—Neches river, above the junction of Angelina river.

LEWELLYL, *Ark.*—Mississippi river, above Greenville, not above Memphis.

LEWIS' LANDING, *La.*—Bayou Macon, 20 miles from its mouth, not above Monticello.

LEWIS', M. LANDING, *Ala.*—Tombigbee river, not above Demopolis.

LEWIS', N., *Ala.*—Tombigbee river, not above Demopolis.

LEWISBURG, *Ark.*—Arkansas river, 351 miles above Napoleon, above Little Rock, not above Norristown.

LEWISBURG, *La.*—Lake Pontchartrain.

LEXINGTON LANDING, *Ala.*—Alabama river, not above Selma.

LEXINGTON, *Mo.*—Missouri river, 337 miles above its mouth, above Jefferson City.

LINDEN.—Yazoo river, above Yazoo City, not above Leflore.

LIMERICK.—Yazoo river, not above Yazoo City.

LINE BAYOU.—260 miles up Sunflower river.

LIND GROVE.—Bayou Bartholomew, above Point Pleasant, not above Arkansas line.

L'HOMOND'S LANDING, *La.*—Ouachita river, above Trenton, not above Alabama Landing.

LIBERTY, *Ill.*—Mississippi river, 1083 miles above New Orleans, above the mouth of the Ohio river, not above Alton.

LIBERTY, *Ark.*—White river, 347 miles from the Mississippi river, above Batesville.

LIBERTY, *Texas.*—Trinity river, not above.

LIBERTY LANDING, *Mo.*—Missouri river, 388 miles above its mouth, above Lexington, not above Iatan.

LICKING RIVER, *Ohio.*—Ohio river, 542 miles above its mouth, above Paducah, not above Cincinnati.

LIDDEL'S LANDING, *La.*—Black river, La.

LILE'S, JNO., LANDING, *La.*—Ouachita river, above Harrisonburg, not above Trenton.

LIMA LANDING.—Mississippi river, above Greenville, not above Memphis.

LIMAN'S, BEN., LANDING, *Miss.*—Mississippi river, above Grand Gulf, not above Greenville.

LINHOOP.—Mississippi river, 1118 miles above New Orleans, above Memphis.

LINSEY'S, JAS., LANDING, *La.*—Atchafalaya river, below Simmsport.

LINDSAY'S, DR., LANDING, *Ala.*—Alabama river, not above Selma.

LINDSAY'S FERRY, *Miss.*—Tombigbee river, above Gainesville, not above Columbus.

LINEPORT, *Tenn.*—Cumberland river, not above Nashville.

LINWOOD'S LANDING, *Ark.*—Mississippi river, above Greenville, not above Memphis.

LINWOOD'S, M., LANDING, *La.*—Mississippi river, not above Bayou Sara.

LIPSCOMB'S LANDING, *Ark.*—Arkansas river, 203 miles above Napoleon, above Pine Bluff, not above Little Rock.

LISBON, *Ala.*—Alabama river, not above Selma.

LISSO'S LANDING, *La.*—Red river, above Grand Ecore, not above Shreveport.

LITTLE MISSOURI, *La.*—Atchafalaya river, below Simmsport.

LITTLE ISLAND, *Ark.*—White river, 335 miles above its mouth, below the junction of Black river.

LITTLE PRAIRIE LANDING, *La.*—Black river, La.

LITTLE RED RIVER, *Ark.*—White river, 251 miles above its mouth, below the junction of Black river.

LITTLE HILL, *Ark.*—White river, 188 miles above its mouth, below the junction of Black river.

LITTLE ROCK, *Mo.*—Mississippi river, 1275 miles above New Orleans, above the mouth of the Ohio river, not above Alton.

LITTLE ROCK, *Ark.*—Arkansas river, 280 miles above Napoleon, above Pine Bluff.

LITTLE PRAIRIE LANDING, *Ark.*—Red river, 190 miles above Shreveport, above Carolina Bluff, not above Fulton.

LITTLE PRAIRIE LANDING, *Ark.*—Black river, above the junction of White river.

LITTLE PRAIRIE.—Mississippi river, 933 miles above New Orleans, above Greenville, not above Memphis.

LINWOOD.—Ouachita river, above Harrisonburg, not above Trenton.

LISLE.—Ouachita river, above Harrisonburg, not above Trenton.

LITTLE BAY.—Ouachita river, above Alabama Landing, not above Camden.

LITTLE BLACK.—Yazoo river, above Yazoo City, not above Leflore.

LITTLE HOPE LANDING.—119 miles up Sunflower river.

LITTLE PRAIRIE.—Red river, not above Alexandria.

LITTLE PRAIRIE.—Black river, La., not above Trinity.

LITTLE PASS (ALBON).—Red river, above Shreveport, not above Carolina Bluff.

LITTLE RIVER (MOUTH OF).—Red river, above Cane river, not above Grand Ecore.

LIVINGSTON (OLD PLACE).—Bayou Bartholomew, above Point Pleasant, not above Arkansas line.

LLANADA, *La.*—Black river, not above Harrisonburg.

LITTLE MIAMIE RIVER, *Ohio.*—Ohio river, 539 miles above its mouth, above Cincinnati.

LITTLE KENAWHA RIVER, *Va.*—Ohio river, 539 miles above its mouth, above Cincinnati.

LITTLE BAY.—Ouachita river, above Alabama Landing, not above Camden.

LITTLE RIVER, *La.*—Not above the mouth of Old river.

LITTLE PLATTE RIVER, *Ia.*—Missouri river, 419 miles above its mouth, above Lexington, not above Iatan.

LITTLE DETROIT, *Ill.*—Illinois river, 179 miles above its mouth, above Beardstown, not above the mouth of Fox river.

LITCHFIELD, *Ark.*—White river, below the junction of Black river.

LITTLE FORK BAYOU, *La.*—Bayou Macon, 110 miles from its mouth, not above Monticello.

LIVE OAK LANDING, *Ala.*—Alabama river, not above Selma.

LIVE OAK LANDING, *La*—Black river, La., not above Harrisonburg.

LIVERPOOL, *Ohio.*—Obio river, 957 miles above its mouth, above Cincinnati.

LIVERPOOL, *Miss.*—Yazoo river, 74 miles from Vicksburg, not above Yazoo City.

LIVERPOOL, *Ill*—Illinois river, 131 miles from its mouth, above Beardstown, not above the mouth of Fox river.

LIVINGSTON, *Mo.*—Missouri river, 383 miles above its mouth, above Lexington, not above Iatan.

LIVINGSTON, *Ill.*—Wabash river, above Terre Haute.

LLOYD'S PLANTATION, *La.*—Tensas river, 44 miles from Trinity, not above Bayou Macon.

LLOYD'S BRIDGE, *La.*—Bayou Bœuf.

LOCK PLACE.—Red river, above Fulton, not above Lanesport.

LOCUST GROVE.—Ouachita river, above Alabama Landing, not above Camden.

LOCUST GROVE.—Yazoo river, not above Yazoo City.

LOCUST GROVE.—Ouachita river, above Harrisonburg, not above Trenton.

LODE —Yazoo river, above Yazoo City, not above Leflore.

LOE DES MUIR.—Red river, above Grand Ecore, not above Shreveport.

LOFLORE'S LANDING.—Arkansas river, above Fort Smith, not above Fort Gibson.

LOBDELL'S STORE, *La.*—Mississippi river, above New Orleans, not above Bayou Sara.

LOCHLEMOND, *La.*—Ouachita river, above Harrisonburg, not above Trenton.

LOCKPORT, *La.*—Bayou Lafourche, below Thibodeaux.

LOCKPORT, *Ind.*—Wabash river, above the Rapids, not above Terre Haute.

LODI LANDING, *Ala*—Alabama river, above Selma, not above Wetumpka..

LOFTIN'S LANDING, *Ala.*—Alabama river, above Selma, not above Wetumpka.

LOGGY BAYOU, *La.*—Red river, 590 miles above New Orleans, above Grand Ecore, not above Shreveport.

LOGAN'S PORT, *Ind.*—Wabash river, above the Rapids, not above Terre Haute.

LOGAN'S PORT, *Texas.*—Sabine river, above Hamilton.

LOGREE'S SPRING, *Ark.*—White river, below the junction of Black river.

LOGAN'S, Z. LANDING, *Ala.*—Warrior river, not above Tuscaloosa.

LOGAN'S LANDING, *Ala.*—Warrior river, not above Tuscaloosa.

LOGAN'S, LEROY LANDING, *Ala.*—Warrior river, not above Tuscaloosa.

LOGTOWN, *La.*—Ouachita river, above Harrisonburg, not above Trenton.

LONGMEYER'S, R. LANDING, *Ala.*—Alabama river, not above Selma.

LONGMEYER'S, J. LANDING, *Ala.*—Alabama river, not above Selma.

LONGBRIDGE'S LANDING, *Miss.*—Tombigbee river, above Columbus, not above Cotton Gin Port.

LONE PINE, *Ark.*—Ouachita river, above Alabama Landing.

LONG'S, O. P. LANDING, *La.*—Atchafalaya river, below Simmsport.

LONGUEVILLE, *La.*—Bayou Lafourche.

LORENZO'S, JAMES LANDING, *Ala.*—Alabama river, not above Selma.

LOST BEND, *La.*—Black river, La., not above Harrisonburg.

LOTT'S LANDING, *Ala.*—Tombigbee river, not above Demopolis.

LOUISVILLE, *Ky.*—Ohio river, 383 miles above its mouth, above Paducah, not above Cincinnati.

LOUISIANA & MISSISSIPPI LINE.—Mississippi river, 207 miles above New Orleans, above Bayou Sara, not above Grand Gulf.

LOUISIANA LINE.—Mississippi river, 498 miles above New Orleans, above Grand Gulf, not above Greenville.

LOUISIANA, *Mo.*—Mississippi river, above the foot of first not above the foot of the second Rapids.

LOURS, *La.*—Morgan railroad, 70 miles from New Orleans,

LOVE'S LANDING, *Ark.*—Arkansas river, 374 miles above Napoleon, above Little Rock, not above Norristown.

LONE POINT (or SQUIRREL POINT).—Red river, above Grand Ecore, not above Shreveport.

LONG POINT.—Red river, above foot of Raft, not above Fulton.

LONG LAKE.—Ouachita river, above Harrisonburg, not above Trenton.

LONG WOOD (or FUQUA).—Yazoo river, not above Yazoo City.

LONG'S LANDING.—Mississippi river, above Grand Gulf, not above Greenville.

LOOKOUT (STATION).—34 miles from New Orleans, on Mobile railroad.

LOTUS PLACE.—Red river, above Grand Ecore, not above Shreveport.

LOUISIANA LINE.—Bayou Bartholomew, above Point Pleasant, not above Arkansas line.

LOURNE, J.—Red river, above Cane river, not above Grand Ecore.

LOUSY LEVEL.—Yazoo river, above Yazoo City, not above Leflore.

LOWEN PIGEON HILL.—Ouachita river, above Alabama Landing, not above Camden.

LOWERRIES, MRS. *La.*—Mississippi river, above Grand Gulf, not above Greenville.

LOWRY PL. (L. TEMPLEMAN'S).—Red river, above Grand Ecore, not above Shreveport.

LOVE'S LANDING, *Ala.*—Alabama river, above Selma, not above Wetumpka.

LOVETT'S LANDING, *Ala.*—Alabama river, not above Selma.

LOWE'S LANDING, *Ala.*—Tombigbee river, above Demopolis, not above Gainesville.

LOW PEACH TREE LANDING, *Ala.*—Alabama river, 152 miles above Mobile, not above Selma.

LOWELL, *Ga.*—Chattahoochie river, not above Columbus.

LOWE'S LANDING —Mississippi river, 1045 miles above New Orleans, above the mouth of the Ohio river, not above Alton.

LOWER SWAN LAKE, *Ark.*—Arkansas river, 118 miles above Napoleon, above Arkansas Post, not above Pine Bluff.

LOWND'S PORT, *Ala.*—Alabama river, 329 miles above Mobile above Selma, not above Wetumpka.

LOWNDESVILLE, *Miss.*—Tombigbee river, above Gainesville, not above Columbus.

LUCAS' LANDING, *Mo.*—Mississippi river, above Memphis, not above mouth of Ohio.

LUCKETT'S LANDING, *La.*—Red river, above Alexandria, not above Cane river.

LUCY'S LANDING, *La.*—Ouachita river, above Harrisonburg, not above Trenton.

LUCKETT'S, DR. (ASHBURN).—Red river, above Alexandria, not above Cane river.

LUM'S LANDING.—Mississippi river, above Bayou Sara, not above, Grand Gulf.

LUM'S LANDING, *La.*—Black river, La.

LUNA LANDING, *Ark.*—Mississippi river, 637 miles above New Orleans, above Greenville, not above Memphis.

LUSKS.—Yazoo river, above Yazoo City, not above Leflore.

LYNCH PLACE.—Yazoo river, above Yazoo City, not above Leflore.

LYNCHBURG, *Tenn.*—Cumberland river, not above Nashville.

LYNN GROVE LANDING, *La.*—Bayou Bartholomew, above Point Pleasant, not above Arkansas line.

LYNN GROVE, *Ind.*—Wabash river, not above the Rapids.

LYON'S, *Iowa.*—Mississippi river, 1561 miles above New Orleans, above the second Rapids, not above Galena.

LYNXVILLE, *Ill.*—Mississippi river, 1686 miles above New Orleans, above Galena.

LYON'S LANDING, *La.*—Atchafalaya river, below Simmsport.

Mc

McALLISTER'S.—Bayou Bartholomew, above Portland.
McALLISTER'S LANDING, *La.*—Mississippi river, 396 miles above New Orleans, above Grand Gulf, not above Greenville.
McALPIN'S LANDING, *Ala.*—Tombigbee river, above Demopolis, not above Gainesville.
McALPIN'S FERRY, *Ala.*—Warrior river, not above Tuscaloosa.
McBRADE'S LANDING, *La.*—Atchafalaya river, below Simmsport.
McBEE LANDING (MRS. BARKHOW'S).—Yazoo river, above Yazoo City, not above Leflore.
McCARTY'S FERRY, *Ala.*—Tombigbee river, not above Demopolis.
McCARTY'S, JOE LANDING, *Ala.*—Tombigbee river, not above Demopolis.
McCARTY'S BLUFF, *Miss.*—Tombigbee river, above Gainesville, not above Columbus.
McCARTHY'S LANDING, *Ark.*—White river, 218 miles from its mouth, below the junction of Black river.
McCABE'S LANDING, *La.*—Black river, La.
McCLURE'S, MRS. L. L. LANDING, *La.*—Black river, La., not above Harrisonburg.
McCLURE'S, MRS. M. L. LANDING, *La.*—Black river, La., not above Harrisonburg.
McCOWAN'S BLUFF, *Ala.*—Warrior river, not above Tuscaloosa.
McCREA'S, J. J. LANDING, *La.*—Atchafalaya river, below Simmsport.
McCUTCHEON'S POINT, *La.*—Mississippi river, 25 miles above New Orleans, not above Bayou Sara.
McCUNNINSBY LANDING (or McCONNAUGHEY'S), *Ark.*—Arkansas river, 264 miles above Napoleon, above Pine Bluff, not above Little Rock.
McCLINTOCK'S LANDING, *Ark.*—Red river, 154 miles above Shreveport, above Carolina Bluff, not above Fulton.
McCARTHY'S.—Yazoo river, not above Yazoo City.
McCALEB.—Tallahatchie river, not above Cassidy Bayou.
McCANE'S.—Red river, above foot of Raft, not above Fulton.
McCOMBS & EASTMAN.—Bayou Bartholomew, above Portland.

McCLANAHAN.—89 miles up Bœuf river, above Thomas' Landing

McCLINTOCK, J. (or CALIFORNIA PLANTATION).—Red river, above foot of Raft, not above Fulton.

McCLINTOCK, STONE.—Red river, above foot of Raft, not above Fulton.

McCREIGHT, DR. (PAXTON).—Bayou Bartholomew, above Point Pleasant, not above Arkansas line.

McDANIELS, J. B.—77 miles up Bœuf river, above Thomas' Landing.

McDANIELS.—81 miles up Bœuf river, above Thomas' Landing.

McDONALD'S.—73 miles up Bœuf river, above Thomas' Landing.

McDONALD'S, TOM.—74 miles up Bœuf river, above Thomas' Landing.

McDONALD LANDING.—Ouachita river, above Alabama Landing, not above Camden.

McDONALD, A.—Ouachita river, above Harrisonburg, not above Trenton.

McDANIEL'S LANDING, *Ala.*—Warrior river, not above Tuscaloosa.

McDANIEL'S, JUDGE LANDING, *Ark.*—Little Red river, 26 miles from its mouth, below the junction of Black and White rivers.

McDAVID'S WOODYARD, *Ala.*—Alabama river, not above Selma.

McDUFFY'S LANDING, *Ala.*—Alabama river, not above Selma.

McDOWELL'S LANDING, *Ala.*—Tombigbee river, not above Demopolis.

McDONALD'S LANDING, *La.*—Black river, La.

McDONALD'S, MRS. LANDING, *La.*—Ouachita river, above Harrisonburg, not above Trenton.

McDONALD'S LANDING, *Ala.*—Alabama river, not above Selma.

McECKRIDGE'S LANDING, *Ala.*—Tombigbee river, not above Demopolis.

McFADDEN.—Ouachita river, not above Harrisonburg.

McFARLAND'S, DR. LANDING, *La.*—Red river, above Grand Ecore, not above Shreveport.

McGAVOCK'S LANDING, *Ark.*—Mississippi river, 866 miles from New Orleans, above Greenville, not above Memphis.

McGREGOR'S FLOUR LANDING, *Ark.*—Arkansas river, above Pine Bluff, not above Little Rock.

McGEE'S.—Red river, above foot of Raft, not above Fulton.

McGEE, DR. (or WILLOW POINT).—Red river, above foot of Raft, not above Fulton.

McGEHEE.—Ouachita river, above Harrisonburg, not above Trenton.

McGREGGOR'S LANDING.—156 miles up Sunflower river.

McGILL (or BEN. HAWKINS).—Red river, above Fulton, not above Lanesport.

McGREGOR'S LANDING.—Mississippi river, 533 miles above St. Louis, above Galena.

McGUIRE'S LANDING, *Ark*.—White river, not above Batesville.

McGUYRE'S LANDING, *Ala*.—Alabama river, not above Selma.

McGIFFORD'S LANDING, *Ala*.—Warrior river, not above Tuscaloosa.

McINTOSH'S LANDING, *Ala*.—Alabama river, not above Selma.

McINTYRE'S LANDING, *La*.—Red river, above Grand Ecore, not above Shreveport.

McINTOCH, DR.—Bœuf river, above Thomas' Landing.

McJEMISON'S LANDING, *Ala*.—Warrior river, not above Tuscaloosa.

McKAIN'S LANDING, *Ala*.—Red river, 16 miles above Shreveport, not above Carolina Bluff.

McKEE.—Yazoo river, not above Yazoo City.

McKENZIE LANDING.—Arkansas river, not above Pine Bluff.

McKEY'S LANDING.—Bœuf river, above Thomas' Landing.

McKINNEY, WIDOW.—Red river, above Grand Ecore, not above Shreveport.

McKINNEY, E. P.—Red river, above Grand Ecore, not above Shreveport.

McKNEELEY'S LANDING, *Ark*.—Red river, 322 miles above Shreveport, above Fulton, not above Lanesport.

McKNIGHT'S LANDING, *La*.—Red river, above Grand Ecore, not above Shreveport.

McLEOD.—212 miles up Sunflower river.

McLEOUD'S.—95 miles up Bœuf river, above Thomas' Landing.

McLEROY, DR.—118 miles up Bœuf river, above Thomas' Landing.

McLENDER'S LANDING, *Ark*.—Red river, 279 miles above its mouth, above Shreveport, not above Carolina Bluff.

McLEAD'S FERRY, *Ala*.—Alabama river, not above Selma.

McLAURAN'S LANDING, *La.*—Red river, above Cotile, not above Grand Ecore.

McMAHAN.—Ouachita river, above Alabama Landing, not above Camden.

McNEALD (or JNO. DEYSON PLANTATION).—Red river, above foot of Raft, not above Fulton.

McLAURAN'S LANDING, *Miss.*—Tombigbee river, above Gainesville, not above Columbus.

McMASTER'S (or LAKE GEORGE).—81 miles up Sunflower river.

McNEILL'S GIN, *Ala.*—Alabama river, not above Selma.

McNEILL'S LANDING, *Ala.*—Alabama river, not above Selma.

McNEILL'S LANDING, *Miss.*—Mississippi river, above Greenville, not above Memphis.

McNEILL'S LANDING, *Ark.*—Arkansas river, 219 miles above Napoleon, above Pine Bluff, not above Little Rock.

McOWEN'S LANDING, *Ark.*—Red river, 346 miles above Shreveport, above Fulton, not above Lanesport.

McPHERSON'S WOODYARD, *Ark.*—Mississippi river, 718 miles above New Orleans, above Greenville, not above Memphis.

McPIPE'S LANDING, *Mo.*—Mississippi river, 1161 miles from New Orleans, above the Ohio river, not above Alton.

McRAE.—Bayou Bartholomew, not above Point Pleasant.

McRAY PLACE.—109 miles up Bœuf river, above Thomas' Landing.

McSWAINS.—Ouachita river, above Harrisonburg, not above Trenton.

McTYRE, RANNY.—Red river, above Grand Ecore, not above Shreveport.

McWILLIAMS, MATTHEWS.—Bayou Bartholomew, not above Point Pleasant.

McSWEENEY'S LANDING, *Ala.*—Tombigbee river, not above Demopolis.

McWILLIAMS' WOODYARD, *Ala.*—Alabama river, not above Selma.

M

MABIN'S LANDING, *Miss.*—76 miles up Sunflower river.

MACKEQUETA RIVER, *Iowa.*—Mississippi river, 1593 miles above New Orleans, above the second Rapids, not above Galena.

MACE'S, COL. W.—Red river, above Alexandria, not above Cane river.

MACKVILLE, *Miss.*—122 miles up Big Deer Creek.

MADISON, *Ind.*—Ohio river, 441 miles above its mouth, above Paducah, not above Cincinnati.

MADISON.—St. Francois river, not above Wettsburg.

MADISON, *Ill.*—Mississippi river, 1194 miles above New Orleans, above mouth of the Ohio, not above Alton.

MADISON, *Texas.*—Sabine river, above Sabine City, not above Belgrade.

MADISONVILLE, *La.*—Lake Pontchartrain.

MADDEN ROCK CITY.—Mississippi river, 279 miles above St. Louis, above Galena.

MADDOX BAY, *Ark.*—White river, 97 miles from its mouth, below the junction of Black river.

MAES LANDING.—123 miles up Bœuf river, above Thomas' Landing.

MAGENTA.—Yazoo river, above Yazoo City, not above Leflore.

MAGNOLIA GROVE, *Miss.*—115 miles up Big Deer Creek.

MAGEE'S, JACOB, LANDING, *Ala.*—Alabama river, not above Selma.

MAGNOLIA, *Ala.*—Tombigbee river, not above Demopolis.

MAGNOLIA BLUFF, *Ala.*—Alabama river, not above Selma.

MAGNOLIA LANDING, *Texas.*—Trinity river.

MAGNOLIA, *Miss.*—Jackson railroad, 98 miles from New Orleans.

MAGNOLIA, *La.*—Black river, not above Harrisonburg.

MAGNOLIA (or HUTCHINSON).—Red river, above Grand Ecore, not above Shreveport.

MAGRUDER, DR. (or DR. HALL).—Red river, above Alexandria, not above Cane river.

MAGNESSY, *Ark.*—White river, not above Batesville.

MAGGINNIS, MORGAN, *Ark.*—White river, not above Batesville.

MAHEE, P., *La.*—Mississippi river, above Grand Gulf, not above Greenville.

MALIFORD, LAYSARD.—Red river, above Alexandria, not above mouth of Cane river.

MALONE'S, S. LANDING, *Ala.*—Tombigbee river, not above Demopolis.

MALONE'S, G. B. LANDING.—Tombigbee river, not above Demopolis.

MALONE'S COTTON SHED, *Miss.*—Tombigbee river, above Columbus, not above Cotton Gin Port.

MALLORY'S LANDING, *La.*—Mississippi river, 354 miles above New Orleans, above Grand Gulf, not above Greenville.

MANCHESTER.—Yazoo river, above Yazoo City, not above Leflore.

MANCHESTER, *Ohio.*—Ohio river, 606 miles above its mouth, above Cincinnati.

MANCHESTER, *Tenn.*—Ohio river, 1003 miles above its mouth, above Cincinnati.

MANEPORT, *Ind.*—Ohio river, above Paducah, not above Cincinnati.

MANFERT, A. (CEDAR BLUFF.—Red river, above Shreveport, not above Carolina Bluff.

MANY, *La.*—(Interior) Shipping port, Grand Ecore, on the Red river.

MANNYVILLE, *Va.*—Ohio river, 899 miles above its mouth, above Cincinnati.

MANCHAC, *La.*—Iberville river, below Bayou Sara, 131 miles above New Orleans, on the Mississippi river.

MANCHAC, *La.*—Jackson railroad, 37 miles from New Orleans.

MANDEVILLE, *La.*—Lake Pontchartrain.

MANSFIELD LANDING.—Bayou Pierre, DeSoto parish, La.

MARCY'S ISLAND, L. (Cut-off).—Red river, above Grand Ecore, not above Shreveport.

MARSHALL'S, JACOB.—Red river, above Grand Ecore, not above Shreveport.

MARSHALL'S LANDING.—Mississippi river, above Grand Gulf, not above Greenville.

MARDIS, OLD LANDING.—Black river, La.

MAPLE SHADE.—Tallahatchie river, not above Cassidy Bayou.

MARION.—Missouri river, above Jefferson City, not above Lexington.

MANOMIN, *Minn.*—Mississippi river, 1878 miles above New Orleans, above Galena.

MANSFIELD'S LANDING.—Ouachita river, above Harrisonburg, not above Trenton.

MANNY'S BEND, *Mo.*—Missouri river, 250 miles above its mouth, above Jefferson City, not above Lexington.

MANLEY'S LANDING, *Mo.*—Missouri river, 524 miles from St. Louis, above Iatan.

MANTANZAS, *Ill.*—Illinois river, 181 miles from St. Louis, above Beardstown, not above the mouth of Fox river.

MANNING'S PLANTATION, *La.*—Mississippi river, 73 miles above New Orleans, not above Bayou Sara.

MANNING'S LANDING, *Mo.*—Mississippi river, 1091 miles above New Orleans, above the Ohio river, not above Alton.

MANITEAU, *Mo.*—Missouri river, 171 miles above its mouth, above Jefferson City, not above Lexington.

MARBLE, R. D. (WEST BEND.—Bayou Bartholomew, not above Point Pleasant.

MARCOFF'S.—Red river, not above Alexandria.

MARCELLA.—Yazoo river, above Yazoo City, not above Leflore.

MARCH BANK.—Tallahatchie river, not above Cassidy Bayou.

MARCH PRAIRIE.—Tallahatchie river, not above Cassidy Bayou.

MARSHALL, *Texas.*—In Harrison county.

MARSHALL'S, J. (Woodyard.—Red river, not above Alexandria.

MARKS' LOWER PLACE (or MATTOCK.—Red river, above Shreveport, not above foot of Raft.

MARKS (or BROFIOLD).—Red river, above Shreveport, not above foot of Raft.

MARKS (or CEDAR BLUFF).—Red river, above foot of Raft, not above Fulton.

MARKS' UPPER PLACE.—Red river, above foot of Raft, not above Fulton.

MARINE SALINE LANDING, *Ark.*—Ouachita river, 375 miles above the mouth of Old river, above Alabama Landing, not above Camden.

MARSHALL'S LOWER LANDING, *Ala.*—Alabama river, not above Selma.

MARSHALL'S GIN, *Ala.*—Alabama river, not above Selma.

MARSHALL'S UPPER LANDING, *Ala.*—Alabama river, not above Selma.

MARSH'S LANDING, *Ala.*—Alabama river, not above Selma.

MARBIN'S, DR. LANDING, *Ala.*—Alabama river, not above Selma.

MARSTON'S, MRS. LANDING, *Ala.*—Alabama river, not above Selma.

MARTIN'S LANDING, *Ark.*—Mississippi river, above Greenville, not above Memphis.

MARTIN'S LANDING, *Mo.*—Mississippi river, 972 miles above New Orleans, above Memphis, not above the mouth of the Ohio.

MARTIN'S LANDING.—Mississippi river, 62 miles above St. Louis, above Alton, not above first Rapids.

MARTINSBURG, *Ky.*—Cumberland river, above Gainesboro.

MARTINSVILLE, *Ohio.*—Ohio river, 912 miles above its mouth, above Cincinnati.

MARYLAND'S LANDING, *Miss.*—Mississippi river, above Grand Gulf, not above Greenville.

MARION, *Ark.*—Ouachita river, above Alabama Landing, not above Camden.

MARION, *Mo.*—Missouri river, 165 miles above its mouth, above Jefferson City, not above Lexington.

MARION, *Texas.*—Angelina river, above Bevil Port, not above Partonia.

MARION CITY, *Mo*—Mississippi river, above the first not above the second Rapids.

MARION ISLAND, *Mo.*—Missouri river, 151 miles from its mouth, above Jefferson City, not above Lexington.

MARIETTA, *Ohio.*—Ohio river, 836 miles above its mouth, above Cincinnati.

MARY'S RIVER, *Ill.*—Mississippi river, 1099 miles above New Orleans, above Ohio river, not above Alton.

MARR'S, MRS. LANDING, *Ala.*—Warrior river, not above Tuscaloosa.

MARTIN'S, ISAAC LANDING.—Tombigbee river, not above Demopolis.

MARTIN'S, F. LANDING, *Ala.*—Tombigbee river, not above Demopolis.

MARTIN'S BLUFF, *Miss.*—Tombigbee river, above Columbus, not above Cotton Gin Port.

MARTIN'S LANDING.—Tombigbee river, above Demopolis, not above Gainesville.

MARIPOSA LANDING, *Ark.*—Mississippi river, above Greenville, not above Memphis.

MARIPOSA, *Ark.*—Mississippi river, 639 miles above New Orleans, above Greenville, not above Memphis.

MARDIS & BRO.—Black river, La., not above Harrisonburg.

MARKSVILLE, *Ind.*—Wabash river, above Rapids, not above Terre Haute.

MARSH, *Ill.*—Mississippi river, 1140 miles above New Orleans, above the Ohio river, not above Alton.

MARSH'S LANDING, *La.*—Ouachita river, above Harrisonburg, not above Trenton.

MARTIN'S, JOHN (STONEWALL) LANDING.—Red river, not above Alexandria.

MARTIN, WIDOW.—Red river, not above Alexandria.

MARTINSVILLE.—Yazoo river, above Yazoo City, not above Leflore.

MARIE SELINE.—Ouachita river, above Alabama Landing, not above Camden.

MARTINSBURG.—Neches river, Texas.

MARKSVILLE.—Yazoo river, above Yazoo City, not above Leflore.

MARSHES.—Ouachita river, above Harrisonburg, not above Trenton.

MARSTON, B. W. (ASHLAND.—Red river, above Grand Ecore, not above Shreveport.

MATLEY'S.—Bayou Macon, not above Monticello.

MATLOCK (or MARKS' LOWER PLACE.—Red river, above Shreveport, not above foot of Raft.

MATTHEW'S PLACE.—325 miles up Sunflower river.

MATTISON'S.—Ouachita river, above Trenton, not above Alabama Landing.

MAXWELL'S LANDING.—Big Deer Creek, 109 miles from Vicksburg.

MAXWELL'S.—Yazoo river, above Yazoo City, not above Leflore.

MAYBERRY.—Ouachita river, above Alabama Landing, not above Camden.

MAYAUX, PIERRE.—Red river, not above Alexandria.

MAY DAY.—Yazoo river, above Yazoo City, not above Leflore.

MAY FLOWER LANDING.—138 miles up Sunflower river.

MABERY'S LANDING, *La.*—Ouachita river, above Harrisonburg, not above Trenton.

MARENGO, *La.*—Mississippi river, 286 miles above New Orleans, above Bayou Sara, not above Grand Gulf.

MARSHALL'S LANDING, *La.*—Mississippi river, 421 miles above New Orleans, above Grand Gulf, not above Greenville.

MARSDEN, *La.*—Red river, above Grand Ecore, not above Shreveport.

MASON'S LANDING.—Mississippi river, 44 miles above St. Louis, above Alton, not above the first Rapids.

MASON'S, L. W., LANDING, *Ala.*—Alabama river, not above Selma.

MATHESON'S, MRS., LANDING.—Alabama river, not above Selma.

MATTHEWS,' S. B., UPPER LANDING.—Alabama river, not above Selma.

MATTHEWS,' L. W., LANDING, *Ala.*—Alabama river, not above Selma.

MATTHEWS,' P. E., LOWER LANDING, *Ala.*—Alabama river, not above Selma.

MATTHEWS,' P. E., LANDING, *Ala.*—Alabama river, not above Selma.

MATTHEWS,' T. M., LANDING, *Ala.*—Alabama river, not above Selma.

MATTHEWS,' J. E., LANDING, *Ala.*—Alabama river, not above Selma.

MATAMOROS, *Ohio.*—Ohio river, 870 miles above its mouth, above Cincinnati.

MATISON'S LANDING, *La.*—Ouachita river, above Trenton, not above Alabama Landing.

MAWARA.—Mississippi river, above Grand Gulf, not above Greenville.

MAXVILLE, *Ind.*—Ohio river, 254 miles above its mouth, above Paducah, not above Cincinnati.

MAXWELL'S LANDING, *Mo.*—Missouri river, 419 miles above its mouth, above Lexington, not above Iatan.

MAYBURN'S STATE BANK, *Texas.*—Red river, 550 miles above Shreveport, above Mound City.

MALTRIES (or J. E. ADGUS).—Red river, above Shreveport, not above foot of Raft.

MAYNARD'S BAYOU, *Ark.*—Arkansas river, 672 miles above Napoleon, above Fort Smith.

MAYNARD'S LANDING, *Ark.*—Arkansas river, 38 miles above Napoleon, not above Arkansas Post.

MAYSVILLE, *Ky.*—Ohio river, 594 miles above its mouth, above Cincinnati.

MAY'S, P., LANDING, *Ala.*—Tombigbee river, not above Demopolis.

MAY'S MILLS, *Ala.*—Tombigbee river, above Gainesville, not above Columbus.

MAY'S, JOE, LANDING, *Miss.*—Tombigbee river, above Columbus, not above Cotton Gin Port.

MEAD, CAPT. (AVOCA).—Red river, above Alexandria, not above Cane river.

MEANS.—Ouachita river, not above Harrisonburg.

MEAHER'S WHARF, *Ala.*—Alabama river, not above Selma.

MEAN'S LANDING, *La.*—Atchafalaya river, below Simmsport.

MECHANICSBURG, *Ohio.*—Ohio river, 567 miles above its mouth, above Cincinnati.

MEDICINE CREEK.—Missouri river, 1489 miles from St. Louis, above Iatan.

MEDLOCK'S.—Bayou Bartholomew, above Portland.

MEDORA.—Missouri river, not above Jefferson City.

MEIGSVILLE, *Tenn.*—Cumberland river, above Gainesboro.

MELTON, *Miss.*—Tallahatchie river, above Belmont.

MELROSE LANDING, *Miss.*—Mississippi river, 595 miles above New Orleans, above Greenville, not above Ohio river.

MELBOURNE.—Mississippi river, above Grand Gulf, not above Greenville.

MELROSE.—Yazoo river, not above Yazoo City.

MELANCON, *La.*—Bayou Courtableau, usual navigation.

MEMPHIS, *Tenn.*—Mississippi river, 839 miles above New Orleans, not above the mouth of the Ohio.

MEMPHIS, *Ala.*—Tombigbee river, above Gainesville, not above Columbus.

MENDOTA, *Wis.*—Mississippi river, 1656 miles above New Orleans, above Galena.

MENDOTA, *Minn.*—Mississippi river, 1861 miles above New Orleans, above Galena.

MENNY.—Mississippi river, above Grand Gulf, not above Greenville.

MERIDOSIA, *Ill.*—Illinois river, 72 miles above its mouth, not above Beardstown.

MERIN, *Ind.*—Wabash river, above Terre Haute.

MERRILL & DARDEN'S LANDING, *Ala.*—Alabama river, above Selma, not above Wetumpka.

MERRICK'S FERRY, *Texas.*—Sabine river, above Hamilton.

MERRIWEATHER'S LANDING, *Ala.*—Warrior river, not above Tuscaloosa.

MERRYWEATHER'S ISLAND TEN, *Ky.*—Mississippi river, 986 miles above New Orleans, above Memphis, not above the Ohio.

MERRIWETHER (D. S. HOOKS).—Red river, above Grand Ecore, not above Shreveport.

MERRIWETHER, MRS. A. J.—Red river, above Grand Ecore, not above Shreveport.

MERBOURNE, *La.*—Red river, above Cotile, not above Grand Ecore.

MEREDITH'S (EAGLE BEND.)—Mississippi river, above Grand Gulf, not above Greenville.

MERRIMECK'S RIVER.—Mississippi river, 1154 miles above New Orleans, above the Ohio river, not above Alton.

MESSICK.—Yazoo river, above Yazoo City, not above Leflore.

METROPOLIS, *Ill.*—Ohio river, 36 miles above its mouth, not above Paducah.

METAMORA, *Tenn.*—Hatchee river, not above Bolivar.

METCALF LANDING, *Miss.*—Mississippi river, 266 miles above New Orleans, above Bayou Sara, not above Grand Gulf.

MIAMI, *Mo.*—Missouri river, 281 miles above its mouth, above Jefferson City, not above Lexington.

MIDDLETON, *Penn.*—Ohio river, 994 miles above its mouth, above Cincinnati.

MIDWAY'S LANDING, *Ala.*—Alabama river, not above Selma.

MILLER'S FERRY, *Ala.*—Alabama river, not above Selma.

MICHIE.—Bayou Bartholomew, above Point Pleasant, not above Arkansas line.

MICHORE (STATION).—Mobile railroad, 15 miles from New Orleans.

MILAN, *Texas*.—Above White Oak Shoals.

MILK RIVER.—Missouri river, 2202 miles from its mouth, above Iatan.

MILL PORT.—143 miles up Sunflower river.

MILLES, WM.—Ouachita river, above Harrisonburg, not above Trenton.

MILLER WAREHOUSE.—Bayou Bartholomew, above Point Pleasant, not above Arkansas line.

MILLER PLACE.—Bayou Bartholomew, above Point Pleasant, not above Arkansas line.

MILLER'S BLUFF, *Ark*.—White river, 165 miles from its mouth, below junction of Black river.

MILLER'S BLUFF.—Ouachita river, 459 miles above the mouth of Old river, above Alabama Landing, not above Camden.

MILLER'S, MRS., LANDING, *La*.—Black river.

MILLER'S, MRS., LANDING, *La*.—Atchafalaya river, below Simmsport.

MILLER'S LANDING, *La*.—Bayou Macon, 35 miles from its mouth, below Monticello.

MILLER'S LANDING, *Mo*.—Missouri river, 77 miles above its mouth, not above Jefferson City.

MILLER'S LANDING, *Ark*.—Red river, 78 miles above Shreveport, above Carolina Bluff, not above Fulton.

MILLER'S FERRY, *Ala*.—Alabama river, 311 miles, above Mobile, above Selma.

MILLER'S POINT, *Tenn*.—Mississippi river, above Grand Gulf, not above Greenville.

MILLERSBURG, *Ind*.—Ohio river, 495 miles above its mouth, above Paducah, not above Cincinnati.

MILLERSPORT, *Ohio*.—Ohio river, 710 miles above its mouth, above Cincinnati.

MILLERSVILLE, *Mo*.—Missouri river, 790 miles from St. Louis, above Iatan.

MILLWOOD.—Little river, not above Hood's Landing.

MILLIKEN STORE.—Mississippi river, above Grand Gulf, not above Greenville.

MILLER'S BLUFF, *Ala.*—Tombigbee river, not above Demopolis.

MILLWOOD, *Ala.*—Warrior river, not above Tuscaloosa.

MILL'S LANDING, *Ala.*—Tombigbee river, not above Demopolis.

MILL POINT, *La.*—Bayou Macon, 78 miles from its mouth, below Monticello.

MILL POINT, *Mo.*—Mississippi river, 1016 miles above New Orleans, above Memphis, not above Ohio river.

MILL BAYOU, *Ark.*—Mississippi river, above Greenville, not above Memphis.

MILL CREEK, *Texas.*—Red river, 384 miles above Shreveport, above Lanesport, not above Mound City.

MILL CREEK, *Ark.*—White river, 328 miles from its mouth, below junction of Black river.

MILE'S POINT, *Mo.*—Missouri river, 332 miles above its mouth, above Jefferson City, not above Lexington.

MILL'S, J. Y., LANDING, *La.*—Atchafalaya river, below Simmsport.

MILLIKEN'S BEND, *La.*--Mississippi river, 478 miles above New Orleans, above Grand Gulf, not above Greenville.

MILK RIVER.—Missouri river, 2579 miles from St. Louis, above Iatan.

MILTON, *Ky.*—Ohio river, 442 miles above its mouth, above Paducah, not above Cincinnati.

MILTON, *Ala.*—Tennessee river, 280 miles above its mouth, above Florence.

MILROSE LANDING, *Miss.*—Mississippi river, 595 miles above New Orleans, above Greenville, not above the Ohio river.

MIMM'S, *Texas.*—Red river, 512 miles above Shreveport, above Mound City.

MINAKA CITY, *Mo.*—Missouri river, 674 miles from St. Louis, above Iatan.

MINER'S VILLE, *Ohio.*—Ohio river, 752 miles above its mouth, above Cincinnati.

MINDEN, *La.*—Lake Bistenau.

MIND HALL, *La.*—Ouachita river, above Harrisonburg, not above Trenton.

MINDENHALL.—Ouachita river, above Harrisonburg, not above Trenton.

MINNEAPOLIS, *Minn.*—Mississippi river, 1869 miles above New Orleans, above Galena.

MINNENGER.—Mississippi river, 770 miles above St. Louis, above Galena.

MINNESOTA RIVER.—Mississippi river. 770 miles above St. Louis, above Galena.

MINNESOTA CITY, *Minn.*—Mississippi river, 1751 miles above New Orleans, above Galena.

MINNIESKA —Mississippi river, 680 miles above St. Louis, above Galena.

MINNOWA.—Mississippi river, 651 miles above St. Louis, above Ga-Galena.

MINTER'S LANDING, *Ala.*—Alabama river, above Selma, not above Wetumpka.

MIRBEAU (W. S. CALHOUN'S).—Red river, above Alexandria, not above mouth of Cane river.

MISSOURITON, *Mo.*—Missouri river, 47 miles above its mouth, not above Jefferson City.

MISSOURI CITY, *Mo.*—Missouri river, 376 miles above its mouth, above Lexington, not above Iatan.

MISSISSIPPI LINE.—Mississippi river, 796 miles above New Orleans, above Greenville, not above Memphis.

MISSISSINEWA, *Ind.*—Wabash river, above the Rapids, not above Terre Haute.

MITCHELL'S BEND.—Missouri river, 2508 miles from St. Louis, above Iatan.

MITCHELL'S POINT, *Tenn.*—Mississippi river, above Memphis, not above the mouth of the Ohio river.

MITCHELL'S, B. H. LANDING, *Ala.*—Alabama river, not above Selma.

MITCHELL'S, MRS. LANDING, *Ala.*—Tombigbee river, not above Demopolis.

MIXON'S LANDING, *Ala.*—Alabama river, not above Selma. Demopolis.

MOCCASSINVILLE, *Mo.*—Mississippi river, 1117 miles above New Orleans, above the mouth of the Ohio, not above Alton.

MIXON & CLAY'S LANDING, *Ala.*—Tombigbee river, not above
MOBLEY'S LANDING, *Ala.*—Tombigbee river, above Gainesville, not above Columbus.
MOHERLEY'S LANDING.—Missouri river, 327 miles above its mouth, above Jefferson City, not above Lexington.
MONTGOMERY'S PLACE.—Yazoo river, above Yazoo City, not above Leflore.
MONTGAY'S FERRY.—Yazoo river, above Yazoo City, not above Leflore.
MONTEREY.—Yazoo river, above Yazoo City, not above Leflore.
MOLINE, *Ill.*—Mississippi river, 1518 miles above New Orleans, above the second Rapids, not above Galena.
MOLINE, *Miss.*—Tallahatchie river, above Belmont.
MOLETT'S, JOHN A. LANDING, *Ala.*—Alabama river, not above Selma.
MOLETT'S, W. P. LANDING, *Ala.*—Alabama river, not above Selma.
MOLINO DEL REY, *Ark*—White river, below the junction of Black river.
MONNETT'S FERRY, *La.*—Cane river (old Red river).
MONROE, *La.*—Ouachita river, 285 miles from the mouth of Old river, above Harrisonburg, not above Trenton.
MONTANA, *La.*—Red river, above Cotile, not above Grand Ecore.
MONTGOMERY, *Ala.*—Alabama river, 355 miles above Mobile, above Selma.
MONTGOMERY HILL, *Ala.*—Alabama river, not above Selma.
MONTGOMERY'S LANDING, *Ala.*—Alabama river, above Selma, not above Wetumpka.
MONTGOMERY, *Ark.*—Mississippi river, 643 miles above New Orleans, above Greenville, not above Memphis.
MONTGOMERY, *La.*—Red river, 436 miles above New Orleans, above Cane river, not above Grand Ecore.
MONTGOMERY'S LANDING, *Miss.*—Yazoo river, 161 miles from Vicksburg, above Yazoo City, not above Leflore.
MONTGOMERY'S LANDING, *La.*—Ouachita river, above Harrisonburg, not above Trenton.

MONTGOMERY'S LANDING, *La.*—Bayou Macon, 107 miles above the mouth, below Monticello.

MONTICELLO, *Miss.*—Pearl river, above Columbia.

MONTICELLO, *La.*—(Not above) On Bayou Macon.

MONTEREY, *Ark.*—Mississippi river, above Greenville, not above Memphis.

MONTEREY, *Ill.*—Illinois river, 13 miles above the mouth, not above Beardstown.

MONTEREY LANDING, *La.*—Black river, La., not above Harrisonburg.

MONARCH'S LANDING, *Ark.*—Mississippi river, 579 miles above New Orleans, above Greenville, not above Memphis.

MONTROSE, *Iowa.*—Mississippi river, 1389 miles above New Orleans, above the first, not above the second Rapids.

MONTEZUMA, *Ill.*—Illinois river, 49 miles above its mouth, not above Beardstown.

MONTEZUMA, *Ind.*—Wabash river, above the Rapids, not above Terre Haute.

MOON'S, R. H. LANDING, *Ala.*—Alabama river, not above Selma.

MOONSVILLE, *La.*—Mississippi river, 272 miles above New Orleans, above Bayou Sara, not above Grand Gulf.

MOORE'S BLUFF, *Miss.*—Tombigbee river, above Gainesville, not above Columbus.

MOORE'S ROCK, *Ark.*—Arkansas river, 513 miles above its mouth, above Norristown, not above Fort Smith.

MOORE'S LANDING, *Ark.*—Sulphur river, 60 miles above its mouth (Sulphur river is a tributary of Red river).

MOORE'S LANDING, *Mo.*—Missouri river, 172 miles above its mouth, above Jefferson City, not above Lexington.

MOORE'S (MRS.) LANDING, *La.*—Mississippi river, 448 miles above New Orleans, above Grand Gulf, not above Greenville.

MOORE & PRICE'S LANDING, *La.*—Mississippi river, 98 miles above New Orleans, below Bayou Sara.

MOORE MILL.—Ouachita river, above Alabama Landing, not above Camden.

MOORE, DANE.—100 miles up Bœuf river, above Thomas' Landing.

MOORE, LAURENCE.—Bayou Bartholomew, above Point Pleasant, not above Arkansas line.

MOORE'S (W. L. BALL'S).—Red river, above Grand Ecore, not above Shreveport.

MOORE'S LANDING (or JOHNSON'S STORE).—Red river, above Rowland and Mound City.

MOORING'S PORT, *La.*—Lake Caddo, above Jefferson.

MORANTINE, J. J.—Red river, above Alexandria, not above mouth of Cane river.

MORANCY, *La.*—Mississippi river, above Grand Gulf, not above Greenville.

MORENCIE.—Mississippi river, above Grand Gulf, not above Greenville.

MORCAN, LESTON.—Red river, not above Alexandria.

MOREHOUSE, BRUCE.—259 miles up Sunflower river.

MOREHOUSE POINT.—Bayou Bartholomew, not above Point Pleasant.

MOREHOUSE POINT.—Ouachita river, above Alabama Landing, not above Camden.

MOREHOUSE.—Ouachita river, above Trenton, not above Alabama Landing.

MORGAURA.—Yazoo river, above Yazoo City, not above Leflore.

MORGAN'S LANDING, *Ala.*—Alabama river, above Selma, not above Wetumpka.

MORNING'S PORT.—Red river, above Shreveport, not above Carolina Bluffs.

MORO.—Ouachita river, above Alabama Landing, not above Camden.

MORROW'S LANDING, *Ala.*—Warrior river, not above Tuscaloosa.

MORROW'S, E. LANDING, *Ala.*—Alabama river, not above Selma.

MORRISON'S BLUFF, *Ark.*—Arkansas river, 434 miles above Napoleon, above Norristown, not above Fort Smith.

MORRISON'S LANDING, *Miss.*—Mississippi river, 247 miles above New Orleans, above Bayou Sara, not above Grand Gulf.

MORRISON'S LANDING, *Mo.*—Mississippi river, 978 miles above New Orleans, above Memphis, not above the Ohio river.

MORGAN'S, CYRUS, LANDING, *Ark.*—Red river, 162 miles above Shreveport, not above White Oak Shoals.

MORGAN'S BEND.—Mississippi river, not above Bayou Sara.

MORGAN'S FERRY, *La.*—Atchafalaya river, below Simmsport.

MORGAN'S HOUSES.—Missouri river, 2619 miles from St. Louis, above Iatan.

MORGAN'S POINT, *Ark.*—Mississippi river, 851 miles above New Orleans, above Greenville, not above Memphis.

MORGAN, MAGINNIS, *Ark.*—White river, not above Batesville.

MORGANZA, *La.*—Mississippi river, 177 miles above New Orleans, above Bayou Sara, not above Grand Gulf.

MORIS,' F., LANDING, *Ark.*—Red river, 191 miles above Shreveport, above Carolina Bluff, not above Fulton.

MORIS' LANDING, *La.*—Mississippi river, not above Bayou Sara.

MORISETTE'S LANDING, *Ala.*—Alabama river, not above Selma.

MORO, *La.*—Mississippi river, 274 miles above New Orleans, above Bayou Sara, not above Grand Gulf.

MORO LANDING, *Ark.*—Ouachita river, above Alabama Landing, not above Camden.

MOROBAY.—Ouachita river, 417 miles above the mouth of Old river, above Alabama Landing, not above Camden.

MORRANCY, *La.*—Mississippi river, 243 miles above New Orleans, above Grand Gulf, not above Greenville.

MORRISON'S (or WHITE OAK SHOALS.—Red river, above Fulton, not above Lanesport.

MORRIS.—Mississippi river, above Grand Gulf, not above Greenville.

MORRIS' FERRY.—Angelina river, Texas.

MORRIS' GIN.—Bayou Bartholomew, above Point Pleasant, not above Arkansas line.

MORRIS HOUSE.—Bayou Bartholomew, above Point Pleasant, not above Arkansas line.

MORRISON'S BLUFF.—Arkansas river, above Dardanelle, not above Roseville.

MORSE, P. A. (LACK MINACK'S).—Red river, above Grand Ecore, not above Shreveport.

MORSON, DR. LANDING.—Mississippi river, 159 miles up Big Deer Creek.

MORTON'S LANDING, *Ala.*—Alabama river, above Selma, not above Wetumpka.

MOSELEY'S, A. W. LANDING, *Miss*—144 miles up Big Deer Creek.

MOSES, F.—Ouachita river, above Harrisonburg, not above Trenton.

MOSS PLANTATION (or SHAM'S).—Red river, above Lanesport, not above Mound City.

MOSS'—Tallahatchie river, not above Cassidy Bayou.

MOSS PRESS.—Red river, not above Alexanpria.

MOSCOW, *Ohio.*—Ohio river, 562 miles above its mouth, above Cincinnati.

MOSCOW, *La.*—Red river, above Grand Ecore, not above Shreveport.

MOSCOW, *Ala.*—Tombigbee river, not above Demopolis.

MOSCOW, *La.*—Lake Bisteneau.

MOSCOW, *Ill.*—Illinois river, 173 miles from St. Louis, above Beardstown, not above Fox river.

MOSS, J., LANDING, *Texas.*—Red river, 378 miles above Shreveport, above Lanesport, not above Mound City.

MOSELLE, *Ill.*—Mississippi river, 1601 miles above New Orleans, above the second Rapids, not above Galena.

MOSSIER'S LANDING, *Ark*—Little Red river, 32 miles above its mouth, below junction of Black and White rivers.

MOSSY GROVE LANDING, *La.*—Black river, not above Harrisonburg.

MOTLEY'S LANDING, *La.*—Bayou Macon, 200 miles above its mouth, above Monticello.

MOUND CITY, *Ark.*—Mississippi river, 747 miles above New Orleans, above Greenville, not above Memphis.

MOUND CITY, *Ill.*—Ohio river, 6 miles from its mouth, below Paducah.

MOUNDVILLE, *Va.*—Ohio river, 898 miles above its mouth, above Cincinnati.

MOUND BAYOU, *La.*—Tensas river, above the mouth of Bayou Macon.

MOUND CITY.—Red river, 10 miles above Rowland, above Lanesport.

MOUND GROVE.—Arkansas river, above Arkansas Post, not above Pine Bluff.

MOUND PLACE.—Bayou Bartholomew, above Point Pleasant, not above Arkansas line.

MOUND FLAT.—Red river, above Grand Ecore, not above Shreveport.

MOUNGER'S LANDING, *Ala.*—Tombigbee river, not above Demopolis.

MOUNT CARMEL, *Ind.*—Wabash river, above Terre Haute.

MOUNT GILEAD, *Ark.*—Arkansas river, above Norristown, not above Fort Smith.

MOUNT GROVE, *Ark.*—Arkansas river, 68 miles above Napoleon, above Arkansas Post, not above Pine Bluff.

MOUNT VERNON, *Miss.*—Mississippi river, above Grand Gulf, not above Greenville.

MOUNT VERNON, *Ind.*—Ohio river, 151 miles above its mouth, above Paducah, not above Cincinnati.

MOUNT VERNON, *Mo.*—Missouri river, 182 miles above its mouth, Jefferson City, not above Lexington.

MOUNT VERNON.—Mississippi river, 678 miles from St. Louis, above Galena.

MOUNT PLEASANT, *Ala.*—Alabama river, not above Selma.

MOUNT STERLING, *Texas.*—Angelina river, above Bevilport.

MOUNT PLEASANT, *Mo.*—Missouri river, 56 miles above its mouth, not above Jefferson City.

MOUNT OLIVE, *Ark.*—White river, 316 miles from the Mississippi river, above Batesville.

MOUNT VERNON WHARF, *Ala.*—Alabama river, not above Selma

MOUNETTE'S FERRY, *La.*—Cane river (old Red river).

MOUNTVILLE, *Minn.*—Mississippi river, 1749 miles above New Orleans, above Galena.

MOUTH'S, J. C. LANDING, *Ala.*—Tombigbee river, not above Demopolis.

MOUTH OF TENSAS, *Ala.*—Alabama river, not above Selma.

MOUTH BLACK RIVER.—Red river, not above Alexandria.

MOUTH COCODRIA.—Red river, not above Alexandria.

MOUTH BAYOU BŒUF RIVER.—Ouachita river, above Harrisonburg, not above Trenton.

MOUTH BUSHLEY.—Ouachita river, not above Harrisonburg.

MOUTH BAYOU BARTHOLOMEW.—Ouachita river, above Trenton, not above Alabama Landing.

MOUTH DESAIRD.—Bayou Bartholomew, not above Point Pleasant.

MOUTH DARRO (N. BUSH).—Red river, above Alexandria, not above mouth Cane river.

MOUTH OF MILL CREEK (or MRS. BOYCE).—Red river, above Lanesport, not above Mound City.

MOUTH OF KIOMITTIA.—Red river, above Mound City.

MOUTH OF PECAN BAYOU (or COL. AIKENS).—Red river, above Lanesport, not above Mound City.

MOUTH OF TCHULA —Yazoo river, above Yazoo City, not above Leflore.

MOUTH OF QUIVER—199 miles up Sunflower river.

MOUTH OF YALLABUSHA.—Yazoo river, above Yazoo City, not above Leflore.

MOUTH OF HUSHPUCKANCE.—298 miles up Sunffower river.

MOUTH OF NOXABEE, *Ala.*—Tombigbee river, above Gainesville, not above Columbus.

MOUTH OF SIPSEY, *Ala.*—Tombigbee river, above Gainesville, not above Columbus.

MOUTH OF COALFIRE, *Miss.*—Tombigbee river, above Gainesville, not above Columbus.

MOUTH OF CANE RIVER, *La.*—Red river, 400 miles above New Orleans, above mouth of Cane river, not above Grand Ecore.

MOUTH OF FOURCHE, *Ark.*—Arkansas river, above Little Rock, not above Norristown.

MOUTH OF BAYOU ROUGE, *La.*—Below Simmsport, on the Atchafalaya river.

MOUTH OF BLACK BAYOU, *La.*—Red river, 50 miles above Shreveport, not above Carolina Bluff.

MOUTH OF SANDY RIVER, *Tenn.*—Not above Eastport, on Tennessee river.

MOUTH OF PINE RIVER.—Mississippi river, 231 miles from St. Louis, above the first, not above the second Rapids.

MOUTH OF OHIO RIVER, *Ill.*—Mississippi river, 1040 miles above New Orleans.

MOUTH OF RED RIVER, *La.*—Mississippi river, 210 miles above New Orleans, above Grand Gulf, not above Greenville.

MOUTH OF BULL RIVER, *Ark.*—White river, above Batesville.

MOUTH OF WHITE RIVER, *Ark.*—Mississippi river, 635 miles above New Orleans, above Greenville, not above Memphis.

MOUTH OF BAYOU MACON, *La.*—Tensas river, La., 53 miles from Trinity.

MOUTH OF WABASH RIVER, *Ind.*—Ohio river, 139 miles above its mouth, above Paducah, not above Cincinnati.

MOUTH OF YAZOO RIVER, *Miss.*—Mississippi river, 413 miles above New Orleans, above Grand Gulf, not above Greenville.

MOUTH OF HATCHEE RIVER, *Tenn.*—Mississippi river, 880 miles above New Orleans, above Memphis, not above the mouth of the Ohio.

MOUTH OF TENNESSEE RIVER.—Ohio river, 48 miles above its mouth, not above Paducah.

MOUTH OF CUMBERLAND RIVER, *Ky.*—Ohio river, 60 miles above its mouth, above Paducah, not above Cincinnati.

MOUTH OF FOX RIVER.—Illinois river, 262 miles above its mouth.

MOUTH OF MISSISSIPPI RIVER, *La.*—102 miles below New Orleans.

MOUTH OF MISSOURI RIVER, *Mo.*—Mississippi river, 18 miles above St. Louis, not above Alton.

MOUTH OF ST. FRANCIS RIVER.—Mississippi river, 1738 miles above New Orleans, above Greenville, not above Memphis.

MOUTH OF ARKANSAS RIVER, *Ark.*—Mississippi river, 620 miles above New Orleans, above Greenville, not above Memphis.

MOUTH OF SULPHUR RIVER, *Ark.*—Red river, 114 miles above Shreveport, above Black Bayou, not above White Oak Shoals.

MOUTH OF SABINE RIVER, *Texas.*—Sabine Lake.

MOUTH OF CURRANT RIVER, *Ark.*—A tributary of Black and White rivers.

MOUTH OF LITTLE TENSAS, *La.*—Tensas river, 31 miles from Trinity, not above the mouth of Bayou Macon.

MOUTH OF STRAWBERRY RIVER, *Ark.*—Black river, Arkansas.

MOUTH FOOL RIVER, *La.*—Tensas river, 46 miles from Trinity, not above the mouth of Bayou Macon.

MOUTH JOE BAYOU, *La.*—Bayou Macon, 117 miles from mouth below Monticello.

MOUTH MOREAU RIVER, *Mo.*—Missouri river, 130 miles above its mouth, below Jefferson City.

MOUTH MOREAU.—Missouri river, 1686 miles from St. Louis, above Iatan.

MOUTH CEDAR RIVER, *Mo.*—Missouri river, 138 miles above its mouth, above Jefferson City, not above Lexington.

MOUTH FISHING RIVER, *Mo.*—Missouri river, 376 miles above mouth, above Lexington, not above Iatan.

MOUTH YELLOW STONE RIVER.—Missouri river, 1996 miles from St. Louis, above Iatan.

MOUTH MARIA RIVER.—Missouri river, 3085 miles from St. Louis, above Iatan.

MOUTH PINEY RIVER, *Ark.*—Arkansas river, above Norristown, not above Fort Smith.

MOUTH GRAND RIVER, *Ark.*—Arkansas river, above Fort Smith, not above Fort Gibson.

MOUTH ROCK RIVER.—Mississippi river, 345 miles from St. Louis above the first, not above the second Rapids'

MOUTH LAKE PEKIN.—Mississippi river, 331 miles from St. Louis, above Galena.

MOUTH OF LITTLE SUNFLOWER.—Yazoo river, not above Yazoo City.

MOUTH OF BIG SUNFLOWER.—Yazoo river, not above Yazoo City.

MOUTH OF LITTLE MUDDY.—Missouri river, 2016 miles above its mouth, above Iatan.

MOUTH OF BIG MUDDY.—Missouri river, 2020 miles above its mouth, above Iatan.

MOUTH OF LITTLE RIVER.—Upper Red river, above Fulton, not above Lanesport.

MOUTH OF LITTLE RIVER.—Red river, above Cane river, not above Grand Ecore.

MOUTH OF ROLLING FORK.—104 miles up Sunflower river.

MUCK PORT, *Ky.*—Ohio river, 343 miles above its mouth, above Paducah, not above Cincinnati.

MUDDY RIVER, *Ill.*—Mississippi river, 1099 miles above New Orleans, above Ohio river, not above Alton.

MUDDY BAYOU.—64 miles up Bœuf river, above Thomas' Landing.

MUD HOUSE (M. LATTIER'S.—Red river, above Grand Ecore, not above Shreveport.

MULBERRY PLANT.—Red river, above Grand Ecore, not above Shreveport.

MUMFORD'S.—Ouachita river, above Alabama Landing, not above Camden.

MURPHY, JUDGE.—Red river, above foot of Raft, not above Fulton.

MURPHY, PAT (OLD JONES PLACE).—Red river, above Fulton, not above Lanesport.

MURPHY BAYOU.—142 miles up Sunflower river.

MURRAY'S, P. H.—Red river, above Grand Ecore, not above Shreveport.

MURRAY'S (or HART'S).—Red river, above Grand Ecore, not above Shreveport.

MURRAY'S, *Ind. Terr.*—Red river, above Fulton, not above Lanesport.

MURRELL, BEN.—Bayou Bartholomew, above Point Pleasant, not above Arkansas line.

MUD LAKE, *Ark.*—Arkansas river, 109 miles above Napoleon, above Arkansas Post, not above Pine Bluff.

MULBERRY, *Ark.*—Arkansas river, 496 miles above Napoleon, above Norristown, not above Fort Smith.

MULBERRY GROVE, *Ark.*—Arkansas river, 136 miles above Napoleon, above Arkansas Post, not above Pine Bluff.

MULLEN'S LANDING, *Miss.*—Tombigbee river, above Columbus, not above Cotton Gin Port.

MURPHY'S BLUFF, *Ala.*—Tombigbee river, not above Demopolis.

MURRAYSVILLE, *Va.*—Ohio river, 799 miles above its mouth, above Cincinnati.

MURRELL'S, ISAAC, LANDING, *La.*—Red river, above Grand Ecore, not above Shreveport.

MUSELO SHOALS, *Ala.*—Tennessee river, 218 miles above its mouth, above Eastport, not above Florence.

MUSCATINE, *Iowa.*—Mississippi river, 1487 miles above New Orleans, above the secoad Rapids, not above Galena.

MUSGROVE, *Ark.*—Mississippi river, 912 miles above New Orleans, above Greenville, not above Memphis.

MUSCLE SHELL RIVER.—Missouri river, 2789 miles from St. Louis, above Iatan.

MUSHINGUM RIVER, *Ohio.*—Ohio river, 836 miles above its mouth, above Cincinnati.

MYRE'S BLUFF, *Ala.*—Warrior river, not above Tuscaloosa.

MYERS, S.—Ouachita river, above Harrisonburg, not above Trenton.

MYETTE LANDING.—Mississippi river, not above Bayou Sara.

MYRTLE GROVE.—Red river, not above Alexandria.

N

NASH'S LANDING, P.—Red river, above Black Bayou, not above White Oak Shoals.

NATCHITOCHES BAYOU.—Red river, not above Alexandria.

NAPOLEON, *Ark.*—At the mouth of the Arkansas river, 620 miles above New Orleans, above Greenville, not above the mouth of the Ohio river.

NAPOLEON, *Ky.*—Ohio river, 28 miles above its mouth, not above Paducah.

NAPOLEON, *Mo.*—Missouri river, 356 miles above its mouth, above Lexington, not above Iatan.

NAPOLEONVILLE, *La.*—Bayou Lafourche.

NAPLES, *Ill.*—Illinois river, 65 miles above its mouth, not above Beardstown.

NASHVILLE, *Tenn.*—Cumberland river, 203 miles above its mouth.

NASHVILLE.—Mississippi river, 1385 miles above New Orleans, above the first, not above the second Rapids.

NASHVILLE, *Mo.*—Missouri river, 174 miles above its mouth, above Jefferson City, not above Lexington.

NASHVILLE, *Miss.*—Tombigbee river, above Gainesville, not above Columbus.

NATCHEZ, *Miss.*—Mississippi river, 277 miles above New Orleans, above Bayou Sara, not above Grand Gulf.

NATURAL STEPS, *Ark*—Arkansas river, 298 miles above Little Rock, not above Norristown.

NATCHITOCHES, *La*—Cane river (Red river) 418 miles from New Orleans.

NAUVOO, *Ill*—Mississippi river, 1385 miles above New Orleans, above first, not above second Rapids.

NAVIGATOR LANDING.—Red river, above Grand Ecore, not above Shreveport.

NEAL'S LANDING, *Ala*—Tombigbee river, above Gainesville, not above Columbus.

NEAL SMITH'S LANDING, *Ala.*—Alabama river, below Selma.

NEBRASKA CITY, *Neb.*—Missouri river, 632 miles above its mouth, above Iatan.

NEBRASKA WOODYARD, *Tenn.*—Mississippi river, above Memphis, not above the mouth of the Ohio river.

NECHES RIVER, *Texas.*—Above the junction of Angelina river.

NECHES SALINE, *Texas.*—Neches river, above the junction of Angelina river.

NECO'S, DR., LANDING, *La.*—Mississippi river, above Bayou Sara, not above Grand Gulf.

NEEDHAM'S CUT-OFF, *Tenn.*—Mississippi river, 844 miles above New Orleans, above Memphis, not above the mouth of the Ohio.

NEELEY'S LANDING, *Mo.*—Mississippi river, above the mouth of the Ohio river, not above Alton.

NEGRO HILL, *Ark.*—White river, 239 miles above its mouth, below the junction of Black river.

NELSON'S BLUFF, *Miss.*—Tallahatchie river, above Cold Water, not above Belmont.

NELSON'S, MRS., LANDING, *La.*—Atchafalaya river, below Simmsport.

NESBITT'S, MRS., LANDING, *La.*—Red river, above Grand Ecore, not above Shreveport.

NEVILLE, *Ohio.*—Ohio river, 564 miles above its mouth, above Cincinnati.

NEW ALBANY, *Ind.*—Ohio river, 380 miles above its mouth, above Paducah, not above Cincinnati.

NEW ALBANY, *Miss.*—Tallahatchie river, above Belmont.

NEW BRITON, *Ill.*—Mississippi river, 1461 miles above New Orleans, above the second Rapids, not above Galena.

NEALLY WOODYARD.—Ouachita river, above Alabama Landing, not above Camden.

NEAL'S LANDING, *Fla.*—Chattahoochie river, not above Eufaula.

NEALS, THOS.—Red river, not above Alexandria.

NEALES.—Ouachita river, above Harrisonburg, not above Trenton.

NEBRASKA, *La.*—Mississippi river, above Grand Gulf, not above Greenville.

NEGRO.—Ouachita river, above Harrisonburg, not above Trenton.

NEIGHBORS.—93 miles up Bœuf river, above Thomas' Landing.

NELSON'S.—Yazoo river, not above Yazoo City.

NELSON, L. C. (CRAWSER).—Red river, above Grand Ecore, not above Shreveport.

NELSON, G. A.—Red river, above Grand Ecore, not above Shreveport.

NETHERLY.—Ouachita river, above Harrisonburg, not above Trenton

NETTLES.—Red river, above Grand Ecore, not above Shreveport.

NEW BERLIN.—162 miles up Sunflower river.

NEWBURGER LANDING.—Mississippi river, not above Bayou Sara.

NEW COMERS.—Bayou Macon, not above Monticello.

NEW ERA.—Sunflower river.

NEW FOUNDLAND.—Red river, above Grand Ecore, not above Shreveport.

NEW HOPE.—Tallahatchie river, not above Cassidy Bayou.

NEW HOPE (SPYKER BROS).—Bayou Bartholomew, not above Point Pleasant.

NEW HOPE GIN.—Bayou Bartholomew, not above Point Pleasant.

NEW HOPE (BRINGHURST).—Red river, not above Alexandria.

NEW HOPE (R. SCOTT).—Red river, above Grand Ecore, not above Shreveport.

NEW HOPE (WIDOW ATKINS).—Red river, above Grand Ecore, not above Shreveport.

NEWBURG, *Ohio.*—Ohio river, 943 miles above its mouth, above Cincinnati.

NEWBURG, *Ind.*—Ohio river, 203 miles above its mouth, above Paducah, not above Cincinnati.

NEWBURG, *Tenn.*—Tennessee river, not above Eastport.

NEW CARTHAGE, *La.*—Mississippi river, 381 miles above New Orleans, above Grand Gulf, not above Greenville.

NEW CHARLESTON, *Ind.*—Wabash river, not above the Rapids.

NEW CORYDENS, *Ind.*—Wabash river, not above the Rapids.

NEW COLUMBUS, *Texas.*—Sabine river, above Belgrade, not above Hamilton.

NEW GASCONY, *Ark.*—Arkansas river, 134 miles above Napoleon, above Arkansas Post, not above Pine Bluff.

NEW HAMPTON, *La.*—Mississippi river, 100 miles above New Orleans, not above Bayou Sara.

NEW HOPE LANDING, *La.*—Red river, 635 miles above New Orleans, above Grand Ecore, not above Shreveport.

NEW HOPE, *Ala.*—Tennessee river, above Florance.

NEW HOPE, *La.*—Red river, above Alexandria, not above Cane river.

NEW IBERIA, *La.*—Bayou Teche.

NEW LONDON, *Ind.*—Ohio river, 431 miles above its mouth, above Paducah, not above Cincinnati.

NEW MADRID, *Mo.*—Mississippi river, 1003 miles above New Orleans, above Memphis, not above the mouth of the Ohio.

NEW MARTINSVILLE, *Va.*—Ohio river, 873 miles above its mouth, above Cincinnati.

NEW ORLEANS, JACKSON AND GREAT NORTHERN R. R.

NEW PORT, *Ky.*—Ohio river, 542 miles above its mouth, above Paducah, not above Cincinnati.

NEW PORT, *Ohio.*—Ohio river, 854 miles above its mouth, above Cincinnati.

NEW PORT, *Ala.*—Tennessee river, above Eastport, not above Florance.

NEW PORT, *Ark.*—White river, 351 miles above its mouth, below the junction of Black river.

NEW PORT, *Mo.*—Missouri river, not above Jefferson City.

NEW PORT, *Ill.*—Illinois river, 35 miles above its mouth, not above Beardstown.

NEW PORT, *Ind.*—Wabash river, above the Rapids, not above Terre Haute.

NEW PORT, *Ala.*—Tombigbee river, above Gainesville, not above Columbus.

NEWPORT.—Ouachita river, above Alabama Landing, not above Camden.

NEWPORT, *Franklin County, Ala.*—Alabama river, above Montgomery, not above Wetumpka.

NEW PHILADELPHIA, *Mo.*—Mississippi river, 1021 miles above New Orleans, above the mouth of the Ohio river, not above Alton.

NEW PORTLAND, *Tenn.*—Tennessee river, not above Eastport.

NEW PROVIDENCE, *Tenn.*—Cumberland river, not above Nashville.

NEW RICHMOND, *Ohio.*—Ohio river, 562 miles above its mouth, above Cincinnati.

NEW RIVER LANDING, *La.*—Mississippi river, 87 miles above New Orleans, not above Bayou Sara.

NEW TEXAS LANDING, *La.*—Mississippi river, not above Bayou Sara.

NEWTON, *Ga.*—Flint river.

NEWTON.—Yazoo river, above Yazoo City, not above Leflore.

NEWTON, *Miss.*—Chickasaha river.

NEWTON, *Texas.*—Sabine river, above Belgrade, not above Hamilton

NEW VILLE, *Ind.*—Wabash river, not above the Rapids.

NEW YORK, *Mo.*—Mississippi river, 1031 miles above New Orleans, above the mouth of the Ohio, not above Alton.

NEW YORK, *Ind.*—Ohio river, 472 miles above its mouth, above Paducah, not above Cincinnati.

NEW YORK, *Tenn.*—Cumberland river, not above Nashville.

NIBLETT'S, DR. LANDING, *Miss.*—Mississippi river, above Greenville, not above Memphis.

NICCOTOO, *Ark.*—Arkansas river, 111 miles above Napoleon, above Arkansas Post, not above Pine Bluff.

NICHOLAS' LANDING, *Ark.*—Arkansas river, 141 miles above Napoleon, above Arkansas Post, not above Pine Bluff.

NICHOL'S, JOE LANDING, *Ark.*—Arkansas river, above Pine Bluff, not above Little Rock.

NICOLIN'S LANDING, *La.*—Black river, La.

NIGGER POINT, *Ill*—Mississippi river, 1133 miles above New Orleans, above the mouth of the Ohio, not above Alton.

NINE MILE BLUFF, *La*—Red river, 13 miles above Shreveport, not above Carolina Bluff.

NIBLETT'S BLUFF, *Texas.*—Sabine river.

NICK VILLIAN.—Red river, above Alexandria, not above Cane river.

NICHOLA, *La.*—Black river, not above Harrisonburg.

NIGGER POINT (FRANK CLAVERIE).—Red river, not above Alexandria.

NIGGER.—Ouachita river, above Harrisonburgh, not above Trenton.

NOBLES.—Bayou Bartholomew, above Portland.

NOBLE.—Ouachita river, above Harrisonburg, not above Trenton.

NOBLE'S, E. LANDING, *La.*—Ouachita river, above Harrisonburg, not above Trenton.

NODWAY CITY, *Mo.*—Missouri river, 532 miles above its mouth, above Iatan.

NORMA, *La.*—Black river, not above Harrisonburg.

NORMAND'S, J. J.—Red river, not above Alexandria.

NORMAN'S, C. C.—Red river, not above Alexandria.

NORRIS' LANDING.—Ouachita river, above Alabama Landing, not above Camden.

NORFOLK, *Mo.*—Mississippi river, 729 miles above New Orleans, above Memphis, not above mouth of the Ohio.

NORMAN'S LANDING.—Red river, 293 miles from New Orleans, not above Alexandria.

NORMANDY'S LANDING, *La.*—Black river, not above Harrisonburg.

NORTH POINT, *Ark.*—Arkansas river, above Little Rock, not above Norristown.

NORTH FORK, *Ark.*—White river, above Batesville.

NORTHAMPTON, *Ky.*—Ohio river, 330 miles above its mouth, above Paducah, not above Cincinnati.

NORTH BEND.—Ohio river, 525 miles above its mouth, above Paducah, not above Cincinnati.

NORRISTOWN, *Ark.*—Arkansas river, 304 miles above Napoleon.

NOTREBE PLACE, *Ark.*—Arkansas river, 54 miles above Napoleon, not above Arkansas Post.

NOYES' LANDING.—Black river, La., not above Trinity.

NOTT'S LANDING, *Ark.*—Arkansas river, 146 miles above Napoleon, above Arkansas Post, not above Pine Bluff.

NUNNABY'S LANDING, *Texas.*—Red river, 334 miles above Shreveport, above Fulton, not above Lanesport.

NUNNALEE'S LANDING, *Ala.*—Alabama river, not above Selma.

NUTT'S, L. M., LANDING, *La.*—Red river, above Grand Ecore, not above Shreveport.

NUTT'S, DR.—Mississippi river, above Grand Gulf, not above Greenville.

NYTHAYUMS, *Miss.*—126 miles up Big Deer Creek.

O

OAK GROVE LANDING.—Bayou Macon, not above Monticello.

OAKLAND.—Red river, above Alexandria, not above mouth of Cane river.

OAK VALLEY.—Yazoo river, not above Yazoo City.

OAK WOOD.—Yazoo river, above Yazoo City, not above Leflore.

OAK WOOD.—Bayou Macon, not above Monticello.

OAKVILLE, *Mo.*—Mississippi river, 1208 miles above New Orleans, above mouth of the Ohio, not above Alton.

OAK GROVE, *La.*—Morgan railroad, 46 from above New Orleans.

OAKLAND, or GEN. CLAWTON, *Ark.*—Arkansas river, 131 miles above Napoleon, above Arkansas Post, not above Pine Bluff.

OAKLAND LANDING, *La.*—Black river, not above Harrisonburg.

OAKLEY'S LANDING, *Ark.*—Arkansas river, 78 miles above Napoleon, above Arkansas Post, not above Pine Bluff.

OAKLEY, *La.*—Bayou Macon, not above Monticello.

OAKLEY, *Miss.*—Mississippi river, above Grand Gulf, not above Greenville.

OAK BLUFF, *Ala.*—Tombigbee river, not above Demopolis.

OAK CHEE BLUFF, *Ala.*—Tombigbee river, not above Demopolis.

OBANIUS, *Miss.*—Mississippi river, above Greenville, not above Memphis.

OBIONVILLE, *Tenn.*—Mississippi river, 979 miles above New Orleans, above Memphis, not above mouth of the Ohio.

OBION RIVER.—Any point.

OBREA, *Miss.*—Mississippi river, above Bayou Sara, not above Grand Gulf.

O'BRIEN, *Miss.*—Mississippi river, 210 miles above New Orleans, above Bayou Sara, not above Grand Gulf.

OCH LEVEN, *Miss.*—Mississippi river, above Bayou Sara, not above Grand Gulf.

ODD FELLOWS, (WOODYARD).—Red river not above Alexandria.

ODOM'S LANDING, *Ala.*—Tombigbee river, not above Demopolis.

ODOM'S, J. T., LANDING, *Ala.*—Alabama river, not above Selma.

OFFELE, MRS., *Ark.*—Mississippi river, above Greenville, not above Memphis.

OGDEN'S LANDING, *La.*—Ouachita river, not above Harrisonburg.

OGDEN PLACE.—Red river, not above Alexadrina.

OGDEN, SAM.—Red river, above Fulton, not above Lanesport.

OHIO LANDING.—Ouachita river, above Trenton, not above Alabama Landing.

OHIO CITY, *Mo.*—Mississippi river, 1067 miles above New Orleans opposite Cairo.

OIL TROUGH, *Ark.*—White river, not above Batesville.

O. K. PLANTATION, *La.*—Tensas river, 33 miles from Trinity, not above Bayou Macon.

O. K. LANDING, *La.*—Red river, 446 miles from New Orleans, above Cane river, not above Grand Ecore.

OLD FORT GEORGE, *Mo.*—Missouri river, 1511 miles above its mouth, above Iatan.

OLD TOWN, *Ark.*—Mississippi river, above Greenville, not above Memphis.

OLD TOWN LANDING, *Ark.*—Mississippi river, above Greenville, not above Memphis.

OLD JOHN'S LANDING, *Ala.*—Alabama river, not above Selma.

OLD FIELD'S LANDING, *Ark.*—Arkansas river, 266 miles above Napoleon, above Pine Bluff, not above Little Rock.

OLD JEFFERSON, *Mo.*—Mississippi river, 243 miles above its mouth, above Jefferson City, not above Lexington.

OLD RIVER, *Ark.*—Mississippi river, above Greenville, not above mouth of the Ohio.

OLD RIVER, *La.*—Mississippi river, near Railroad Landing.

OLD FRANKLIN, *Mo.*—Missouri river, 202 miles above its mouth, above Jefferson City, not above Lexington.

OLD REE VILLAGE, *Mo.*—Missouri river, 1726 miles above its mouth, above Iatan.

OLD CARR PLACE.—Red river, above Fulton not above Lanesport.

OLD FORT PIERRE. (Black Hill's Landing.)—Missouri river, 1330 miles up, above Iatan.

OLD MARDIS LANDING.—Black river, La., not above Trinity.

OLD TAYLOR.—Ouachita river, above Alabama Landing, not above Camden.

OLDEN, *Ark.*—Mississippi river, above Greenville, not above Memphis.

OLDHAM.—Mississippi river, above Memphis, not above the mouth of the Ohio.

OLWER'S LANDING, *Ala.*—Alabama river, not above Selma.

OMEGA LANDING.—Red river, above Alexandria, not above Cane river.

OMEGA.—Tallahatchie river, not above Cassidy Bayou.

OMEGA.—Yazoo river, above Yazoo City, not above Leflore.

OMAHA CITY, *Neb.*—Missouri river, 686 miles above its mouth, above Iatan.

OMEGA, *La.*—Mississippi river, 427 miles above New Orleans, above Grand Gulf, not above Greenville.

OX BOWS.—Yazoo river, above Yazoo City, not above Leflore.

ONAWA, *Mo.*—Missouri river, above Iatan.

ONECHO, *Tenn.*—Cumberland river, not above Nashville.

O'NEALS CREEK.—Yazoo river, above Yazoo City, not above Leflore.

ONWARD, *Tenn.*—Tennessee river, not above Eastport.

ORANGE, *Texas.*—Sabine river, not above Niblett's Bluff.

OREGON.—Yazoo river, above Yazoo City, not above Leflore.

ORCHARD PLANTATION, *La.*—Red river, not above Alexandria.

OSBURN (or M. WELSH'S).—Red river, not above Alexandria.

OSWEGO.—Yazoo river, above Yazoo City, not above Leflore.

OWENS.—Red river, above Shreveport, not above Carolina Bluffs.

OPELOUSAS, *La.*—Parish of St. Landry.

OPELOUSAS RAILROAD.—Now called Morgan railroad.

OPON POND.—Chattahoochie river, not above Columbus.

OSARK, *Ark*—Arkansas river, 476 miles above Napoleon, above Norristown, not above Fort Smith.

OSAGE RIVER, *Mo.*—Missouri river, 156 miles above its month, not above Jefferson City.

OSAGE, *Ala.*—Alabama river, not above Selma.

OSCEOLA, *Ark.*—Mississippi river, 895 miles above New Orleans, above Greenville, not above the mouth of the Ohio.

OSCEOLA, *Miss.*—Pearl river, above Columbia.

OSBORN'S LANDING, *La*—Bayou Macon, above Monticello.

OSBORN'S LANDING, *La.*—Bayou Macon, 50 miles from its mouth, not above Monticello.

OSWALT, *La.*—Black river, La., not above Harrisonburg.

OSYKA, *Miss.*—Jackson railroad, 88 miles from New Orleans.

OTTO CITY, *Mo.*—Missouri river, 714 miles above its mouth, above Iatan.

OTTOWA, *Ill.*—Illinois river, 262 miles above its mouth, above Beardstown, not above the mouth of Fox river.

OTT'S LANDING, *La*—Ouachita river, not above Harrisonburg.

OVEN BLUFF, *Ala.*—Tombigbee river, not above Demopolis.

OVEN'S BURG, *Ky.*—Ohio river, 233 miles above its mouth, above Paducah, not above Cincinnati.

OWAWA BLUFF, *Mo.*—Missouri river, above Iatan.

OWENSBORO, *Ky.*—Ohio river, 220 miles above its mouth, above Paducah, not above Cincinnati.
not above Rosville.

OZMENT'S LANDING.—Sabine river.

OZARK.—Arkansas river, 476 miles above Napoleon, above Norristown,

OWEN'S LANDING, *Mo.*—Missouri river, 382 miles above its mouth, above Lexington, not above Iatan.

OX BOWS, *Ark.*—White river, 29 miles above its mouth, below the junction of Black river.

OXFORD, *Miss.*—Jackson railroad, 341 miles from New Orleans.

P

PACE & MURPHY, *La.*—Ouachita river, above Trenton, not above Alabama Landing.

PACE'S LANDING, *La.*—Ouachita river, above Trenton, not above Alabama Landing.

PACE'S LANDING, *Ala.*—Tombigbee river, not above Demopolis.

PACE'S PLACE, *Miss.*—163 miles up Big Deer Creek.

PACKERY.—Red river, above Shreveport, not above Carolina Bluff.

PADUCAH, *Ky.*—Ohio river, 44 miles above its mouth.

PAINCOURTVILLE, *La.*—Bayou Lafourche.

PALESTINE, *Ohio.*—Ohio river, 550 miles from its mouth, above Cincinnati.

PALMYRA, *Tenn.*—Cumberland river, not above Nashville.

PALMYRA, *Miss.*—Mississippi river, 393 miles above New Orleans, above Grand Gulf, not above Greenville.

PALMETTO, *Miss.*—Mississippi river, above Bayou Sara, not above Grand Gulf.

PALMETTO CREEK, *Texas.*—Trinity river, above Smithville, not above Magnolia Landing.

PALMETTO PLANTATION (D. ALLEN), *La*—Red river, above Cotile, not above mouth of Cane river.

PALMETTO POINT, *Miss.*—Mississippi river, above Bayou Sara, not above Grand Gulf.

PALMERMO; *Mo.*—Missouri river, above Iatan.

PALIWAIRE, *Tenn.*—Cumberland river, not above Nashville.

PALLOWAY'S LANDING, *La.*—Bayou Macon, 100 miles from its mouth, not above Monticello.

PALAHALTO LANDING.—Tallahatchie river, not above Cold Water.

PALESTINE.—Anderson City, Texas.

PALMETTO HOME.—Yazoo river, above Yazoo City, not above Leflore.

PALMETTO PLACE.—Red river, above Alexandria, not above mouth of Cane river.

PALO ALTO.—Black river, La., not above Trinity.

PALMA VISTA.—Bayou Mason, not above Monticello.

PANTHER BURN, *Miss.*—133 miles up Big Deer Creek.

PARADISE A.—112 miles up Big Deer Creek, not above Yazoo City.

PALO ALTO—Tallahatchie river, not above Cassidy Bayou.

PANOLA, *Miss.*—Tallahatchie river, above the mouth of Cold Water, not above Belmont.

PANOLA (or T. C. WALMSLEY), *La.*—Red river, above Grand Ecore, not above Shreveport.

PANDORA LANDING, *La.*—Black river, La.

PANNEL'S LANDING, *Mo*—Missouri river, not above Jefferson City.

PARGOUD'S, F. LANDING, *La.*—Ouachita river, above Harrisonburg, not above Trenton.

PARGOUD'S, N. LANDING, *La.*—Ouachita river, above Trenton, not above Alabama Landing.

PARKVILLE, *Mo.*—Missouri river, 417 miles above its mouth, above Lexington, not above Iatan.

PARK'S LANDING, *La.*—Ouachita river, above Trenton, not above Alabama Landing.

PARK'S LANDING, *Ala.*—Alabama river, not above Selma.

PARKERSBURG, *Ohio.*—Ohio river, 823 miles above its mouth, above Cincinnati.

PARKER'S, D. LANDING, *Ala.*—Alabama river, not above Selma.

PARKER'S LANDING, *Miss*—Tombigbee river, above Columbus, not above Cotton Gin Port.

PARGETTS LANDING, *La.*—Ouachita river, above Harrisonburg, not above Trenton.

PARKER'S BAYOU.—Yazoo river, above Yazoo City, not above Leflore.

PARKER'S GIN.—Bayou Bartholomew, above Point Pleasant not above Arkansas line.

PARKER, TOM --Bayou Bartholomew, above Point Pleasant, not above Arkansas line.

PARKER'S LANDING.—Bayou Macon, not above Monticello.

PARKS, T. G., *Miss.*—116 miles up Big Deer Creek.

PARSONS, JONES.—Boeuf river, not above Thomas' Landing.

PARSON & JONS.—Bayou Bartholemew, not above Point Pleasant.

PARTONIA.—Angelina river, Texas.

PARISH'S.—Tallahatchie river, not above Cassidy Bayou.

PARKHURST, *Iowa.*—Mississippi river, 1537 miles above New Orleans, above second Rapids, not above Galena.

PARMAVISTA, *La.*—Bayou Macon, 58 miles from its mouth, not above Monticello.

PARSON'S LANDING, *Ark.*—Red river, 190 miles above Shreveport, above Carolina Bluff, not above Fulton.

PARIS LANDING, *Tenn.*—Tennessee river, not above Eastport.

PARVIS, *La.*—Bayou Macon, 135 miles above its mouth, not above Monticello.

PARRSVILLE, *Miss.*—Tombigbee river, above Columbus, not above Cotton Gin Port.

PASCAGOULA.—Station on the Mobile Railrod, 100 miles from New Orleans.

PASCAGOULA PLACE.—Red river, above Grand Ecore not above Shreveport.

PASS CHRISTIAN, *Miss.*—52 miles from New Orleans, by Mobile Railroad.

PATENT LANDING.—Ouachita river, not above Harrisonburg.

PATRIA LANDING.—Mississippi river, above Greenville not above Memphis.

PASCAGOULA RIVER, *Miss.*—Any point.

PASTORIA, *Ark.*—Arkansas river, 191 miles above Napoleon, above Pine Bluff, not above Little Rock.

PATEE'S LANDING, *Ark.*—Arkansas river, 232 miles above Napoleon, above Pine Bluff, not above Little Rock.

PATRIARCH, *Ky.*—Ohio river, 510 miles above its mouth, above Paducah, not above Cincinnati.

PATRIOT, *Ind*—Ohio river, 490 miles above its mouth, above Paducah, not above Cincinnati.

PATRIOT, *Tenn.*—Tennessee river, not above Eastport.

PATTERSONVILLE, *La.*—Bayou Teche, Attakapas.

PATTERSON'S BLUFF, *Ark.*—Arkansas river, 453 miles above Napoleon, above Norristown, not above Fort Smith.

PATTERSON'S FERRY, *Mo.*—Missouri river, 40 miles from its mouth, not above Jefferson City.

PATTERSON'S FERRY, *Texas.*—Sabine river, above Belgrade, not above Hamilton.

PATTERSON'S LANDING, *Ark.*—Mississippi river, above Greenville, not above Memphis.

PATTERSON'S FERRY, *Tenn.*—Tennesee river, not above Eastport.

PATTERSON'S WOODYARD, *Ala.*—Warrior river, not above Tuscaloosa.

PATRICK'S FERRY, *Texas.*—Trinity river, above Smithville, not above Magnolia Landing.

PAUL'S LANDING, *Miss.*—Yazoo river, not above Yazoo City.

PAXTON LANDING.—Yazoo river, not above Yazoo City.
PAXTON'S LANDING, *Miss.*—166 miles up Big Deer Creek.
PAXTON'S BRIDGE, *Miss.*—168 miles up Big Deer Creek.
PAXTON'S LANDING, *Ark.*—Red river, 336 miles above Shreveport, above Fulton, not above Lanesport.
PAYNE'S LANDING, *Ala.*—Alabama river, not above Selma.
PAYNE'S, R. O., LANDING, *Ala.*—Tombigbee river, not above Demopolis.
PEACE POINT (or HODGES), *La.*—Red river, above Grand Ecore, not above Shreveport.
PEACH ORCHARD BLUFF, *Ark.*—White river, 234 miles from its mouth, not above the junction of Black river.
PEARL RIVER, *Miss.*—Above Columbia.
PEARL RIVER ISLAND, *Miss.*—Pearl river, above Gainesville, not above Columbia.
PEARLINGTON, *Miss.*—Pearl river, not above Gainesville.
PEARTS, T. L. (WOODYARD).—Red river, not above Alexandria.
PEBBLES BLUFFS.—Tallahatchie river, not above Cassidy Bayou.
PECAN POINT, *La.*—Mississippi river, 446 miles above New Orleans, above Grand Gulf, not above Greenville.
PECAN POINT, *Texas.*—Red river, 438 miles above Shreveport, above Lanesport, not above Mound City.
PECANTY LANDING, *La.*—Black river, La.
PECAN POINT (or WATSON PLANTATION.—Red river, above Lanesport, not above Mound City.
PECAN POINT, *La.*—Red river, above Grand Ecore, not above Shreveport.
PECAN POINT.—Tallahatchie river, not above Cassidy Bayou.
PEDROU.—Ouachita river, above Alabama Landing, not above Camden.
PEELER, R.—Mississippi river, above Grand Gulf, not above Greenville.
PEEBLE'S WOODYARD, *Ala.*—Alabama river, not above Selma.
PEGGY WATSON'S LANDING, *Ky.*—Mississippi river, above Memphis, not above the Ohio river.
PEKIN, *Ill.*—Illinois river, 163 miles from its mouth, above Beardstown, not above the mouth of Fox river.

PELCHER'S POINT, *La.*—Mississippi river, 490 miles above New Orleans, above Grand Gulf, not above Greenville.

PELLY'S LANDING.—Mississippi river, 700 miles above New Orleans, above Greenville, not above the mouth of the Ohio.

PEMBERTON'S LANDING, *Ark.*—Arkansas river, 268 miles above Napoleon, above Pine Bluff, not above Little Rock.

PENDLETON, *Ohio.*—Ohio river, 536 miles above its mouth, above Cincinnati.

PENDLETON, *Texas.*—Sabine river, not above Grand Bluff.

PENNINGTON'S, W. Q. LANDING, *Ark.*—Arkansas river, 258 miles above Napoleon, above Pine Bluff, not above Little Rock.

PENNINGTON'S, M. LANDING, *Ark.*—Arkansas river, 246 miles above Napoleon, above Pine Bluff, not above Little Rock.

PENITENTIARY LANDING, *Ill.*—Mississippi river, above the mouth of the Ohio, not above Alton.

PENN'S, DR. WOOD LANDING, *Mo.*—Missouri river, 33 miles above its mouth, not above Jefferson City.

PEORIA, *Ill.*—Illinois river, 174 miles from its mouth, above Beardstown, not above the mouth of Fox river.

PEORIA LAKE, *Ill.*—Illinois river, 196 miles above its mouth, above Beardstown, not above the mouth of Fox river.

PERU, *Ill.*—Illinois river, above Beardstown, not above the mouth of Fox river.

PERU, *Iowa.*—Mississippi river, 1630 miles above New Orleans, above Galena.

PERU, *Ind.*—Wabash river, above the Rapids, not above Terre Haute.

PERU.—Missouri river, 690 miles above its mouth, above Iatan.

PERRYVILLE, *Ind.*—Wabash river, above the Rapids, not above Terre Haute.

PERRYVILLE, *Tenn.*—Tennessee river, 131 miles from its mouth, not above Eastport.

PERRY'S LANDING, *Ala.*—Alabama river, above Selma, not above Wetumpka.

PERRY'S LANDING, *Ala.*—Warrior river, not above Tuscaloosa.

PEROTTE CYNAQUE.—Red river, above Grand Ecore, not above Shreveport.

PERROTT, JAMES MAD.—Red river, above Grand Ecore, not above Shreveport.

PERCY PLACE, *Miss.*—182 miles up Big Deer Creek.

PEROTT, JOHN LOUIS.—Red river, above Grand Ecore, not above Shreveport.

PEROT, CHS.—Red river, above Cane river, not above Grand Ecore.

PERRE, AUGUSTE.—Ouachita river, above Alabama Landing, not above Camden.

PERRY, G.—83 miles up Bœuf river, above Thomas' Landing.

PERKINS.—Bayou Bartholomew, above Portland.

PERSON, L. K. (or LITTLE PRAIRIE.—Red river, above foot of Raft, not above Fulton.

PERRY'S LANDING, *Ill.*—Illinois river, not above Beardstown.

PERROT'S LANDING, *La.*—Red river, above Grand Ecore, not above Shreveport.

PERKIN'S, JR. LANDING, *Miss.*—Mississippi river, above Greenville, not above Memphis.

PERKIN'S LANDING, *Ala.*—Warrior river, not above Tuscaloosa.

PERKIN'S LANDING, *Ark.*—Arkansas river, 260 miles above Napoleon, above Pine Bluff, not above Little Rock.

PETERSBURG, *Ky.*—Ohio river, 509 above its mouth, above Paducah, not above Cincinnati.

PETIT JEAN LANDING, *Ark.*—Arkansas river, 368 miles above Napoleon, above Little Rock, not above Norristown.

PETTY CLAIRE, *Ark.*—White river, 319 miles above its mouth, not above the junction of Black river.

PETERSBURG, *Mo.*—Missouri river, 546 miles above its mouth, above Iatan.

PETERKIN'S.—Bayou Bartholomew, above Point Pleasant, not above Arkansas line.

PETERS.—Mississippi river, above Grand Gulf, not above Greenville.

PETTICORE WOODYARD.—Red river, above Cane river, not above Grand Ecore.

PETTIWAY'S LOWER LANDING, *Ala.*—Alabama river, not above Selma.

PETER'S, DR. LANDING, *Ark.*—Mississippi river, above Greenville, not above Memphis.

PETTY CAILLOU BAYOU, *La*—Any point.

PETTY'S BLUFF, *Miss.*—Tombigbee river, above Gainesville, not above Columbus.

PEVEY'S LANDING, *Ala.*—Tombigbee river, not above Demopolis.

PEYTON.—Mississippi river, 746 miles above New Orleans, above Greenville, not above Memphis.

PEYTONIA LANDING, *Tenn.*—Cumberland river, not above Nashville.

PHARE'S LOWER GIN, *Ala.*—Tombigbee river, above Demopolis, not above Gainesville.

PHILADEPHIA, *Mo.*—Mississippi river, above the mouth of the Ohio, not above Alton.

PHILADELPHIA, *Miss.*—Pearl river, above Columbia.

PHILIP'S, P. LANDING, *Ark.*—Red river, 261 miles above Shreveport, above Fulton, not above Lanesport.

PHILIP'S, W. Y. LANDING, *La.*—Ouachita river, above Trenton, not above Alabama Landing.

PHILIP'S LANDING, *Mo.*—Mississippi river, above Memphis, not above the mouth of the Ohio.

PHILIP'S, D. JR. LANDING, *Mo.*—Mississippi river, above Memphis, not above the mouth of the Ohio.

PHILIP'S, MRS. LANDING, *Ala.*—Tombigbee river, above Demopolis, not above Gainesville.

PHILIP'S SHIP, *Mo.*—Mississippi river, above Memphis, not above the mouth of the Ohio.

PHILIPTOWN, *Ind.*—Wabash river, above Terre Haute.

PHILLIPOT'S LANDING, *La.*—Ouachita river, above Harrisonburg, not above Trenton.

PIERRE BAYOU, *Miss.*—Mississippi river, above Grand Gulf, not above Greenville.

PIERCE'S LANDING, *La.*—Red river, 325 miles above New Orleans, not above Alexandria.

PIERCE'S LANDING, *Ala.*—Alabama river, not above Selma.

PICKETT'S LANDING, *La.*—Red river, one mile above Shreveport, not above Carolina Bluff.

PIGEON MILLS.—Ouachita river, 416 miles above Old river, above Alabama Landing, not above Camden.

PEYTON'S WOODYARD.—Red river, not above Alexandria.

PEYTON'S, WIDOW LANDING.—Red river, not above Alexandria.

PFEIFFER GIN (MAXWELL).—Bayou Bartholomew, not above Point Pleasant.

PHELPS LANDING.—Ouachita river, above Harrisonburg, not above Trenton.

PHILIPS PLANTATION.—Red river, above Fulton, not above Lanesport.

PHILIPS, HAYGOOD.—Yazoo river, above Yazoo City, not above Leflore.

PHILLIPS, MRS.—113 miles up Bœuf river, above Thomas' Landing.

PHELPSTON.—Yazoo river, above Yazoo City, not above Leflore.

PHŒNIX MILLS.—Yazoo river, above Yazoo City, not above Leflore.

PIERRE'S, MAYOUX LANDING.—Red river, not above Alexandria.

PICKETT'S, J. A. LANDING (or LAST CHANCE), *La.*—Red river, above Grand Ecore, not above Shreveport.

PICKEN'S LANDING, *Ala.*—Warrior river, not above Tuscaloosa.

PICKENSVILLE, *Ala.*—Tombigbee river, above Gainesville, not above Columbus.

PIERCE, A. LANDING.—Ouachita river, above Harrisonburg, not above Trenton.

PIERCE, C. LANDING.—Ouachita river, above Harrisonburg, not above Trenton.

PIERCE.—Bayou Bartholomew, not above Point Pleasant.

PIERSON'S, C. A.—Red river, above Cane river, above Grand Ecore.

PIERSON'S, A. A. (WOODYARD).—Red river, above Cane river, not above Grand Ecore.

PICKETT BLUFF.—Bayou Bartholomew, above Arkansas line, not above Portland.

PICKET'S (or CASH POINT).—Red river, above Shreveport, not above foot of Raft.

PICKETT'S, JOHN (or HURRICANE BLUFF.)—Red river, above Shreveport, not above foot of Raft.

PICKETT, ESTATE OF.—Red river, above Grand Ecore, not above Shreveport.

PIGEON HILL (UPPER AND LOWER).—Ouachita river, above Alabama Landing, not above Camden.

PIKE'S PEAK.—Red river, above Cane river, not above Grand Ecore.

PILES, JOHN.—Ouachita river, above Alabama Landing, not above Camden.

PINE BLUFF.—Little river, not above Woods' Landing.

PINE PRAIRIE.—Ouachita river, above Alabama Landing, not above Camden.

PIONEER.—Red river, above Fulton, not above Lanesport.

PIPES, D. (or HIGH DIE).—Red river, above Cane river, not above Grand Ecore.

PIPPINS.—Ouachita river, above Harrisonburg, not above Trenton.

PIGEON CREEK, *Ala.*—Alabama river, not above Selma.

PILCHER'S POINT, *La.*—Mississippi river, 490 miles above New Orleans, above Grand Gulf, not above Greenville.

PILLARD'S LANDING.—Mississippi river, above Grand Gulf, not above Greenville.

PINE BLUFF, *Ark.*—Arkansas river, 172 miles above Napoleon.

PINE BLUFF, *Texas*—Red river, above Carolina Bluff, not above Fulton.

PINE BLUFF, *La.*—Ouachita river, above Harrisonburg, not above Trenton.

PINE BLUFF, *Ky.*—Tennessee river, not above Eastport.

PINE BLUFF, *Texas.*—Red river, 540 miles above Shreveport, above Mound City.

PINE BLUFF, *Texas.*—Trinity river, above Magnolia Landing.

PINE BLUFF, *La.*—Lake Bisteneau.

PINEY LANDING, *Ark.*—Arkansas river, 414 miles above its month, above Norristown, not above Fort Smith.

PINE BAYOU, *Ark.*—White river, above Batesville.

PINEVILLE, *La.*—Red river, 360 miles from New Orleans, opposite Alexandria.

PINE BEND.—Mississipp, river, above Galena.

PIN HOOK, *Miss.*—Tombigbee river, above Gainesville, not above Columbus.

PINE PRAIRIE, *Ark.*—Red river, 300 miles above Shreveport, above Fulton, not above Lanesport.

PINETUCKY, *Miss.*—Pearl river, above Gainesville, not above Columbia.

PINKNEY, *Ky.*—Cumberland river, not above Nashville.

PINE WOODYARD LANDING, *La.*—Mississippi river, above Bayou Sara, not above Grand Gulf.

PINKNEY, *Mo.*—Missouri river, 82 miles above its mouth, not above Jefferson City.

PINKNEYVILLE, *Tenn.*—Cumberland river, not above Nashville.

PITT'S LANDING, *La.*—Lake Caddo.

PITTSBURG, *Penn.*—Ohio river, 1005 miles from its mouth, above Cincinnati.

PITTSBURG, *Ind.*—Wabash river, above the Rapids, not above Terre Haute.

PITTSBURG, *Ark.*—Arkansas river, 426 miles above Napoleon, above Norristown, not above Fort Smith.

PITTSBURG LANDING, *Tenn.*—Tennessee river, 213 miles from its mouth, not above Eastport.

PITTS POINT.—Red river, above Shreveport, not above Carolina Bluff.

PLAISANCE, *La.*—Red river, above Cotile, not above Grand Ecore.

PLAQUEMINE, *La.*—Mississippi river, 122 miles above New Orleans, not above Bayou Sara.

PLATTSMOUTH, *Neb.*—Missouri river, 653 miles above its mouth above Iatan.

PLATTSVILLE, *Iowa.*—Missouri river, 654 miles from its mouth, above Iatan.

PLATTE RIVER.—Missouri river, 658 miles above its mouth, above Iatan .

PLATTEN RIVER, *Mo.*—Mississippi river, 1146 miles above New Orleans, above the mouth of the Ohio, not above Alton.

PLATTE CITY, *Mo.*—Missouri river, above Lexington, not above Iatan.

PLAIN CITY, *Mo.*—Missouri river,-above Jefferson City, not above Lexington.

PLACE, B. (or J. S. YATES).—Red river, above Grand Ecore, not above Shreveport.

PLANTERS' POST.—Ouachita river, above Alabama Landing, not above Camden.

PLANTERSVILLE.—Bayou Bartholomew, above Point Pleasant, not above Arkansas line.

PLEASANT HILL, *Ark.*—White river, not above Batesville.

PLEASANTS, COL —Arkansas river, above Arkansas Post, not above Pine Bluff.

PLEASANT RIDGE.—Yazoo river, above Yazoo City, not above Leflore.

PLEASANT BLUFF, *Ark*—Arkansas river, 618 miles above Napoleon, above Fort Smith.

PLEASANT HILL, *Ark.*—Arkansas river, above Norristown, not above Fort Smith.

PLEASANT ISLAND, *Ark.*—White river, not above Batesville.

PLEASANT VIEW.—Yazoo river, above Yazoo City, not above Leflore.

PLEDGER'S LANDING, *Ala.*—Alabama river, not above Selma.

PLUM BAYOU, *Ark.*—Arkansas river, 224 miles above Napoleon, above Pine Bluff, not above Little Rock.

PLUM POINT, *Tenn.*—Mississippi river, above Memphis, not above the mouth of the Ohio.

PLUNKETT'S PLANTATION, *La.*—Red river, above Grand Ecore, not above Shreveport.

PLYMOUTH, *Miss.*—Tombigbee river, above Columbus, not above Cotton Gin Port.

POCAHONTAS, *Ark.*—Black river, a tributary of White river.

POE'S LANDING, *Ala.*—Tombigbee river, not above Demopolis.

POE'S LANDING, *Ala.*—Alabama river, not above Selma.

POELNITZ'S LANDING, *Ala*—Tombigbee river, not above Demopolis.

PLUM ORCHARD.—109 miles up Sunflower river.

PLUMMERS.—Black river, La., not above Harrisonburg.

PLUNKETT'S (H. H. HUBBARD).—Red river, above Grand Ecore, not above Shreveport.

POINT BRIDGE.—Tensas river, La., above Bayou Macon.

POINT HENDRICK LANDING.—152 miles up Sunflower river.

POINT JEFFERSON.—Bœuf river, above Thomas' Landing.

POINT LOOKOUT.—282 miles up Sunflower river.

POINT PLEASANT.—Yazoo river, above Yazoo City, not above Leflore.

POINT PLEASANT (W. BROS.)—Bayou Bartholomew, not above Point Pleasant.

POINT PLEASANT (UPPER LANDING).—Bayou Bartholomew, not above Point Pleasant.

POINT ISABEL, *Ill.*—Illinois river, above Beardstown, not above the mouth of Fox river.

POINT ISABEL, *Ill.*—Ohio river, 218 miles above its mouth, above Paducah, not above Cincinnati.

POINT PLEASANT, *La.*—Bayou Bartholomew.

POINT PLEASANT, *Ohio.*—Ohio river, 569 miles above its mouth, above Cincinnati.

POINT PLEASANT, *Va.*—Ohio river, 738 miles above its mouth, above Cincinnati.

POINT PLEASANT, *Miss.*—Mississippi river, 975 miles above New Orleans, above Greenville, not above Memphis.

POINT PLEASANT, *La.*—Mississippi river, not above Bayou Sara.

POINTE COUPEE, *La.*—Mississippi river, 165 miles above New Orleans, not above Bayou Sara.

POINTE-A-LA-HACHE, *La.*—Mississippi river, below New Orleans.

POINT PERRY, *Mo.*—Mississippi river, 1096 miles above New Orleans, above the mouth of the Ohio, not above Alton.

POINT DOUGLASS, *Minn.*—Mississippi river, 1830 miles above New Orleans, above Galena.

POINT CHICOT, *Ark.*—Mississippi river, 516 miles above New Orleans, above Greenville, not above Memphis.

POINT MABIN, *La.*—Bayou Macon, 120 miles above its mouth, not above Monticello.

POINT COMFORT, *Ark.*—Mississippi river, above Greenville, not above Memphis.

POINT MASON, *Tenn.*—Tennessee river, not above Eastport.

POKER POINT, *Ark.*—Mississippi river, above Greenville, not above Memphis.

POLKSVILLE, *Miss.*—Tallahatchie river, above the mouth of Cold Water, not above Belmont.

POLK STORES, *Ark.*—Mississippi river, above Greenville, not above Memphis.

POLK, EUGENE.—Bayou Bartholomew, not above Point Pleasant.

POLK, TOM (SANDIDGE).—Bayou Bartholomew, not above Point Pleasant.

POLAND'S, W. H. LANDING, *Ark.*—Red river, 386 miles above Shreveport, above Lanesport, not above Mound City.

POLLARD'S LANDING, *Ala.*—Alabama river, above Selma, not above Wetumpka.

POMROY, *Ohio.*—Ohio river, 751 miles above its mouth, above Cincinnati.

PONKA CREEK.—Missouri river, above Iatan.

PONKA ISLAND.—Missouri river, above Iatan.

PONTCHATOULA, *La.*—Jackson railroad, 48 miles from New Orleans.

PONT AU SUCRE, *Mo*—Mississippi river, 1405 miles above New Orleans, above second Rapids, not above Galena.

POOLE'S CREEK, *Texas.*—Trinity river, above Smithville, not above Magnolia Landing.

POOLE'S, L. B. LANDING, *La.*—Black river, La.

POOL LAKE LANDING.—Ouachita river, above Alabama Landing, not above Camden.

POOLE'S, G. (or BUCK HORN).—Red river, above Grand Ecore, not above Shreveport.

POPE'S, WIDOW LANDING, *Mo.*—Mississippi river, above the Ohio river, not above Alton.

POPE'S, MRS. M. F. LANDING, *Ala.*—Alabama river, above Selma, not above Wetumpka.

POPLAR GROVE, *Tenn.*—Cumberland river, not above Nashville.

POPLAR GROVE, *La.*—Mississippi river, not above Bayou Sara.

POPLAR BLUFF.—Bayou Bartholomew, above Arkansas line, not above Portland.

POPLAR GROVE.—Ouachita river, above Harrisonburg, not above Trenton.

POPLETON'S LANDING.—Mississippi river, above Alton, not above the first Rapids.

PORT VINCENT, *Miss.*—Pearl river, not above Gainesville.

PORT BARRE, *La.*—Parish of St. Landry.

PORT UNION, *La.*—Ouachita river, above Trenton, not above Alabama Landing.

PORT GIBSON, *Miss.*--Bayou Pierre, 28 miles from its mouth; shipping port at Bayou Sara.

PORT CADDO, *La.*—Lake Caddo.

PORT HUDSON, *La.*—Mississippi river, 156 miles above New Orleans, not above Bayou Sara.

PORT WILLIAMS AND MOUTH OF KENTUCKY RIVER.—Ohio river, 453 miles above its mouth, above Paducah, not above Cincinnati.

PORT BOLIVAR, *La.*—Lake Bisteneau.

PORT WORTHINGTON, *Miss.*—Mississippi river, above Grand Gulf, not above Greenville.

PORT LOUISA, *Iowa.*—Mississippi river, 1471 miles above New Orleans, above second Rapids, not above Galena.

PORT BYRON, *Ill.*—Mississippi river, 1536 miles above New Orleans, above the second Rapids, not above Galena.

PORT HICKORY, *La.*—Mississippi river, 218 miles above New Orleans, not above Bayou Sara.

PORT ROYAL, *Mo.*—Missouri river, 45 miles above its mouth, not above Jefferson City.

PORT BARROW, *La.*—Bayou Lafourche.

PORCUPINE CREEK.—Missouri river, 2177 miles above its mouth, above Iatan.

PORT CADDO.—Red river, above Shreveport, not above Carolina Bluff.

PORT EADS, *La.*—Mouth of Mississippi river.

PORT WOOD.—Tallahatchie river, not above Cassidy Bayou.

PORTER BAYOU.—205 miles up Sunflower river.

PORTER'S MRS.—334 miles up Sunflower river.

POSSUM TROTT (DR. SYPE).—Red river, above Alexandria, not above Cane river.

POTT'S, DR.—Bayou Bartholomew, not above Point Pleasant.

POWELL'S, MAD.—Red river, above Grand Ecore, not above Shreveport.

PORT WILLIAMS, *La.*—Old river, (Mississippi river,) not above Bayou Sara.

PORT ANDERSON, *Miss.*—Mississippi river, above Greenville, not above Memphis.

PORT CLARION, *Ala.*—Tombigbee river, not above Demopolis.

PORTUNA, *Mo.*—Missouri river, 57 miles above its mouth, not above Jefferson City.

PORTER'S BLUFF, *Texas.*—Trinity river, above Magnolia Landing.

PORTAGE AUX SIOUX, *Mo.*—Mississippi river, above Alton, not above the first Rapids.

PORTLAND, *Ark.*—Bayou Bartholomew, above Arkansas line.

PORTLAND, *Ky.*—Ohio river, 380 miles above its mouth, above Paducah, not above Cincinnati.

PORTLAND, *Ind.*—Wabash river, above the Rapids, not above Terre Haute.

PORTLAND, *Ala.*—Alabama river, 246 miles from Mobile, not above Selma.

PORTLAND, *Ark.*—Arkansas river, 335 miles above Napoleon, above Little Rock, not above Norristown.

PORTLAND, *Mo.*—Missouri river, 111 miles from its mouth, not above Jefferson City.

PORTSMOUTH, *Ill.*—Mississippi river, 1588 miles above New Orleans, above second Rapids, not above Galena.

PORTSMOUTH, *Ohio.*—Ohio river, 647 miles above its mouth, above Cincinnati.

POST OF ARKANSAS, *Ark.*—Arkansas river, 58 miles above Napoleon.

POTOSI, *Wis.*—Mississippi river, 1637 miles above New Orleans, above Galena.

POVERTY POINT, *Miss*—Mississippi river, above Grand Gulf, not above Greenville.

POVERTY POINT, *La.*—Bayou Macon, 195 miles above its mouth, above Monticello.

POWELL'S LANDING, *La.*—Red river, above Grand Ecore, not above Shreveport.

POWELL'S, DR. LANDING, *La.*—Ouachita river, above Harrisonburg, not above Trenton.

POWELL'S R. LANDING, *Ala.*—Alabama river, not above Selma.

POWHATTAN, *Ark.*—Black river, tributary of White.

POWER'S CUT OFF, *Ark.*—Red river, 211 miles above Shreveport, above Carolina Bluff, not above Fulton.

PRAIRIETOWN, *Ill.*—Wabash river, above Terre Haute.

PRAIRIE BLUFF, *Ala.*—Alabama river, 206 miles from Mobile, not above Selma.

PRAIRIE DU CHIEN, *Wis.*—Mississippi river, 1676 miles above New Orleans, above Galena.

PRAIRIE LACROSSE.—Mississippi river, above Galena.

PRAIRIE LANDING, *Ark.*—White river, 22 miles from its mouth, below the junction of Black river.

PRAIRIE LANDING, *La.*—Black river, La.

PRAIRIE LANDING.—Bœuf river, not above Thomas' Landing.

PRAIRIE LEE, *Texas.*—Caldwelll county, Texas.

PRATT, J. L.—Bayou Bartholomew, above Point Pleasant, not above Arkansas line.

PRATT'S LANDING, *Mo.*—Mississippi river, 1107 miles above New Orleans, above the mouth of the Ohio river, not above Alton.

PRATER'S LANDING, *La.*—Black river, La.

PRENTISS' LANDING, *Miss.*—Mississippi river, above Greenville, not above Memphis.

PRESTON, *Ill.*—Mississippi river, above the mouth of the Ohio, not above Alton.

PRESTON, *Texas.*—Red river, 766 miles above Shreveport, above Mound City.

PRESTON, *Ky.*—Ohio river, 452 miles from its mouth, above Paducah, not above Cincinnati.

PRESCOTT, *Wis.*—Mississippi river, 1830 miles above New Orleans, above Galena.

PRESNALL'S LANDING, *Mo.*—Alabama river, not above Selma.

PRICE'S LANDING, *Mo.*—Mississippi river, 1048 miles from New Orleans, above the mouth of the Ohio, not above Alton.

PRIDE'S LANDING, *Miss.*—Mississippi river, above Greenville, not above Memphis.

PRINCETON, *Texas.*—Sabine river, above Sabine City, not above Belgrade.

PRINCETON, *Miss.*—Mississippi river, 500 miles above New Orleans, above Grand Gulf, not above Greenville.

PRINCETON, *Iowa.*—Mississippi river, 1592 miles above New Orleans, above the second Rapids, not above Dubuque.

PRIANT'S, HARDY.—Red river, above Grand Ecore, not above Shreveport.

PRITCHARD'S FERRY.—Pearl river, not above Columbia.

PRINCE'S LANDING, *Ark.*—Little Red river, below the junction of White and Black rivers.

PRINCE'S, COL. LANDING, *Ark.*—Tombigbee river, not above Demopolis.

PROTHROE'S.—Red river, above Cane river, not above Grand Ecore.

PROCTORVILLE, *La.*—Lake Borgne, by railroad.

PROCTORVILLE, *Ohio.*—Ohio river, 698 miles above its mouth, above Cincinnati.

PROSEA, OGEE.—Red river, above Grand Ecore, not above Shreveport.

PROSPECT BLUFF, *Ark.*—Little Red river, 41 miles above its mouth, below the junction of Black and White rivers.

PROTOW'S LANDING, *La.*—Red river, above Cane river, not above Grand Ecore.

PROTHROE, or GREENOUGH.—Red river, above Cane river, not above Grand Ecore.

PROVIDENCE, *Mo.*—Missouri river, 176 miles above its mouth, above Jefferson City, not above Lexington.

PROVIDENCE, *La.*—Lake Bistenau.

PROVIDENCE, *Ala.*—Alabama river, not above Selma.

PRUDHOMME, G. A.—Red river, above Grand Ecore, not above Shreveport.

PRUDHOMME, G. & E.—Red river, above Grand Ecore, not above Shreveport.

PRUDHOMME, CELESTANS.—Red river, above Cane river, not above Grand Ecore.

PRUDHOMME, T.—Red river, above Cane river, not above Grand Ecore.

PRUDHOMME, ST. ANNE —Red river, above Cane river, not above Grand Ecore.

PRUDHOMME'S, A. LANDING, *La.*—Red river, above Grand Ecore, not above Shreveport.

PRUETT'S.—Bayou Bartholomew, above Portland.

PRYOR'S WOODYARD, *Ark.*—White river, 222 miles from its mouth, below the junction of Black river.

PRYER'S CUT-OFF.—Red river, above foot of Raft, not above Fulton.

PUCKETT, CHAS. J.—Red river, above Grand Ecore, not above Shreveport.

PULASKI.—Sabine river, Texas.

PURVIS.—Yazoo river, not above Yazoo City.

PULLEN'S, R. LANDING, *La.*—Black river, La.

PUGH, R. A. (or WILSON'S).—Bayou Bartholomew, above Arkansas line, not above Portland.

Q

QUAFALONIA.—Yazoo river, above Yazoo City, not above Leflore.

QUAPAW.—Arkansas river, above Pine Bluff, not above Little Rock.

QUITMAN.—Wood county, Texas; if by Sabine, above Hamilton.

QUINCY, *Ills.*—Mississippi river, 1333 miles above New Orleans, above Alton, not above first Rapids.

QUINDARO, *Mo.*—Missouri river, 462 miles above its mouth, above Lexington, not above Iatan.

QUIPAW LANDING, *Ark.*—Arkansas river, 257 miles above Napoleon, above Pine Bluff, not above Little Rock.

R

RABINSON, G. W. (COTTON POINT).—Red river, above Grand Ecore, not above Shreveport.

RABBIT ISLAND (SMARCOTT).—Red river, not above Alexandria.

RACE TRACK.—Tallahatchie river, not above Cassidy Bayou.

RACINE (DUNN'S).—Arkansas river, above Arkansas Post, not above Pine Bluff.

RACONLEY'S, P.—78 miles up Bœuf river, above Thomas' Landing.

RACCOURCI LANDING.—Mississippi river, above Bayou Sara, not above Grand Gulf.

RABBITT'S SHOALS, *Ark.*—Arkansas river, above Fort Smith.

RACELAND, *La.*—Morgan railroad, 40 miles from New Orleans.

RACINE, *Ohio.*—Ohio river, 758 miles above its mouth, above Cincinnati.

RACOON BEND, *La.*—Mississippi river, 205 miles above New Orleans, above Bayou Sara, not above Grand Gulf.

RACOON CUT-OFF, *La.*—Mississippi river, 205 miles above New Orleans, above Bayou Sara, not above Grand Gulf.

RACOON RIVER, *Wis.*—Mississippi river, 1717 miles from New Orleans, above Galena.

RAIR LAND, *La.*—Red river, above Black Bayou, not above White Oak Shoals.

RACHAL'S LANDING, P. *La.*—Red river, 464 miles above New Orleans, above Cane river, not above Grand Ecore.

RALEIGH, *Ky.*—Ohio river, 124 miles above its mouth, above Paducah, not above Cincinnati.

RAMOS, *La.*—Morgan railroad, 76 miles from New Orleans.

RANK'S LANDING, *La.*—Ouachita river, above Trenton, not above Alabama Landing.

RANDOLPH, *Tenn.*—Mississippi river, 874 miles above New Orleans, above Greenville, not above Memphis.

RANDOLPH, *Ills.*—Mississippi river, 1209 miles above New Orleans, above Alton, not above the foot of the first Rapids.

RANDOLPH, *Mo.*—Missouri river, 400 miles above its mouth, above Lexington, not above Iatan.

RAPIDS, *Ind.*—Wabash river.

RATCLIFF'S LANDING, *La.*—Mississippi river, 190 miles above New Orleans, above Bayou Sara, not above Grand Gulf.

RATTLE SNAKE SPRING, *Mo.*—Mississippi river, above the mouth of the Ohio, not above Alton.

RAVENSWOOD, *Ind.*—Ohio river, 787 miles above its mouth, above Cincinnati.

RAVESIE'S LANDING, *Ala.*—Tombigbee river, not above Demopolis.

RAVENSCROFT, *Ill.*—Illinois river, not above Beardstown.

RAYMOND.—Mississippi river, above Grand Gulf, not above Greenville.

RAY'S POINT, *La.*—Ouachita river, above Harrisonburg, not above Trenton.

RAY'S LANDING, *Ala.*—Alabama river, not above Selma.

RAINBOW BEND.—Red river, above Grand Ecore, not above Shreveport.

RAINY DAY.—178 miles up Sunflower river.

RAMSEY, H.—Black river, La.

RANDALL.—Bayou Bartholomew, not above Point Pleasant.

RANDALL.—Yazoo river, above Yazoo City, not above Leflore.

RANDOLPH.—Ouachita river, above Alabama Landing, not above Camden.

RANDOM SHOT.—Yazoo river, above Yazoo City, not above Leflore.
RASBERRY.—Yazoo river, above Yazoo City, not above Leflore.
RAWLINGS, DR.—27 miles up Arkansas river, not above Arkansas Post.
RAVEN CAMP (K. R. HYAMS).—Red river, above Alexandria, not above the mouth of Cane river.
RAY, J. W.—Red river, above Grand Ecore, not above Shreveport.
RAYS.—Tallahatchie river, not above Cassidy Bayou.
RAYNER.—Mississippi river, above Grand Gulf, not above Greenville.
REALTO.—Yazoo river, not above Yazoo City.
RECTOR'S ROCK, *Ark.*—Arkansas river, 534 miles above Napoleon, above Norristown, not above Fort Smith.
RED MOUTH, *La.*—Bœuf river, not above Thomas' Landing.
RED OAK, or BOIS D'ARC CREEK, *Texas.*—Trinity river, above Magnolia Landing.
RED ROCK, *Minn.*—Mississippi river, 1848 miles above New Orleans, above Galena.
RED RIVER LANDING, *La.*—Mississippi river, 210 miles above New Orleans, above Bayou Sara, not above Grand Gulf.
RED BLUFF, *Miss.*—Chichasaba river.
RED CHURCH, *La.*—Mississippi river, 26 miles above New Orleans, not above Bayou Sara.
RED FORK, *Ark.*—Arkansas river, 43 miles above Napoleon, not above Arkansas Post.
RED BAYOU.—Red river, above foot of Raft, not above Fulton.
RED BLUFF.—Bayou Bartholomew, above Point Pleasant, not above Arkansas line.
RED BLUFF, *La.*—Red river, above Grand Ecore, not above Shreveport.
RED BLUFF, *Ark.*—Arkansas river, above Pine Bluff, not above Little Rock.
RED BLUFF.—Red river, above Shreveport, not above Carolina Bluff.
RED CROSS.—Tallahatchie river, not above Cassidy Bayou.
RED HILL (FRAOUKELAN).—Red river, above Grand Gulf, not above Shreveport.
RED LIGHT (WOODYARD)—Red river, not above Alexandria.
RED MOUTH.—120 miles up Bœuf river, above Thomas' Landing.
RED PLAINS.—Red river, above Grand Ecore, not above Shreveport.

RED WING, *Minn*.—Mississippi river, 1812 miles above New Orleans, above Galena.

RED WOOD (B. BLAKES)—Yazoo river, not above Yazoo City.

REDDICK'S LANDING, *La*.—Black river, La.

REED'S BAR, *Ark*.—White river, 348 miles from its mouth, not above junction of Black river.

REESE'S LANDING, *Ala*.—Alabama river, above Selma, not above Wetumpka.

REEVES' GIN, *Ala*.—Alabama river, above Selma, not above Wetumpka.

REEVES' LANDING, *Ark*.—Arkansas river, 101 miles above Napoleon, above Arkansas Post, not above Pine Bluff.

REEVES' LANDING, *Ark*.—Mississippi river, above Greenville, not above Memphis.

REEVELAND, *Miss*.—Big Deer Creek, 123 miles up.

REFUGIO.—Ouachita river, above Harrisonburg, not above Trenton.

REFUGE, *Miss*.—Mississippi river, above Grand Gulf, not above Greenville.

REUB WHITE'S LANDING, *La*.—Red river, 640 miles above New Orleans, above Grand Ecore, not above Shreveport.

REMBERT'S, C. LANDING, *Ala*.—Tombigbee river, not above Demopolis.

REMBERT'S, JUDGE LANDING, *Ala*.—Tombigbee river, not above Demopolis.

RENISON'S, L. K (SUNFLOWER).—Red river, above Grand Ecore, not above Shreveport.

REILLY.—Mississippi river, above Grand Gulf, not above Greenville.

REYNOLDS'.—Red river, above Fulton, not above Lanesport.

REYNOLDS'.—Red river, above Lanesport, not above Mound City.

RHODES' EDDY.—Yazoo river, not above Yazoo City.

RICHARDSON, ED (BEND).—Yazoo river, above Yazoo City, not above Leflore.

REYNOLDS' LANDING, *Miss*.—Tombigbee river, above Columbus, not above Cotton Gin Port.

REYNOLDSBURG, *Tenn*.—Tennessee river, 110 miles from its mouth, not above Eastport.

RIEVE'S, C. LANDING, *Miss*.—15 miles up Big Deer Creek.

RICEVILLE, *Miss.*—Pearl river, above Gainesville, not above Columbia.

RICHLAND, *Ark.*—Arkansas river, 130 miles above Napoleon, above Arkansas Post, not above Pine Bluff.

RICHFIFLD, *Mo.*—Missouri river, 372 miles from its mouth, above Lexington, not above Iatan.

RICHARDS' LANDING, *Ark.*—White river, one mile from its mouth, below junction of Black river.

RICHARDSON'S LANDING, *La.*—Bayou Macon, 175 miles above its mouth, not above Monticello.

RICHARDSON'S BLUFF, *Texas.*—Neches river, above Weisse's Bluff, not above junction of Angelina river.

RICKER'S, R. R. LANDING, *Ark.*—Red river, 140 miles above Shreveport, above Black Bayou, not above White Oak Shoals.

RIDDELL'S POINT, *Miss.*—Mississippi river, 901 miles above New Orleans, above Greenville, not above Memphis.

RIFLE POINT, *La.*—Mississippi river, above Bayou Sara, not above Grand Gulf.

RIFLE DAVE LANDING, *Tenn.*—Cumberland river, not above Nashville.

RIGOLET BON DIEU, *La.*—Red river, above Cane river, not above Grand Ecore.

RINGGOLD BLUFF, *Ala.*—Tombigbee river, above Gainesville, not above Columbus.

RIO FARRELL, *Ark.*—Arkansas river, 29 miles above Napoleon, not above Arkansas Post.

RIPLEY, *Ohio.*—Ohio river, 585 miles above its mouth, above Cincinnati.

RISING SUN, *Miss.*—Yazoo river, 229 miles from Vicksburg, above Yazoo City, not above Leflore.

RISING SUN, *Ind.*—Ohio river, 504 miles from its mouth, above Paducah, not above Cincinnati.

RISING SUN, *Wis.*—Mississippi river, 1734 miles above New Orleans, above Galena.

RIVERTON PLACE, *La.*—Mississippi river, 75 miles above New Orleans, not above Bayou Sara.

RIVERSIDE, *Miss.*—Mississippi river, 210 miles above New Orleans, above Bayou Sara, not above Grand Gulf.

RIVER VIEW, *Tenn.*—Mississippi river, above Gainesville, not above Memphis.

RIVE'S LANDING, *La*—Red river, above Cane river, not above Grand Ecore.

RIVIERE AU CUIVRE, *Minn.*—Mississippi river, 1238 miles from New Orleans, above Alton, not above first Rapids.

RIVERTON, *Miss.*—Above Greenville, not above Memphis.

RIVERSIDE.—Mississippi river, above Grand Gulf, not above Greenville.

RIVERSIDE.—123 miles up Sunflower river.

RIVERSIDE.—Yazoo river, above Yazoo City, not above Leflore.

RIVER VIEW (or BURN'S), *La.*—Mississippi river, above Grand Gulf, not above Greenville.

ROANE'S LANDING, *Ala.*—Alabama river, not above Selma.

ROACHES.—Ouachita river, above Harrisonburg, not above Trenton.

ROARKS.—Ouachita river,above Alabama Landing, not above Camden.

ROB ROY, *Ind.*—Wabash river, above the Rapids, not above Terre Haute.

ROB ROY, *Ark.*—Arkansas river, 154 miles above Napoleon, above Arkansas Post, not above Pine Bluff.

ROBB'S, DR.—Arkansas river, above Arkansas Post, not above Pine Bluff.

ROBB'S LANDING, *Miss.*—Mississippi river, above Bayou Sara, not above Grand Gulf.

ROBB'S, MRS. LANDING, *La.*—Mississippi river, above Grand Gulf, not above Greenville.

ROBERTS & RAPPS, *Ark.*—Mississippi river, above Greenville, not above Memphis.

ROBIN'S FERRY, *Texas.*—Trinity river, above Smithville, not above Magnolia Landing.

ROBINSON'S LANDING, *Ala.*—Tombigbee river, not above Demopolis.

ROBINSON'S LANDING, *Ala.*—Alabama river, above Selma, not above Wetumpka.

ROBINSON'S, E (GIN).—Red river, above Grand Ecore, not above Shreveport.

ROBINSON, E (WILLOW PLANTATION).—Red river, above Grand Ecore, not above Shreveport.

ROBINSON'S LANDING, *Ala.*—Warrior river, not above Tuscaloosa.
ROBINSON, JACK LANDING.—130 miles up Sunflower river.
ROBINSON, J. W.—Bayou Bartholomew, above Arkansas line, not above Portland.
ROBINSON, P. C (CROSS LANDING).—Bayou Bartholomew, above Point Pleasant, not above Arkansas line.
ROBINSON'S, JERRY.—Yazoo river, above Yazoo City, not above Leflore.
ROBINSON, MRS.—Tallahatchie river, not above Cassidy Bayou.
ROBINSON'S.—Ouachita river, above Harrisonburg, not above Trenton.
ROBSEN'S LANDING, *Miss.*—Mississippi river, 687 miles above New Orleans, above Greenville, not above Memphis.
ROCHELL, PINK.—Red river, above Fulton, not above Lanesport.
ROCHELL, J. H.—Red river, above Fulton, not above Lanesport.
ROCKEY COMFORT, *Ark.*—The landing is Lanesport, Red river.
ROCK ISLAND (L. BAILEY).—Red river, above Cane river, not above Grand Ecore.
ROCK ROW.—Ouachita river, above Trenton, not above Alabama Landing.
ROCK PORT, *Ind.*—Ohio river, 230 miles from its mouth, above Paducah, not above Cincinnati.
ROCK PORT, *Miss.*—Tallahatchie river, above Belmont.
ROCK PORT, *Mo.*—Missouri river, 190 miles above its mouth, above Jefferson City, not above Lexington.
ROCK CASTLE, *Ky.*—Cumberland river, 6 miles from its mouth, not above Nashville.
ROCK HAVEN, *Ky.*—Ohio river, 367 miles from its mouth, above Paducah, not above Cincinnati.
ROCK ISLAND. *Ill.*—Illinois river, 262 miles above its mouth, above Beardstown, not above the mouth of Fox river.
ROCK ISLAND, *Ill.*—Mississippi river, 1518 miles above New Orleans, above the first, not above the second Rapids.
ROCK ISLAND CITY, *Ill.*—Mississippi river, 1515 miles from New Orleans, above the first, not above the second Rapids.
ROCK FERRY, *Ky.*—Cumberland river, not above Nashville.

ROCK RIVER, *Ill.*—Mississippi river, 1513 miles above New Orleans, above the first, not above the second Rapids.

ROCK ROE FERRY, *Ark.*—White river, below the junction of Black river.

ROCK CREEK, *Ark.*—White river, above Batesville.

ROCKAWAY, *Ky.*—Ohio river, above Paducah, not above Cincinnati.

ROCK HILL, *Miss.*—Mississippi river, 215 miles above New Orleans, above Bayou Sara, not above Grand Gulf.

ROCK LANDING, *Ark.*—White river, 126 miles from its mouth, below the junction of Black river.

ROCKVILLE, *Ohio.*—Obio river, 629 miles above its mouth, above Cincinnati.

ROCK SPRING, *Ky.*—Ohio river, 571 miles above its mouth, above Cincinnati.

ROCHE'S LANDING, *La.*—Ouachita river, above Harrisonburg, not above Trenton.

ROCHESTER, *Tenn.*—Ohio river, 976 miles above its mouth, above Cincinnati.

RODNEY, *Miss.*—Mississippi river, 340 miles above New Orleans, above Bayou Sara, not above Grand Gulf.

RODNEY'S LANDING, *Mo.*—Mississippi river, 1039 miles above New Orleans, above the mouth of the Ohio, not above Alton.

RODNEY KING, *Miss.*—Mississippi river, above Bayou Sara, not above Grand Gulf.

ROE BUCK.—Yazoo river, above Yazoo City, not above Leflore.

ROGERS', O. T. LANDING, *La.*—Atchafalaya river, below Simmsport.

ROGERS' LANDING, *Miss.*—Tombigbee river, above Columbus, not above Cotton Gin Port.

ROGERS' LANDING, *Ala.*—Mississippi river, above Greenville, not above Memphis.

ROGER'S, H. M. LANDING.—Red river, not above Alexandria.

ROGER'S LANDING.—Ouachita river, above Alabama Landing, not above Camden.

ROKEBY.—Yazoo river, not above Yazoo City.

ROKEY POINT.—Red river, above Shreveport, not above Carolina Bluff.

ROLLING FORK.—Sunflower river.

ROLAND'S RAFT.—Ouachita river, above Alabama Landing, not above Camden.

ROLLING FORK.—Big Deer Creek, Miss., 104 miles from Vicksburg.

ROLLING FORK POINT.—Big Deer Creek, Miss., 110 miles from Vicksburg.

ROME, *Ill.*—Illinois river, 192 miles above its mouth, above Beardstown, not above the mouth of Fox river.

ROME, *Ark.*—Ouachita river, above Camden, not above Ross' Landing.

ROME, *Ind.*—Ohio river, 282 miles above its mouth, above Paducah, not above Cincinnati.

ROME, *Ohio.*—Ohio river, 620 miles above its mouth, above Cincinnati.

ROME, *Tenn.*—Cumberland river, above Nashville, not above Gainesboro.

ROME FERRY, *Ky.*—Cumberland river, above Nashville, not above Gainesboro.

RONOAKE, *Ga.*—Chattahoochie river, not above Columbus.

RONARD'S LANDING, *La.*—Atchafalaya river, below Simmsport.

ROPER'S WOODYARD, *Ala.*--Alabama river, not above Selma.

ROSS PLANTATION.—Red river, above Grand Ecore, not above Shreveport.

ROSS, E. W.—Bayou Bartholomew, not above Point Pleasant.

ROSS, J. N. (SANDIDGE).—Bayou Bartholomew, not above Point Pleasant.

ROSS.—Yazoo river, not above Yazoo City.

ROSS, WM.—Yazoo river, not above Yazoo City.

ROSS' LANDING, *Ark.*—Ouachita river, above Camden.

ROSA LANDING, *Ark.*—Mississippi river, above Greenville, not above Memphis.

ROSA'S LANDING, *La.*—Ouachita river, above Harrisonburg, not above Trenton.

ROSA PLANTATION, *La.*—Red river, above Grand Ecore, not above Shreveport.

ROSE, H. LANDING, *Ala.*—Alabama river, above Selma, not above Wetumpka.

ROSE BLUFF.—Sabine river, Texas, not above Grand Bluff.

ROSEVILLE, *Ark.*--Arkansas river, 464 miles above Napoleon, above Norristown, not above Fort Smith.

ROSE BANK.—Yazoo river, above Yazoo City, not above Leflore.

ROSE BOWER.—Yazoo river, above Yazoo City, not above Leflore.

ROSEDALE, *Miss.*—Mississippi river, above Greenville, not above the mouth of the Ohio.

ROSEDALE (or BLEDSOE).—Tallabatchie river, not above Cassidy Bayou.

ROSEDALE (BAGLEY'S).—Red river, above Grand Ecore, not above Shreveport.

ROUBIEN, FRANCOIS.—Red river, above Grand Ecore, not above Shreveport.

ROUBIEN, MAD.—Red river, above Grand Ecore, not above Shreveport.

ROUGH AND READY.—Red river, above Shreveport, not above foot of Raft.

ROUGH AND READY.—Yazoo river, not above Yazoo City.

ROUND BUTE.—Missouri river, 2304 miles from its mouth, above Iatan.

ROUTHS, *La.*—Black river, not above Harrisonburg.

ROUTENS.—Ouachita river, not above Harrisonburg.

ROWLAND.—Red river, above Lanesport, not above Mound City.

ROWLAND (UPPER).—Red river, above Lanesport, not above Mound City.

ROWLAND'S RAFT.—Ouachita river, above Alabama Landing, not above Camden.

ROWLETT, B. A. LANDING.—Red river, above mouth of Cane river, not above Grand Ecore.

ROW'S LANDING, *Ala.*—Tombigbee river, above Demopolis, not above Gainesville.

ROW'S LANDING.—Mississippi river, 190 miles above New Orleans, above Bayou Sara, not above Grand Gulf.

ROW'S LANDING, *La.*—Mississippi river, above Bayou Sara, not above Grand Gulf.

ROWENA, *Ky.*—Cumberland river, above Nashville, not above Gainesboro.

ROWLAND'S LANDING, *Ark.*—Arkansas river, 303 miles above Little Rock, not above Norristown.

ROWLAND'S LANDING, *Texas.*—Red river, 458 miles above Shreveport, above Lanesport, not above Mound City.

ROZIER'S LANDING, *Mo.*—Mississippi river, above the mouth of the Ohio, not above Alton.

RUCKER'S LANDING, *Ark.*—Arkansas river, 30 miles above Napoleon, not above Arkansas Post.

RUCKERSVILLE, *Miss.*—Hatchee river, not above Bolivar.

RUDDY'S LANDING, *Ark.*—Mississippi river, above Greenville, not above Memphis.

RULO.—Missouri river, above Iatan.

RUM RIVER, *Minn.*—Mississippi river, 1888 miles above New Orleans, above Galena.

RUNNELL'S, E. LANDING, *Texas.*—Red river, 369 miles above Shreveport, above Lanesport, not above Mound City.

RUNNELL'S LANDING, *Texas.*—Red river, 329 miles above Shreveport, above Fulton, not above Lanesport.

RUSH TOWER, *Mo.*—Mississippi river, 1139 miles above New Orleans, above the mouth of the Ohio river, not above Alton.

RUSH'S LANDING, *Ala.*—Tombigbee river, not above Demopolis.

RUSH, GEN. LANDING, *La.*—Ouachita river, above Harrisonburg, not above Trenton.

RUSHVILLE.—Missouri river, above Iatan.

RUSHBOTTOM.—Missouri river, above Iatan.

RUST.—Ouachita river, above Harrisonburg, not above Trenton.

RUSH POINT.—Red river, above Shreveport, not above foot of Raft.

RUSH BAYOU (WOODLAWN).—Red river, above Grand Ecore, not above Shreveport.

RUSH ISLAND (M. LATTIER).—Red river, above Grand Ecore, not above Shreveport.

RUSK.—Cherokee county, Texas.

RUST'S.—Bayou Barthôlomew, above Portland.

RUSSELL.—Red river, above foot of Raft, not above Fulton.

RUSSELL.—Bayou Bartholomew, not above Point Pleasant.

RUTHERFORD, S. LANDING.—Red river, not above Alexandria.

RUTH'S.—Mississippi river, above Grand Gulf, not above Greenville.

RUTHLAND'S, DR.—Tallahatchie river, not above Cassidy Bayou.

RUTY, MRS. (WALNUT PRAIRIE).—Red river, above Lanesport, not above Mound City.

RUTLAND'S.—Ouachita river, above Harrisonburg, not above Trenton.

RUTLAND'S BAR.—Ouachita river, above Harrisonburg, not above Trenton.

RUTCHEE'S POINT, *Tenn.*—Mississippi river, above Greenville, not above Memphis.

RUTH'S FRANK LANDING, *La.*—Black river, La.

RUTHLAND'S LANDING, *La.*—Ouachita river, above Harrisonburg, not above Trenton.

RYAN'S, M.—Red river, not above Alexandria.

S

SABINE CITY, *Mo.*—Missouri river, 223 miles above its mouth, above Jefferson City, not above Lexington.

SABINE CITY, *Texas.*—Sabine Lake.

SABINE TOWN, *La.*—Red river, above Grand Ecore, not above Shreveport.

SABINE TOWN, *Texas.*—Sabine river, above Belgrade, not above Hamilton.

SABULA, *Iowa.*—Mississippi river, 1576 miles above New Orleans, above the second Rapids, not above Galena.

SADLER, DR.—Bayou Bartholomew, above Point Pleasant, not above Arkansas line.

SAILOR'S REST, *Tenn.*—Cumberland river, not above Nashville.

SAKERFIELD'S, DR. LANDING, *La.*—Atchafalaya river, below Simmsport.

SALEM, *Texas.*—Sabine river, above Sabine City, not above Belgrade.

SALINE RIVER.—Any point.

SALISAS LANDING, *Ark.*—Arkansas river, 602 miles above Napoleon, above Fort Smith.

SALT RIVER, *Ky.*—Ohio river, 369 miles above its mouth, above Paducah, not above Cincinnati.

SALT RIVER, *Mo.*—Mississippi river, 1290 miles above New Orleans, above Alton, not above the first Rapids.

SALT WORKS, *Ala.*—Tombigbee river, not above Demopolis.

SALTILLO, *Tenn.*—Tennessee river, not above Eastport.

SALINE BAYOU.—Red river, not above Alexandria.

SALINE, MARIE.—Ouachita river, above Alabama Landing, not above Camden.

SALLY MOUND.—Tallahatchie river, not above Cassidy Bayou.

SAMPLE'S BLUFF, *Ala.*—Warrior river, not above Tuscaloosa.

SAMPAYROCK, A. B. LANDING.—Red river, above Cane river, not above Grand Ecore.

SANDRIGE, OLD (or SOUTH BEND).—Red river, above Shreveport, not above foot of Raft.

SANDFORD, J. S (HAMBURG LANDING).—Bayou Bartholomew, above Arkansas line, not above Portland.

SANDIGE.—Ouachita river, above Harrisonburg, not above Trenton.

SANDIGE, J. G —Bayou Bartholomew, not above Point Pleasant.

SANDIGE, CAPT. GEO.—Bayou Bartholomew, not above Point Pleasant.

SANDY POINT (J. E. SMITH).—Bayou Bartholomew, above Arkansas line, not above Portland.

SANDY RIDGE.—Tallahatchie river, not above Cassidy Bayou.

SANDY BAYOU.—Red river, not above Alexandria.

SANDFORD, *La.*—Ouachita river, above Harrisonburg, not above Trenton.

SANFORD'S CAMP, *Ala.*—Warrior river, not above Tuscaloosa.

SANDER'S FERRY, *Ala.*—Warrior river, not above Tuscaloosa.

SANDIFORS, *Miss.*—Pearl river, above Columbia.

SANDY HOOK, *Mo.*—Missouri river, 149 miles above its mouth, above Jefferson City, not above Lexington.

SANSAMON, *Ill.*—Illinois river, 96 miles above its mouth, above above Beardstown, not above the mouth of Fox river.

SANS BOIS LANDING, *Ark.*—Arkansas river, 595 miles above Napoleon, above Fort Smith.

SANTA FE.—Mississippi river, 1056 miles above New Orleans, above the mouth of the Ohio, not above Alton.

SARDSCRABLE, *La.*—Atchafalaya river, below Simmsport.

SATARTIA, *Miss.*—Yazoo river, 61 miles from Vicksburg, not above Yazoo City.

SATTERFIELD'S, DR. LANDING, *Miss.*—149 miles up Big Deer Creek.

SAVAGES.—Mississippi river, above Grand Gulf, not above Greenville.

SAWILSKI, OTTO LANDING.—157 miles up Sunflower river.

SATTERWHITE'S LANDING, *Ala.*—Alabama river, not above Selma.

SAUNDERS' LANDING, *Miss.*—Tombigbee river, above Columbus, not above Cotton Gin Port.

SAVANNAH, *Tenn.*—Tennessee river, above Eastport, not above Florence.

SAVANNAH, *Ill.*—Mississippi river, above the second Rapids, not above Galena.

SAVANNAH, *Tenn.*—Tennessee river, not above Eastport.

SAVERTIN, *Mo.*—Mississippi river, 1308 miles above New Orleans, above Alton, not above first Rapids.

SCANLIN'S LANDING, *Ark.*—Mississippi river, above Greenville, not above Memphis.

SCARBOROUGH GIN.—Bayou Bartholomew, not above Point Pleasant.

SCHERSON RIVER, *Tenn.*—Cumberland river, not above Nashville.

SCHOEFIELD.—Red river, above foot of Raft, not above Fulton.

SCHOLARS.—Bayou Bartholomew, above Point Pleasant, not above Arkansas line.

SCHOONERS' POINT, *Ind.*—Above Paducah, not above Cincinnati.

SCIOTOVILLE, *Ohio.*—Ohio river, 656 miles above its mouth, above Cincinnati.

SCIOTO RIVER, *Ohio.*—Ohio river, 647 miles above its mouth, above Cincinnati.

SCOTIA LANDING, *Ark.*—Arkansas river, 411 miles above Napoleon, above Norristown, not above Fort Smith.

SCOPINAS, *La.*—Red river, above Grand Ecore, not above Shreveport.

SCOTLAND LANDING, *La.*—Mississippi river, not above Bayou Sara.

SCOTLAND, *Ark.*—Mississippi river, above Grand Gulf, not above Greenville.

SCOTT, MAHALA LANDING, *Miss.*—150 miles up Big Deer Creek.

SCOTT'S LANDING, *Ala.*—Tombigbee river, not above Demopolis.

SCOTT'S.—Yazoo river, above Yazoo City, not above Leflore.

SCOTT, JOE LANDING, *Miss.*—123 miles up Big Deer Creek.

SCOTT'S, R.—Ouachita river, not above Harrisonburg.

SCOTT, R. (NEW HOPE).—Red river, above Grand Ecore, not above Shreveport.

SCOTT LANDING.—Mississippi river, above Grand Gulf, not above Greenville.

SCOTT'S FERRY, *Ala*—Alabama river, not above Selma.

SCOTT'S LANDING, *Ala.*—Alabama river, not above Selma.

SCOTTSVILLE, *Ala*—Tennessee river, above Florence, not below Eastport.

SCROPINA, ADOLPH.—Red river, above Grand Ecore, not above Shreveport.

SCRUG'S LANDING, *Ala.*—Tombigbee river, not above Demopolis.

SCREWS & WILSONS.—Yazoo river, not above Yazoo City.

SCRIBER, P. (or ISAAC COLE.—Bayou Bartholomew, not above Point Pleasant.

SCROGGIN'S.—192 miles up Sunflower river.

SCULLYVILLE, *Ark.*—Arkansas river, 575 miles above Napoleon, above Fort Smith.

SEARCEY LANDING, *Ark.*—Little Red river, 48 miles from its mouth, below the junction of Black and White rivers.

SEARY LANDING, *Ala.*—Warrior river, not above Tuscaloosa.

SEBASTOPOL.—Mississippi river, above Grand Gulf, not above Greenville.

SECOND RAPIDS.—Mississippi river.

SECURITY, *La.*—Black river, La., not above Harrisonburg.

SEDGEFIELD.—Yazoo river, above Yazoo City, not above Leflore.

SELBYVILLE.—In Selby County, Texas.

SELLERS.—Ouachita river, above Harrisonburg, not above Trenton.

SELMA, *Ala.*—Alabama river.

SELMA, *Mo.*—Mississippi river, 1210 miles from New Orleans, above the mouth of the Ohio, not above Alton.

SELLERS LANDING, *Ala.*—Tombigbee river, not above Demopolis.

SELLEMAN CREEK, *Ark.*—White river, above Batesville.

SENAPEE, *Wis.*—Mississippi river, above Galena.

SENTELL'S (or LAKE POINT).—Red river, above foot of Raft, not above Fulton.

SENTELL'S, STORE JNO.—Red river, above foot of Raft, not above Fulton.

SESSION.—Yazoo river, not above Yazoo City.

SEYMOUR'S BLUFF, *Ala.*—Tombigbee river, not above Demopolis.

SHADE RIVER, *Ohio.*—Ohio river, 798 miles above its mouth, above Cincinnati.

SHADELL'S LANDING, *La.*—Atchafalaya river, below Simmsport.

SHADRICK POINT.—Red river, not above Alexandria.

SHADY GROVE (or VANCE).—Red river, above Shreveport, not above foot of Raft.

SHANNON'S.—Red river, not above Alexandria.

SHANNONDALE.—Tallahatchie river, not above Cassidy Bayou.

SHANCETOWN (or R. M. JONES).—Red river, above Rowland and Mound City.

SHARP'S, PETER.—18 miles up Sunflower river.

SHARP'S LANDING.—331 miles up Sunflower river.

SHARP'S LANDING, *Ill.*—Illinois river, above Beardstown, not above the mouth of Fox river.

SHARKEY'S.—Tallahatchie river, above Cassidy Bayou.

SHAWS (or MOSS PLANTATION).—Red river, above Lanesport, not above Moond City.

SHAW'S PLANTATION.—Red river, above Fulton, not above Lanesport.

SHAWNEETOWN, *Texas*.—Red river, above Fulton, not above Lanesport.

SHAWNEETOWN, *Ohio.*—Ohio river, 128 miles above its mouth, above Paducah, not above Cincinnati.

SHAW'S LANDING, *Tenn.*—Mississippi river, above Greenville, not above the mouth of the Ohio river.

SHEARERS (or GRAND VIEW).—125 miles up Sunflower river.

SHEARER, DR.—Bayou Bartholomew, above Arkansas line, not above Portland.

SHEGOGG.—Tallahatchie river, not above Cassidy Bayou.

SHELL MOUND.—Tallahatchie river, not above Cassidy Bayou.

SHELL RIDGE.—171 miles up Sunflower river.

SHEFFIELD, *Ohio.*—Ohio river, 749 miles above its mouth, above Cincinnati.

SHEFFIELD, *Mo.*—Mississippi river, above the mouth of the Ohio, not above Alton.

SHELL CREEK, *Ala.*—Alabama river, not above Selma.

SHELL BLUFF, *Miss.*—Yazoo river, above Yazoo City, not above Leflore.

SHELBY'S LANDING, *Tenn.*—Cumberland river, not above Nashville.

SHEPARD TOWN, *Ala.*—Warrior river, not above Tuscaloosa.

SHEPARD'S LANDING, *Ark.*—Arkansas river, 151 miles above Napoleon, above Arkansas Post, not above Pine Bluff.

SHEPHERD'S LANDING, *Ill.*—Mississippi river, above the mouth of the Ohio river, not above Alton.

SHEPPARDSTOWN.—Yazoo river, above Yazoo City, not above Leflore.

SHERRARD'S.—Yazoo river, not above Yazoo City.

SHERRODY, O. W.—Red river, above Grand Ecore, not above Shreveport.

SHIELDSBOROUGH (or BAY ST. LOUIS), *Miss.*—48 miles, by rail, from New Orleans.

SHIPS.—Yazoo river, above Yazoo City, not above Leflore.

SHINEY, *La.*—Ouachita river, above Harrisonburg, not above Trenton.

SHIP BAYOU, *La.*—Mississippi river, above Grand Gulf, not above Greenville.

SHIP ISLAND, *Miss.*—Mississippi river, 750 miles above New Orleans, above Greenville, not above Memphis.

SHIPPENSPORT, *Ohio.*—Ohio river, 381 miles above its mouth, above Paducah, not above Cincinnati.

SHIPLEY'S LANDING, *Mo.*—Missouri river, 119 miles above its mouth, not above Jefferson City.

SHIPLAND'S LANDING, *Miss*—Mississippi river, above Grand Gulf, not above Greenville.

SHILOH, *Ark.*—Bayou D'Arbonne, above Farmersville.

SHILOH BATTLE-FIELD, *Tenn.*—Tennessee river, 213 miles above its mouth, not above Eastport.

SHOAL CREEK, *Ark.*—Arkansas river, 421 miles above Napoleon, above Norristown, not above Fort Smith.

SHORTWAY CUT-OFF.—Red river, above Grand Ecore, not above Shreveport.

SHORT MOUNTAIN, *Ark.*—Arkansas river, 454 miles above Napoleon, above Norristown, not above Fort Smith.

SHOUSES' TOWN, *Pa.*—Ohio river, 1002 miles from its mouth, above Cincinnati.

SHREVEPORT, *La.*—Red river, 700 miles from New Orleans.

SHUBUTH, *Miss.*—Chicasaha river.

SIBLEY, *Mo.*—Missouri river, 362 miles from its mouth, above Lexington, not above Iatan.

SIBLEY'S LANDING, *Ala.*—Alabama river, not above Selma.

SIDON, *Miss.*—Yazoo river, 234 miles from Vicksburg, above Yazoo City, not above Leflore.

SIDNEY'S LANDING, *Mo.*—Missouri river, 700 miles above its mouth, above Iatan.

SIEWICKLEYVILE, *Pa.*—Ohio river, 992 miles its mouth, above Cincinnati.

SILVER TOP, *Tenn.*—Mississippi river, above Memphis, not above mouth of the Ohio.

SILVER'S LANDING, *Ark.*—Arkansas river, 227 miles above Napoleon, above Pine Bluff, not above Little Rock.

SILLAN'S LANDING, *La.*—Red river, above Cane river, not above Grand Ecore.

SILENT SHADE. Yazoo river, above Yazoo City, not above Leflore.

SILVER POINT (C. R. GRISWOLD).—Red river, above Shreveport, not above foot of Raft.

SILLAMORE, *Ark.*—White river, above Batesville.

SILVER'S WOODYARD, *Ala.*—Alabama river, not above Selma.

SILVER'S LANDING, *Ala.*—Alabama river, not above Selma.

SILVER'S, JOE LANDING, *Ala.*—Alabama river, not above Selma.

SILVER CREEK, *Miss.*—Yazoo river, above Yazoo City, not above Leflore.

SIM'S LANDING, *Miss.*—170 miles up Big Deer Creek.

SIMMONS' LANDING, *Ark.*—Red river, 206 miles above Shreveport, above Carolina Bluff, not above Fulton.

SIMMONS' LANDING, *Ala.*—Tombigbee river, not above Demopolis.

SIMME'S LANDING, *Ala.*—Warrior river, not above Tuscaloosa.

SIMM'S B. B. LANDING, *La.*—Atchafalaya river, above Simmsport.

SIMMONS.—Ouachita river, above Harrisonburg, not above Trenton.

SIMMSPORT, *La.*—Atchafalaya river.

SIMPSON'S, J. W. *Ark.*—Arkansas river, 120 miles above Napoleon, above Arkansas Post, not above Pine Bluff.

SIMPSON'S, J. D.—Bayou Bartholomew, above Arkansas line, not above Portland.

SIMPSON'S, HY.—Arkansas river, above Arkansas Post, not above Pine Bluff.

SINKING CREEK, *Ky.*—Ohio river, 285 miles from its mouth, above Paducah, not above Cincinnati.

SINHOFF'S LANDING, *Mo.*—Mississippi river, above mouth of the Ohio, not above Alton.

SINGLETON'S BLUFF, *Ala.*—Warrior river, not above Tuscaloosa.

SINGLETON'S LANDING, *Ala.*—Tombigbee river, not above Demopolis.

SISLOFF MILLS.—Tallahatchie river, not above Cassidy Bayou.

SIXTEENTH SECTION.—188 miles up Sunflower river.

SIZEMORE.—Ouachita river, above Harrisonburg, not above Trenton.

SIOUX CITY, *Iowa.*—Missouri river, above Jatan.

SISTERVILLE, *Va.*—Ohio river, 866 miles above its mouth, above Cincinnati.

SKIPWITH LANDING, *Mo.*—Mississippi river, 487 miles above New Orleans, above Grand Gulf, not above Greenville.

SKYLARK, *Ark.*—Arkansas river, 409 miles above Napoleon, above Norristown, not above Fort Smith.

SKUNK RIVER, *Iowa.*—Mississippi river, 1412 miles above New Orleans, above second Rapids, not above Galena.

SLADE'S LANDING, *Ala.*—Tombigbee river, not above Demopolis.

SLATER'S LANDING, *Ala.*—Tombigbee river, not above Demopolis.

SLAUGHTER'S, MRS. LANDING, *Ala.*—Alabama river, not above Selma.

SLAUGHTER'S, JNO. *Ala.*—Alabama river, not above Selma.

SLOTE'S LANDING, *La.*—Red river, not above Alexandria.

SLOAN'S, MRS. LANDING, *La.*—Black river, La., not above Harrisonburg.

SMARCOTT'S (RABBIT ISLAND.—Red river, not above Alexandria.

SMITHFIELD (W. S. CALHOUN).—Red river, above Cane river, not above Grand Ecore.

SMITHVILLE, *Texas.*—Trinity river.

SMITHVILLE, *Ark,*—Black river, tributary of White.

SMITH'S LANDING, *Ark.*—Red river, above Carolina Bluff, not above Fulton.

SMITH'S, DENNIS LANDING, *La.*—Red river, above Alexandria, not above Cane river.

SHITH LANDING, *Mo.*—Missouri river, 127 miles above its mouth, not above Jefferson City.

SMITH LANDING, *Texas.*—Red river, above Carolina Bluff, not above Fulton.

SMITH, STERLING LANDING, *Ark.*—Red river, above Carolina Bluff, not above Fulton.

SMITH'S LANDING, *Ala.*—Alabama river, not above Selma.

SMITH'S, R. W., *Ala.*—Alabama river, not above Selma.

SMITH'S, A. M. LANDING, *Ark.*—Arkansas river, 192 miles above Napoleon, above Pine Bluff, not above Little Rock.

SMITH'S, P. LANDING. *La.*—Ouachita river, above Harrisonburg, not above Trenton.

SMITH'S, SAM'L LANDING, *La.* —Ouachita river, above Trenton, not above Alabama Landing.

SMITH'S, MRS. B. LANDING, *Ala.*—Alabama river, above Selma, not above Wetumpka.

SMITH'S, W. D. LANDING, *Ala.*—Alabama river, above Selma, not above Wetumpka.

SMITH'S LANDING, *Ala.*—Tombigbee river, not above Demopolis.

SMITH'S LANDING, *Ala.*—Tombigbee river, above Demopolis, not above Gainesville.

SMITH'S LANDING, *Ill.*—Mississippi river, above the mouth of the Ohio, not above Alton.

SMITH'S, DR. LANDING, *Mo.*—Mississippi river, above the mouth of the Ohio, not above Alton.

SMITH'S, JAS. LANDING, *La.*—Black river, La.

SMITH'S FERRY.—Ohio river, 977 miles above its mouth, above Cincinnati.

SMITH'S FERRY, *Ala.*—Tombigbee river, above Gainesville, not above Columbus.

SMITH, CAROLINE.—Bayou Bartholomew, not above Point Pleasant.

SMITH'S ARKANSAS WOODYARD, *Ala.*—Alabama river, not above Selma.

SMITH, DENIS N. LANDING.—Red river, not above Alexandria.

SMITH, BANKS.—Ouachita river, above Trenton, not above Alabama Landing.

SMITH'S DEADENING.—Yazoo river, above Yazoo City, not above Leflore.

SMITH'S, or EDWARDS'.—Red river, above foot of Raft, not above Fulton.

SMITH'S, or GASTER'S.—80 miles up Bœuf river, above Thomas' Landing.

SMITH'S, MRS.—Red river, above Fulton, not above Lanesport.

SMITH, J. E. (SANDY POINT).—Bayou Bartholomew, above Arkansas line, not above Portland.

SMITH'S LANDING.—156 miles up Sunflower river.

SMITH'S, L. J. (GLOVER BAR).—Red river, not above Alexandria.

SMITH, J. L.—Ouachita river, not above Harrisonburg.

SMITH, TOM K. LANDING.—Red river, not above Alexandria.

SMITH'S.—Ouachita river, above Harrisonburg, not above Trenton.

SMITH'S PLACE.—Yazoo river, above Yazoo City, not above Leflore.

SMITH'S, FLOYD.—Arkansas river, above Arkansas Post, not above Pine Bluff.

SMITH'S POINT, *Mo.*—Missouri river, 66 miles above its mouth, not above Jefferson City.

SMITH'S BAR, *Mo.*—Missouri river, 533 miles above its mouth, above Iatan.

SMITH ISLAND, *Mo.*—Missouri river, 94 miles above its mouth, not above Jefferson City.

SMITH PLACE.—Bayou Bartholomew, not above Point Pleasant.

SMITHLAND, *La.*—Black river, not above Harrisonburg.

SMITHLAND.—Red river, above Shreveport, not above Carolina Bluff

SMITHLAND, *La.*—Cypress Bayou (Lake Caddo).

SMITHLAND, *La.*—Ouachita river, above Harrisonburg, not above Trenton.

SMITHLAND, *Ky.*—Ohio river, 66 miles above its mouth, above Paducah, not above Cincinnati.

SMITHPORT, *La.*—Bayou Pierre, De Sota parish, La.

SMORE'S LANDING.—Mississippi river, above mouth of the Ohio, not above Alton.

SNODDY, WASH.—Red river, not above Alexandria.

SNYDER'S BLUFF.—Yazoo river, not above Yazoo City.

SNAGGY POINT, *La.*—Red river, not above Alexandria.

SOCIAL BEND, *Ark.*—Mississippi river, above Greenville, not above Memphis.

SODA POINT, or DR. WORTHY.—Red river, above Shreveport, not above foot of Raft.

SOLINA, *Miss.*—Above Greenville, not above the mouth of the Ohio.

SOLINA LANDING, *Miss.*—Mississippi river, 637 miles above New Orleans, above Greenville, not above the mouth Ohio river.

SONORA, *Mo.*—Missouri river, 687 miles above its mouth, above Iatan.

SORSBY'S LANDING, *Ala.*—Tombigbee river, above Demopolis, not above Gainesville.

SORRELS.—Ouachita river, above Harrisonburg, not above Trenton.

SOUTH BEND, *La.*—Black river, La., not above Harrisonburg.

SOUTH BEND POST OFFICE, *Ark.*—Arkansas river, 81 miles above Napoleon, above Arkansas Post, not above Pine Bluff.

SOUTH BEND (OLD SANDRIGE).—Red river, above Shreveport, not above foot of Raft.

SPADRA.—430 miles above Napoleon, above Norristown, not above Fort Smith.

SPANISH FORT, or SWEENEY'S.—71 miles up Sunflower river.

SPANISH FORT.—Red river, not above Alexandria.

SPANISH FORT.—Yazoo river, not above Yazoo City.

SPADRA BLUFF, *Ark.*—Arkansas river, 439 miles above Napoleon, above Norristown, not above Fort Smith.

SPANIARD'S CREEK, *Ark.*—Arkansas river, 120 miles above Napoleon, above Fort Smith.

SPANISH BLUFF, *Texas.*—Red river, above Carolina Bluff, not above Fulton.

SPARTA, *La.*—Mississippi river, above Grand Gulf, not above Greenville.

SPENCE, or TELL'S.—110 miles up Bœuf river, above Thomas' Landing.

SPEAR'S, J. J. (WOODYARD).—Red river, above Alexandria, not above the mouth of Cane river.

SPIRA'S LANDING, *Ala.*—Alabama river, not above Selma.

SPINKS.—Ouachita river, above Harrisonburg, not above Trenton.

SPOCIMA CUT OFF, *La.*—Red river, 670 miles from New Orleans above Grand Ecore, not above Shreveport.

SPRING BAY, *Ill.*—Illinois river, 188 miles above its mouth, above Beardstown, not above the mouth of Fox river.

SPREAD EAGLE.—Missouri river, 2121 miles above its mouth, above Iatan.

SPRING BANK, *Ark.*—Red river, 113 miles above Shreveport, above Carolina Bluff, not above Fulton.

SPRING BLUFF, *Ala.*—Tombigbee river, above Demopolis, not above Gainesville.

SPRING COLLEGE, *Miss.*—Pearl river, above Gainesville, not above Columbus.

SPRING COTTAGE, *Miss*—Pearl river, above Gainesville, not above Columbus.

SPRING GATE, *Mo.*—Missouri river, 51 miles above its mouth, not above Jefferson City, not above Lexington.

SPRING HILL, *Mo.*—Mississippi river, above the mouth of the Ohio, not above Alton.

SPRING LAKE, *La.*—Red river, above Cane river, not above Grand Ecore.

SPRING LAKE, *Ill.*—Illinois river, above Beardstown, not above the mouth of Fox river.

SPRING LANDING, *La.*—Lake Bisteneau.

SPRINGVILLE, *Ky.*—Ohio river, 647 miles above its mouth, above Cincinnati.

SPRINGFIELD, *La.*—Mississippi river, not above Bayou Sara.

SPRINGWOOD.—Yazoo river, above Yazoo City, not above Leflore.

SPRINGVILLE (CABIN ROW).—Red river, above Grand Ecore, not above Shreveport.

SPROUL'S (or MYER'S) LANDING.—Red river, above Grand Ecore, not above Shreveport.

SPROUL'S, WM. LANDING.—Red river, above Grand Ecore, not above Shreveport.

SPRULLS.—110 miles up Bœuf river, above Thomas' Landing.

SPRUELS.—Ouachita river, above Harrisonburg, not above Trenton.

SQUAW POINT.—Missouri river, above Iatan.

SQUANKA, *Ill.*—Mississippi river, 1435 miles above New Orleans, above second Rapids, not above Galena.

SQUIRREL POINT, *La.*—Red river, 564 miles from New Orleans, above Grand Ecore, not above Shreveport.

SQUIRES.—Ouachita river, above Harrisonburg, not above Trenton.

ST. LOUIS, *Mo.*—Mississippi river, 1278 miles above New Orleans.

ST. FRANCIS RIVER, *Ark*—Any point.

ST. MAURICE, *La.*—Red river, 459 miles from New Orleans, above Cane river, not above Grand Ecore.

ST. JOSEPH, *La.*—Mississippi river, 327 miles above New Orleans, above Bayou Sara, not above Grand Gulf.

ST. MARTINVILLE, *La.*—Attakapas.

ST. MARY'S LANDING, *Ark*—Arkansas river, 159 miles above Napoleon, above Arkansas Post, not above Pine Bluff.

ST. JOSEPH'S, *Mo.*—Missouri river, 501 miles above its mouth, above Iatan.

ST. ALBAN'S, *La.*—Ouachita river, above Harrisonburg, not above Trenton.

ST. ANDREW'S, *La*—Red river, above Cotile, not above Grand Ecore.

ST. CHARLES, *Mo.*—Missouri river, 22 miles above its mouth, not above Jefferson City.

ST. CHARLES, *Ark.*—White river, 84 miles above its mouth, below the junction of Black river.

ST. CHARLES, *La.*—Morgan railroad, 24 miles from New Orleans.

ST. ALBAN'S, *Mo.*—Missouri river, not above Jefferson City.

ST. MARY'S LANDING, *Mo*—Mississippi river, 1109 miles above New Orleans, above the mouth of the Ohio, not above Alton.

ST. MARY'S, *Mo.*—Missouri river, above Iatan.

ST. CROIX RIVER.—Mississippi river, above Galena.

ST. PAUL'S, *Minn.*—Mississippi river, above Galena.

ST. PETER'S RIVER, *Minn*—Mississippi river, above Galena.

ST. FRANCISVILLE, *La.*—Mississippi river, 165 miles above New Orleans, above Bayou Sara, not above Grand Gulf.

ST. AUGUSTINE.—St. Augustine county, Texas.

ST. CLOUD.—Yazoo river, above Yazoo City, not above Leflore.

ST. MAURICE.—Red river, above Cane river, not above Grand Ecore.

ST. STEPHEN'S, *Ala.*—Tombigbee river, not above Demopolis.

ST. MARTIN'S LANDING, *Ark.*—Arkansas river, 413 miles above Napoleon, above Norristown, not above Fort Smith.

ST. LOUIS PLANTATION, *La.*—Mississippi river, not above Bayou Sara.

ST. THOMAS, *Mo.*—Missouri river, 320 miles above its mouth, above Jefferson City, not above Lexington.

ST. STEPHEN'S, *Mo.*—Missouri river, 653 miles above its mouth, above Iatan.

ST. DERVIN, *Mo.*—Missouri river, 659 miles above its mouth, above Iatan.

STE. GENEVIEVE, *Mo.*—Mississippi river, 1213 miles above New Orleans, above the mouth of the Ohio, not above Alton.

STANDING ROCK AGENCY.—Missouri river, 1535 miles from its mouth, above Iatan.

STAFFORD'S, T. JEFF.—Red river, not above Alexandria.

STAFFORD'S MILL.—Ouachita river, above Harrisonburg, not above Trenton.

STAFFORD'S POINT.—Ouachita river, above Harrisonburg, not above Trenton.

STANDARD, M. LANDING, *Miss.*—153 miles up Big Deer Creek.

STANTON'S (or ALBAN'S GUT).—Red river, above foot of Raft, not above Fulton.

STAR OF THE WEST.—Tallahatchie river, not above Cassidy Bayou.

STAR LANDING (GOXTON).—Bayou Bartholomew, above Point Pleasant, not above Arkansas line.

STARLING, M. H.—Red river, above Grand Ecore, not above Shreveport.

STARK'S LANDING.—Sabine river, Texas.

STATEN'S.—Tallahatchie river, not above Cassidy Bayou.

STANDING STUMP.—250 miles up Sunflower river.

STANLEY'S LANDING, *Ark.*—Arkansas river, 322 miles above Napoleon, above Little Rock, not above Norristown.

STATE ROAD, *Ark.*—Bayou Macon, 235 miles above its mouth, above Monticello.

STATE LINE, *Miss.*—Chickasaha river.

STAFFORD'S LANDING, *La.*—Red river, not above Alexandria.
STARLIGHT, *La.*—Red river, above Grand Ecore, not above Shreveport.
STATEN PLACE (HODGES), *La.*—Red river, above Grand Ecore, not above Shreveport.
STARK'S LANDING, *Ala.*—Alabama river, not above Selma.
STARK'S, COL. LANDING, *Ala.*—Alabama river, not above Selma.
STABLER'S LANDING, *Ala.*—Alabama river, not above Selma.
STABLER'S, MRS. LANDING, *Ala.*—Alabama river, not above Selma.
STANTON'S, D. LANDING, *La.*—Tensas river, not above mouth of Bayou Macon.
START'S LANDING, *La.*—Ouachita river, above Harrisonburg, not above Trenton.
STARK'S LANDING, *Ala.*—Tombigbee river, not above Demopolis.
STALL'S LANDING, *Ala.*—Alabama river, above Selma, not above Wetumpka.
STAMP'S LANDING, *Miss.*—Mississippi river, above Bayou Sara, not above Grand Gulf.
STANFORD'S CAMP, *Ala.*—Warrior river, not above Tuscaloosa.
STEADYSIDE, *Miss.*—Mississippi river, above Greenville, not above Memphis.
STEVENSVILLE.—Ohio river, 946 miles from its mouth, above Cincinnati.
STEDHAM'S LANDING, *Ala.*—Alabama river, not above Selma.
STEDHAM'S WOODYARD, *Ala.*—Alabama river, not above Selma.
STEINERVILLE, *Ohio.*—Ohio river, 890 miles above its mouth, above Cincinnati.
STEELE'S BAYOU.—Yazoo river, not above Yazoo City.
STEIGLER'S LANDING.—267 miles up Sunflower river.
STELLA.—Yazoo river, not above Yazoo City.
STEIGLER'S GIN.—270 miles up Sunflower river.
STENCEL'S, R. M.—Tallahatchie river, not above Cassidy Bayou.
STEPHENS.—Bayou Bartholomew, above Arkansas line, not above Portland.
STEPHENS' BLUFF, *Ala.*—Warrior river, not above Tuscaloosa.
STEUBENVILLE, *Ohio.*—Ohio river, 934 miles above its mouth, above Cincinnati.
STERLING, *Ill.*—Wabash river, above Terre Haute.

STEVENS.—Red river, above Grand Ecore, not above Shreveport.

STEPHENSON, JNO. A.—Red river, above Grand Ecore, not above Shreveport.

STEWART, WIDOW.—Red river, above Grand Ecore, not above Shreveport.

STERLINGTON.—Ouachita river, above Trenton, not above Alabama Landing.

STERLING LANDING, *Ark.*—Ouachita river, above Camden, not above Ross' Landing.

STERLING —Mississippi river, above Greenville, not above mouth of the Ohio.

STERLING'S LANDING, *La.*—Ouachita river, above Trenton, not above Alabama Landing.

STERLING'S LANDING.—Mississippi river, above the mouth of the Ohio, not above Alton.

STEVENSPORT, *Ky.*—Ohio river, 283 miles above its mouth, above Paducah, not above Cincinnati.

STEVENSON, *Ala.*—Tennessee river, above Florence, not above Eastport.

STEVEN'S CREEK. *Texas.*—Trinity river, above Smithville, not above Magnolia Landing.

STEPHEN'S BLUFF, *Ala.*—Warrior river, not above Tuscaloosa.

STEELE'S, D. A. LANDING, *Ala.*—Warrior river, not above Tuscaloosa.

STEELE'S BLUFF, *Ala.*—Warrior river, not above Tuscaloosa.

STEELE'S, GEN'L LANDING, *Ala.*—Alabama river, above Selma, not above Wetumpka.

STEWART'S LANDING, *Ala* —Alabama river, above Selma, not above Wetumpka.

STEWART'S LANDING, *Miss.*—Mississippi river, above Greenville, not above Memphis.

STOUT'S LANDING, *Ark.*—Arkansas river, 359 miles above Napoleon, above Little Rock, not above Norristown.

STONE'S PORT, *Mo.*—Missouri river, 150 miles above its mouth, above Jefferson City, not above Lexington.

STONE'S LANDING, *La.*—Black river, La., not above Harrisonburg.

STONE'S LANDING, *Ala*—Alabama river, above Selma, not above Wetumpka.

STONE'S FERRY, *Ala.*—Tombigbee river, above Gainesville, not above Columbus.

STONE'S LANDING, *Miss.*—170 miles up Big Deer Creek.

STONE, MRS.—Ouachita river, above Alabama Landing, not above Camden.

STONEWALL LANDING, *La.*—Red river, not above Alexandria.

STONEVILLE, *Miss.*—184 miles up Big Deer Creek.

STONEWALL.—Yazoo river, above Yazoo City, not above Leflore.

STOKES' LANDING.—119 miles up Bœuf river, above Thomas' Landing.

STOP LANDING, *Miss.*—Mississippi river, 585 miles above New Orleans, above Greenville, not above Memphis.

STORY'S LANDING, *La.*—Black river, La., not above Harrisonburg.

STOUDMIRE'S LANDING, *Ala.*—Alabama river, above Selma, not above Wetumpka.

STRONG HALL.—Yazoo river, above Yazoo City, not above Leflore.

STRONG'S FERRY.—229 miles up Sunflower river.

STRATHMORE.—Tallahatchie river, not above Cassidy Bayou.

STRIPLINGS.—Ouachita river, above Trenton, not above Alabama Landing.

STRAY HORNE'S LANDING, *Ark.*—Arkansas river, 407 miles above Napoleon, above Norristown, not above Fort Smith.

STRICKLING'S LANDING, *Miss.*—Pearl river, above Columbia.

STRAW HAT LANDING, *Ark.*—Arkansas river, 210 miles above Napoleon, above Pine Bluff, not above Little Rock.

STROTHER'S, G. LANDING, *Ala.*—Alabama river, not above Selma.

STROTHER'S, WIDOW LANDING, *Ala.*—Alabama river, not above Selma.

STRAWHORNE'S LANDING, *Miss.*—Tombigbee river, above Columbus, not above Cotton Gin Port.

STULLVAN'S LANDING, *La.*—Red river, above Grand Ecore, not above Shreveport.

STURDEVANT'S.—Yazoo river, not above Yazoo City.

STYOPA PLACE.—Red river, not above Alexandria.

STYX RIVER.—Ouachita river, above Trenton, not above Alabama Landing.

SUNDERFORD, J. W. (ASH POINT).—Red river, above Grand Ecore, not above Shreveport.

SUMMERS.—Red river, above foot of Raft, not above Fulton.

SUMMERS, P.—99 miles up Bœuf river, above Thomas' Landing.

SUMMERVILLE.—Ouachita river, above Harrisonburg, not above Trenton.

SUMTER.—Ouachita river, above Harrisonburg, not above Trenton.

SUN FLOWER (MOUTH OF BIG).—60 miles from Vicksburg.

SUN FLOWER (L. K. REAISON'S).—Red river, above Grand Ecore, not above Shreveport.

SUNNY SIDE.—Tallahatchie river, not above Cassidy Bayou.

SUNNY SIDE.—124 miles up Sunflower river.

SUGAR LOAF ROCK, *Mo.*—Missouri river, 95 miles above its mouth, not above Jefferson City.

SULLIVAN'S LANDING, *La.*—Red river, above Alexandria, not above Cane river.

SULLIVAN'S LANDING, *La.*—Red river, above Grand Ecore, not above Shreveport.

SULPHUR SPRING, *Ark.*—White river, not above Batesville.

SULPHUR SPRING.—Mississippi river, 1216 miles above New Orleans, above the mouth of the Ohio, not above Alton.

SULTAN'S LANDING, *Mo.*—Missouri river, 590 miles above its mouth, above Iatan.

SUMMER'S LANDING, *Ark.*—Arkansas river, 66 miles above Napoleon, above Arkansas Post, not above Pine Bluff.

SUMMIT, *Miss.*—Jackson railroad, 108 miles above New Orléans.

SUMNER'S LANDING, *Mo.*—Missouri river, 511 miles above its mouth, above Iatan.

SUNFISH.—Ohio river, 896 miles above its mouth, above Cincinnati.

SUNNY POINT (W. CRANE'S), *La.*—Red river, above Grand Ecore, not above Shreveport.

SUN FLOWER RIVER.—Any point.

SUNNY SIDE.—Mississippi river, 530 miles above New Orleans, above Grand Gulf, not above Greenville.

SUN FLOWER, *Miss.*—Mississippi river, above Greenville, not above Memphis.

SUNK RAPIDS, *Miss.*—Mississippi river, above Galena.

SURROUNDED HILL, *Ark.*—White river, 178 miles above its mouth, below the junction of Black river.

SWANSON'S LANDING, *La.*--Lake Caddo.

SWAN LAKE, *Ark.*—Arkansas river, 123 miles above Napoleon, above Arkansas Post, not above Pine Bluff.

SWAN LAKE, *Ark.*—Red river, 257 miles above Shreveport, above Fulton, not above Lanesport.

SWAN RIVER, *Minn.*—Mississippi river, above Galena.

SWAN'S LANDING, *La.*—Ouachita river, above Trenton, not above Alabama Landing.

SWARTWOUT, *Texas.*—Trinity river, above Smithville, not above Magnolia Landing.

SWILEY'S LANDING, *La.*—Red river, above Alexandria, not above Cotile.

SWIMM'S LANDING, *La.*—Ouachita river, above Harrisonburg, not above Trenton.

SWANSON FIELD, *Miss.*—119 miles up Big Deer Creek.

SWANSON'S.—Red river, above Shreveport, not above Carolina Bluff.

SWAN LAKE (or WRIGHT ESTATE).—Red river, above Fulton, not above Lanesport.

SWAN LAKE.—Tallahatchie river, not above Cassidy Bayou.

SWEENEY'S LANDING, or SPANISH FORT, *Miss.*—71 miles up Sunflower river.

SYMMS.—Mississippi river, above Grand Gulf, not above Greenville.

SYKES.—Tallahatchie river, not above Cassidy Bayou.

SYNOPE.—Ouachita river, above Harrisonburg, not above Trenton.

SYPE, DR. (POSSUM TROT).—Red river, above Alexandria, not above Cane river.

SYCAMORE GROVE, *Ark.*—Arkansas river, 139 miles above Napoleon, above Arkansas Post, not above Pine Bluff.

SYCAMORE BLUFF, *Ala.*—Alabama river, not above Selma.

SLAYMORE, *Ark.*—White river, 310 miles above its mouth, above Batesville.

T

TAIT'S FERRY, *Ala.*—Alabama river, not above Selma.
TAIT'S SHOALS, *Ala.*—Alabama river, not above Selma.
TAIT'S LOWER LANDING, *Ala.*—Alabama river, not above Selma
TALLAHATCHEE RIVER.—Not above the mouth of Cold Water.
TALLAWANIE LANDING, *Ark.*—Alabama river, above Selma, not above Wetumpka.
TALLALULAH LANDING, *La.*—Tensas river, above the mouth of Bayou Macon.
TALLALULAH LANDING, *Miss.*—Mississippi river, above Grand Gulf, not above Greenville.
TAMACK, *Miss.*—Mississippi river, above Grand Gulf, not above Greenville.
TANGIPAHOA, *La.*—Jackson railroad, 79 miles from New Orleans.
TALLALAH.—North Louisiana and Texas Railroad.
TALLEQUAH.—Yazoo river, above Yazoo City, not above Leflore.
TANGLE RETREAT.—Yazoo river, above Yazoo City, not above Leflore.
TANGLEWOOD.—112 miles up Bœuf river, above Thomas Landing.
TEAR SHIRT.—Yazoo river, above Yazoo City, not above Leflore.
TATUM'S.—Bayou Bartholomew, above Arkansas line, not above Portland.
TATUM'S.—Ouachita river, above Harrisonburg, not above Trenton.
TAYLOR, C.—Black river, La.
TAYLOR'S JOE.—Yazoo river, not above Yazoo City.
TAYLOR PLACE.—Yazoo river, above Yazoo City, not above Leflore.
TAYLOR, N. C.—117 miles up Sunflower river.
TANLEURIES LANDING, *Ala.*—Alabama river, not above Selma.
TARVER'S LANDING, *Ala.*—Alabama river, above Selma, not above Wetumpka.
TATE'S, FELIX LANDING, *Ala.*—Alabama river, not above Selma.
TATE'S, ROBT. LANDING, *Ala.*—Alabama river, not above Selma.
TATUM'S LANDING, *Ala.*—Alabama river, above Selma, not above Wetumpka.
TAVERN ROCK, *Mo.*—Missouri river, 50 miles above its mouth, not above Jefferson City.
TAYLOR'S BAY, *Ark.*—White river, 286 miles above its mouth, below the junction of Black river.

TAYLOR'S BAR.—Arkansas river, 640 miles above Napoleon, above Fort Smith.

TAYLOR'S LANDING, *La.*—Ouachita river, above Harrisonburg, not above Trenton.

TAYLOR'S, MRS. LANDING, *La.*—Ouachita river, above Trenton, not above Alabama Landing.

TAYLOR'S, J. T. LANDING, *Ala.*—Tombigbee river, not above Demopolis.

TAYLOR'S, MAT. LANDING, *Ala.*—Tombigbee river, above Demopolis, not above Gainesville.

TAYLOR'S, ISAAC LANDING, *Ala.*—Tombigbee river, above Gainesville, not above Columbus.

TAYLOR'S MILLS, *Ky.*—Mississippi river, above Memphis, not above the mouth of the Ohio.

TCHULA LAKE, *Miss.*—Yazoo river, 154 miles from Vicksburg,

TCHULA CITY.—Yazoo river, above Yazoo City, not above Leflore.

TELEGRAM (or H. S. BOSLEY).—Red river, above Grand Ecore, not above Shreveport.

TELL'S (or SPENCE).—110 miles up Bœuf river, above Thomas' Landing.

TEMPLE, J. R.—Bayou Bartholomew, not above Point Pleasant.

TEMPLETON'S.—Yazoo river, not above Yazoo City.

TEMPLETON'S.—Bayou Macon, above Monticello.

TEMPLEMAN'S, L. (LOWRY PLANTATION) —Red river, above Grand Ecore, not above Shreveport.

TEMPLEMAN'S, L. (WHITE HALL).—Red river, above Grand Ecore, not above Shreveport.

TEASERVILLE, *La.*—Atchafalaya river, below Simmsport. above Yazoo City, not above Leflore.

TECKANA, *Neb.*—Missouri river, 740 miles above its mouth, above Iatan.

TELL CITY.—Ohio river, above Paducah, not above Cincinnati.

TEMPLEMAN'S LANDING, *La.*—Red river, above Grand Ecore, not above Shreveport.

TENNESSEE IRONWORKS, *Tenn.*—Cumberland river, not above Nashville.

TENNESSEE LANDING, *Miss.*—Mississippi river, 465 miles above New Orleans, above Grand Gulf, not above Greenville.

TENNESSEE LINE.—Mississippi river, 990 miles above New Orleans, above Memphis, not above the mouth of the Ohio river.

TENNESSEE, *Miss.*—Mississippi river, above Grand Gulf, not above Greenville.

TENSAS LAKE, *La.*—Tensas river, 46 miles from Trinity, below the mouth of Bayou Macon.

TENSAS RIVER, *La.*—Not above the mouth of Bayou Macon.

TENSAS RIVER, *Ala.*—Not above Tensas Landing.

TERRAPIN'S CUT-OFF, *La.*—Mississippi river, above Grand Gulf, not above Greenville.

TERREBONNE, *La.*—Morgan railroad, 51 miles from New Orleans.

TERREBONNE BAYOU, *La.*—Any point.

TERRE HAUTE, *Ind.*—Wabash river.

TERRELL'S BLUFF, *Miss.*—Mississippi river, 400 miles above New Orleans, above Grand Gulf, not above Greenville.

TERRILL'S LANDING, *Ala.*—Warrior river, not above Tuscaloosa.

TERRY'S FERRY, *Ark.*—Arkansas river, 273 miles above Napoleon, above Pine Bluff, not above Little Rock.

TERRY'S, JNO. LANDING, *Ark.*—Little Red river, 30 miles from its mouth, below the junction of Black and White rivers.

TERRY, *Miss.*—Jackson railroad, 79 miles from New Orleans.

TESSIER'S, JNO. M. LANDING, *La.*—Red river, 472 miles from New Orleans, above Cane river, not above Grand Ecore.

TESSIER'S, C. R. LANDING, *La.*—Atchafalaya river, not below Simmsport.

TEXAS, *Tenn.*—Cumberland river, not above Nashville.

TERRAPIN NECK.—Mississippi river,, above Grand Gulf, not above Greenville.

TESTON'S.—96 miles up Bœuf. river, above Thomas' Landing.

TEWS.—Ouachita river, not above Harrisonburg.

THEBES, *Ill.*—Mississippi river, 1071 miles above New Orleans, above the mouth of the Ohio, not above Alton.

THE DECKER.—Red river, not above Alexandria.

THETFORD'S.—Arkansas river, above Arkansas Post, not above Pine Bluff.

THIRD CHICASAW BLUFF, *Tenn.*—Mississippi river, 786 miles above New Orleans, above Memphis, not above the mouth of the Ohio.

THILFORD'S LANDING, *Ark.*—Arkansas river, 79 miles above Napoleon, above Arkansas Post, not above Pine Bluff.

THIRTY-ONE MILE BLUFF, *Ala.*—Tombigbee river, not above Demopolis.

THIBODAUX, *La.*—Bayou Lafourche.

THIERS & BRO. H. H.—Red river, above Grand Ecore, not above Shreveport.

THOMAS, CAPT. (or LAKE PLACE).—Red river, above Shreveport, not above foot of Raft.

THOMAS, J. J.—102 miles up Bœuf river, above Thomas' Landing.

THOMAS, W. P.—91 miles up Bœuf river, above Thomas' Landing.

THOMAS' LANDING.—53 miles up Bœuf river.

THOMAS' POINT, *La.*—Mississippi river, 151 miles above New Orleans, not above Bayou Sara.

THOMAS,' MRS. LANDING, *La.*—Atchafalaya river, below Simmsport.

THOMAS & FRANTHAM'S LANDING, *Ala.*—Tombigbee river, above Gainesville, not above Columbus.

THOMASSON LANDING.—Bœuf river, not above Thomas' Landing.

THOHASSON'S WOODYARD.—Red river, above Cane river, not above Grand Ecore.

THOMPSON'S CREEK, *La.*—Mississippi river, 165 miles above New Orleans, not above Bayou Sara.

THOMPSON'S LANDING, *Miss.*—Mississippi river, above Greenville, not above Memphis.

THOMPSON & CHEWLANDING, *Miss.*—140 miles up Big Deer Creek.

THOMPSON, JULIUS, *Miss.*—141 miles up Big Deer Creek.

THOMPSON'S (ALLIGATOR).—Yazoo river, not above Yazoo City.

THOMPSON'S.—Mississippi river, above Grand Gulf, not above Greenville.

THOMPSON BAYOU.—Ouachita river, above Harrisonburg, not above Trenton.

THOMPSON'S, JOHN LANDING, *Miss.*—Tombigbee river, above Columbus, not above Cotton Gin Port.

THOMPSON'S LANDING, *Ala.*—Tombigbee river, not above Demopolis.

THOMPSON'S BAYOU, *Miss.*—Mississippi river, above Greenville, not above Memphis.

THOMPSON'S LANDING, *Mo.*—Mississippi river, above the mouth of the Ohio, not above Alton.

THORNTON'S LANDING.—Mississippi river, 1051 miles above New Orleans, above the mouth of the Ohio, not above Alton.

THORN'S ESTATE.—Red river, above Grand Ecore, not above Shreveport.

THORNTON PLACE.—Yazoo river, above Yazoo City, not above Leflore.

THORNTON'S LANDING, *Ala.*—Tombigbee river, not above Demopolis.

THORNTON'S, J. W. LANDING, *Ala.*—Tombigbee river, not above Demopolis.

THOUVENIN'S LANDING, *Texas.*—Neches river, above the junction of the Angelina river.

THREE RIVERS, *Ala.*—Tombigbee river, not above Demopolis.

THREE RIVERS.—43 miles up Bœuf river, not above Thomas' Landing.

TICKFAW, *La.*—Jackson railroad, 58 miles from New Orleans.

TIGER ISLAND, *La.*—Red river, 475 miles from New Orleans, above Cane river, not above Grand Ecore.

TIGERVILLE, *La.*—Morgan railroad, 66 miles from New Orleans.

TILGHMAN'S, G. LANDING, *La.*—Tensas river, La., 25 miles from Trinity, below the mouth of Bayou Macon.

TIPTONVILLE, *Tenn*—Mississippi river, above Memphis, not above the mouth of the Ohio.

TIPTON'S PORT, *Ind.*—Wabash river, above the Rapids, not above Terre Haute.

TIPTON'S LANDING, *Ala.*—Alabama river, above Selma, not above Wetumpka.

TIPTON'S LANDING, *Tenn.*—Mississippi river, above Memphis, not above the mouth of the Ohio.

TITTWORTH'S LANDING, *Ark.*—Arkansas river, 462 miles above Napoleon, above Norristown, not above Roseville.

TITTONSVILLE, *Ohio.*—Ohio river, 917 miles above its mouth, above Cincinnati.

TIGER ROCKS.—Red river, above Alexandria, not above moutn of Cane river.

TIBBS, M. C. MRS.—Bayou Bartholomew, above Arkansas line, not above Portland.

TIGNOR, M. E. MRS.—Bayou Bartholomew, above Arkansas line, not above Portland.

TILDEN, L. W.—Red river, not above Alexandria.

TINDALL.—Tallahatchie river, not above Cassidy Bayou.

TOKEBA.—Yazoo river, above Yazoo City, not above Leflore.

TOBACCO PORT, *Tenn.*—Cumberland river, 88 miles from its mouth, not above Nashville.

TOBIN'S PORT, *Ind.*—Ohio river, 275 miles above its mouth, above Paducah, not above Cincinnati.

TOLBERT'S FERRY, *Ark.*—White river, above Batesville.

TOMLIN'S LANDING, *Ala.*—Alabama river, not above Selma.

TOM'S BLUFF, *Ala.*—Tombigbee river, above Demopolis, not above Gainesville.

TOMPKIN'S LANDING, *Miss.*—Mississippi river, 554 miles above New Orleans, above Greenville, not above Memphis.

TOMPKIN'S BLUFF, *Ala*—Tombigbee river, not above Demopolis.

TONEY'S LANDING, *Miss.*—Mississippi river, above Greenville, not above Memphis.

TOOLEY'S LANDING, *La.*—Black river, La.

TOULMIN'S LANDING, *Ala.*—Tombigbee river, not above Demopolis.

TOWER ROCK.—Mississippi river, 1152 miles above New Orleans, above the mouth of the Ohio river, not above Alton.

TOM'S BLUFF.—Neches river, Texas.

TOMMASON'S (WOODYARD), *La.*—Red river, above Cane river, not above Grand Ecore.

TOLEDO, *Texas.*—Sabine river, Texas.

TOUMER'S FT.—Mississippi river, above Grand Gulf, not above Greenville.

TOWN BLUFF.--Neches river, Texas.

TOWNSEND'S.—Bayou Bartholomew, above Portland.

TOWNSEND'S BLUFF.—Angelina river, Texas.

TRACY, *Ind.*—Wabash river, not above the Rapids.

TRADE WATER, *Ky.*—Ohio river, above Paducah, not above Cincinnati.

TRADER'S POINT, *Iowa.*—Missouri river, 668 miles above its mouth, above Iatan.

TRANSYLVANIA.—Mississippi river, above Grand Gulf, not above Greenville.

TRAVIS' LANDING, *La.*—Bayou Macon, 125 miles from its mouth, not above Monticello.

TRANTHAM'S LANDING, *Ala.*—Tombigbee river, above Greenville, not above Columbus.

TREADWELL'S LANDING, *La.*—Red river, above Grand Ecore, not above Shreveport.

TREMPALEAU RIVER, *Miss.*—Mississippi river, 1751 miles above New Orleans, above Galena.

TRENTON, *La.*—Ouachita river, 287 miles above the mouth of Old river.

TRENTON, *Ala.*—Alabama river, 302 miles from Mobile, above Selma, not above Wetumpka.

TRENTON.—Mississippi river, 731 miles above St. Louis, above Galena.

TRIGONIA, *Ala.*—Tennessee river, above Florance.

TRINIDAD, *Texas.*—Trinity river, above Magnolia Landing.

TRINITY, *La.*—Ouachita river, 115 miles from the mouth of Old river, not above Harrisonburg.

TRINITY, *Ala.*—Tennessee river, above Florance.

TRINITY, *Ohio.*—Ohio river, 5 miles from its mouth, not above Paducah.

TRINITY, *La.*—Black river, La.

TRIPLETT'S LANDING, *Ark.*—Arkansas river, 194 miles above Napoleon, above Pine Bluff, not above Little Rock.

TREADAWAY.—Ouachita river, above Alabama Landing, not above Camden.

TREADWELL, W. H.—Red river, above Grand Ecore, not above Shreveport.

TRESHALL, G. L.—Red river, above Grand Ecore, not above Shreveport.

TRIGGS.—Red river, above foot of Raft, not above Fulton.

TROOER POINT.—Missouri river, 2344 miles above its mouth, above Iatan.

TRISLER'S LANDING, *La.*—Black river, La.

TROJIAN, *Ark.*—White river, not above Batesville.

TROY, *Mo.*—Missouri river, above Jefferson City, not above Lexington.

TROY, *Ark.*—Arkansas river, 250 miles above Napoleon, above Pine Bluff, not above Little Rock.

TROY, *Miss.*—Yallabusha river, not above Grenada.

TROY, *Ohio.*—Ohio river, 809 miles above its mouth, above Cincinnati.

TROY, *Ind.*—Ohio river, 266 miles above its mouth, above Paducah, not above Cincinnati.

TROY, *La.*—Black river, above Harrisonburg.

TROY, *Texas.*—Trinity river, above Magnolia Landing.

TROTTER'S LANDING, *Miss.*—Mississippi river, above Greenville, not above Memphis.

TRUELOCK'S, MRS. LANDING, *Ark.*—Arkansas river, 135 miles above Napoleon, above Arkansas Post, not above Pine Bluff.

TRUSSELL'S LANDING, *Ala.*—Tombigbee river, above Demopolis, not above Gainesville.

TRUEMAN'S LANDING, *La.*—Tensas river, 46 miles from Trinity, below the mouth of Bayou Macon.

TULA.—Mississippi river, above Grand Gulf, not above Greenville.

TUHARRILL.—133 miles up Bœuf river, above Thomas' Landing.

TULSOM'S.—Red river, above Grand Ecore, not above Shreveport.

TURKEY CREEK.—5 miles up Bœuf river, not above Thomas' Landing.

TURNBULL'S.—Red river, not above Alexandria.

TURPANS.—Ouachita river, above Trenton, not above Alabama Landing.

TUGALOO, *Miss.*—Jackson railroad, 190 miles from New Orleans.

TULLY, *Mo.*—Mississippi river, above the first, not above the second Rapids.

TUNICA BEND.—Mississippi river, 218 miles above New Orleans, above Bayou Sara, not above Grand Gulf.

TURNIPSEEDS LANDING, *Ala.*—Tombigbee river, above Gainesville, not above Columbus.

TURNER'S.—Tallahatchie river, not above Cassidy Bayou.
TURNER'S FERRY, *Texas.*—Sabine river, above Sabine City, not above Belgrade.
TURNER'S BAYOU, *La.*—Atchafalaya river, below Simmsport.
TURNER'S, MRS. LANDING, *Ala.*—Tombigbee river, not above Demopolis.
TURNER'S SHOALS, *Ala.*—Tombigbee river, not above Demopolis.
TURNER'S, B. L. LANDING, *Ala.*—Tombigbee river, not above Demopolis.
TURNER'S, MRS. LANDING, *Ala.*—Alabama river, above Selma, not above Wetumpka.
TURNER'S LANDING.—Mississippi river, above Alton, not above the first Rapids.
TURNER, J. A. (X. LETARD).—Red river, above Grand Ecore, not above Shreveport.
TURNER, G. S.—Red river, above Grand Ecore, not above Shreveport.
TURNER, LIVINGSTON.—Red river, above Grand Ecore,not above Shreveport.
TURNER, MRS.—626 miles above New Orleans, above Greenville, not above Memphis.
TUSCOMBIA, *Ala.*—Tennessee river, not below Eastport.
TUSCALOOSA, *Ala.*—Warrior river.
TUSCAHOMA, *Miss.*—Yallabusha river, not above Grenada.
TUSCAHOUMA, *Ala.*—Tombigbee river, not above Demopolis.
TUTT'S LANDING, *Ala.*—Tombigbee river, above Demopolis, not above Gainesville.
TWENTY-ONE MILE BLUFF, *Ala.*—Alabama river, not above Selma.
TWENTY-SEVEN MILE BLUFF, *Ala.*—Alabama river, not above Selma.
TWENTY-EIGHT MILE BLUFF, *Ala.*—Alabama river, not above Selma.
TWENTY-ONE MILE BLUFF, *Ala.*—Tombigbee river, not above Demopolis.
TWENTY-SEVEN MILE BLUFF, *Ala.*—Tombigbee river, not above Demopolis.
TWENTY-EIGHT MILE BLUFF, *Ala.*—Tombigbee river, not above Demopolis.

TWIGGS', JOHN LANDING, *Ark.*—Red river, 225 miles above Shreveport, above Carolina Bluff, not above Fulton.

TWO BRANCH LANDING.—Mississippi river, above Alton, not above the first Rapids.

TWO ISLANDS, *Ark.*—Arkansas river, above Little Rock, not above Norristown.

TWELVE MILE BAYOU.—Yazoo river, not above Yazoo City.

TWILIGHT.—Tallahatchie river, not above Cassidy Bayou.

TYLER.—Smith County, Texas.

TYRUS LANDING, *Ala.*—Alabama river, above Selma, not above Wetumpka.

TYPCONE LANDING, *Miss.*—Mississippi river, 655 miles above New Orleans, above Greenville, not above Memphis.

U

UCHEE, ANNA, *Fla.* (W. BRANCH).—Choctawatchee river, not above Geneva.

ULSTER PLACE (R. GOODWYN).—Red river, above Grand Ecore, not above Shreveport.

UNION CHURCH.—112 miles up Bœuf river, above Thomas' Landing.

UNDERHALL'S LANDING, *Ala.*—Alabama river, not above Selma.

UNION POINT, *Ill.*—Mississippi river, 1121 miles above New Orleans, above the mouth of the Ohio, not above Alton.

UNION POINT, *La.*—Mississippi river, 228 miles above New Orleans, above Bayou Sara, not above Grand Gulf.

UNIONTOWN, *Ky.*—Ohio river, 136 miles above its mouth, above Paducah, not above Cincinnati.

UNION BLUFF, *Ala.*—Tombigbee river, above Gainesville, not above Columbus.

UPPER KEECHI CREEK, *Texas.*—Trinity river, above Smithville, not above Magnolia Landing.

UPPER AUDALUSIA.—Ouachita river, above Harrisonburg, not above Trenton.

UPPER FLAGLAND.—Red river, above Alexandria, not above the mouth of Cane river.

UPPER PIGEON HILL.—Ouachita river, above Alabama Landing, not above Camden.

UPPER SWAN LAKE, *Ark.*—Arkansas river, above Arkansas Post, not above Pine Bluff.

URSINO, *Miss.*—Mississippi river, above Grand Gulf, not above Greenville.

UTICA, *Ind.*—Ohio river, 393 miles above its mouth, above Paducah, not above Cincinnati.

UTICA, *Ill.*—Illinois river, 252 miles above its mouth, above Beardstown, not above the mouth of Fox river.

UTICA, *Ind.*—Wabash river, not above the Rapids.

UTOPIA LANDING, *Miss.*—Mississippi river, 655 miles above New Orleans, above Greenville, not above Memphis.

V

VALENTINE'S (ELDORADO).—Yazoo river, not above Yazoo City.

VALLE, JAMES.—Red river, above Alexandria, not above mouth of Cane river.

VALLIE FORGE.—Yazoo river, above Yazoo City, not above Leflore.

VALCOUR'S LANDING, *La.*—Mississippi river, not above Bayou Sara.

VALIE'S LANDING, *La.*—Red river, above Cane river, not above Grand Ecore.

VANCE, S. W. DR. (or BUCK HILL).—Red river, above Shreveport, not above foot of Raft.

VANCE (or SHADY GROVE.—Red river, above Shreveport, not above foot of Raft.

VANCE, W. C. DR. (BATCHELOR'S MISSION.—Red river, above Shreveport, not above foot of Raft.

VANDARRIES, A. A.—Red river, above Grand Ecore, not above Shreveport.

VANHOOK, PHIL. (COL'D).—Bayou Bartholomew, not above Point Pleasant.

VAN WACO LANDING.—136 miles up Sunflower river.

VAN BUREN, *Ark.*—Arkansas river, 538 miles above Napoleon, above Norristown, not above Fort Smith.

VAN BUREN, *Miss.*—Tombigbee river, above Smithville.

VAND LAND.—Yazoo river, above Yazoo City, not above Leflore.

VANCEBURG, *Ky.*—Ohio river, 627 miles above its mouth, above Cincinnati.

VAN'S LANDING, *Ark.*—Arkansas river, 332 miles above Napoleon, above Little Rock, not above Norristown.

VARNER'S LANDING, *Miss.*—Tombigbee river, Columbus, not above Cotton Gin Port.

VARINA LANDING, *Miss.*—Big Black river.

VARNERS, WM.—Ouachita river, above Harrisonburg, not above Trenton.

VASSIER'S LANDING.—Red river, above Grand Ecore, not above Shreveport.

VAUGHN'S LANDING, *Miss.*—Jackson railroad, 220 miles from New Orleans.

VAUGHN'S LANDING, *Ark.*—Arkansas river, above Pine Bluff, not above Little Rock.

VAUGHN'S LANDING, *La.*—Ouachita river, above Harrisonburg, not above Trenton.

VAUGHAN, *Ala.*—Tombigbee river, not above Demopolis.

VAUMATE'S LANDING, *Ark.*—Little Red river, 39 miles above its mouth, below the junction of White and Black rivers.

VAUTER'S LANDING, *Ala.*—Tombigbee river, not above Demopolis.

VAUGHAN, MRS.—Red river, not above Alexandria.

VAUGUS.—Red river, above Fulton, not above Shreveport, not above Lanesport.

VENCIL'S, *Mo.*—Mississippi river, above the mouth of the Ohio, not above Alton.

VENICE, *Ill.*—Mississippi river, 1186 miles above New Orleans, above Alton, not above the first Rapids.

VERA CRUZ, *Miss.*—Tombigbee river, above Columbus, not above Cotton Gin Port.

VERMILLION RIVER, *Minn.*—Mississippi river, 1835 miles above New Orleans, above Galena.

VERMILLIONVILLE, *La.*—Attakapas.

VERMILLION.—Missouri river, 953 miles from its mouth, above Iatan.

VERONA, *Ind.*—Ohio river, 183 miles above its mouth, above Paducah, not above Cincinnati.

VERNON, *Miss.*—Big Black river.

VERNON, *Ala.*—Alabama river, 319 miles above Mobile, above Selma, not above Wetumpka.

VERSAILLES, *Ill.*—Illinois river, not above Beardstown.

VEVEY, *Ind.*--Ohio river, 464 miles above its mouth, above Paducah, not above Cincinnati.

VIAN'S LANDING, *Ark.*—Arkansas river, 612 miles from Napoleon, above Fort Smith.

VICTORIA, *Miss.*—Mississippi river, 644 miles above New Orleans, above Greenville, not above the mouth of the Ohio river.

VICTORIA, *Ark.*—Arkansas river, 144 miles above Napoleon, above Arkansas Post, not above Pine Bluff.

VICKSBURG, *Miss.*—Mississippi river, 401 miles above New Orleans, above Grand Gulf, not above Greenville.

VIDALIA, *La.*—Mississippi river, 277 miles above New Orleans, above Bayou Sara, not above Grand Gulf.

VIENNA, *Va.*—Ohio river, 830 miles above its mouth, above Cincinnati.

VESTER.—Bayou Bartholomew, above Point Pleasant, not above Arkansas line.

VIENNA, *Ala.*—Tombigbee river, above Gainesville, not above Columbus.

VILLAGE CREEK, *Ark.*—White river, 345 miles above its mouth, below the junction of Black river.

VILMONT.—Mississippi river, 565 miles above New Orleans, above Grand Gulf, not above Greenville.

VILLE PLATTE, *La.*—Parish of St. Landry, usual navigation.

VINCENNES, *Ind.*—Wabash river, above Terre Haute.

VISTA, *La.*—Mississippi river, above Grand Gulf, not above Greenville.

VICKERS LANDING.—Lake Bisteneau.

VICKLAND, *Miss.*—131 miles up Big Deer Creek.

VICKLAND BRIDGE.—131 miles up Big Deer Creek.

VICKS.—180 miles up Sunflower river.

VILLA VISTA (or H. HARRIS).—Mississippi river, above Grand Gulf, not above Greenville.

VILLE, C. (or NOBLE'S).—119 miles up Bœuf river, above Thomas' Landing.

VILLIAU, NICK.—Red river, above Alexandria, not above mouth of Cane river.

VINE ISLAND.—Yazoo river, above Yazoo City, not above Leflore.

VININGS.—186 miles up Sunflower river.

VOOIRE'S OLD PLACE.—Red river, not above Alexandria.

VOHLMAN'S LANDING, *Mo.*—Missouri river, 72 miles above its mouth, not above Jefferson City.

W

WABASH, *Ind.*—Wabash river, not above the Rapids.

WABASH, *Ind.*—Wabash river, above the Rapids, not above Terre Haute.

WABASH CITY, *Ohio.*—Wabash river, not above the Rapids.

WABASH RIVER, *Ind.*—Ohio river, 139 miles above its mouth, above Paducah, not above Cincinnati.

WABASHAW, *Mo.*—Mississippi river, 1776 miles above New Orleans, above Galena.

WACO.—Ouachita river, above Harrisonburg, not above Trenton.

WADDIE, WIDOW.—Red river, above Cane river, not above Grand Ecore.

WADE'S, D L. LANDING, *La.*—Ouachita river, above Harrisonburg, not above Trenton.

WADE, DAN.—Ouachita river, above Harrisonburg, not above Trenton,

WADE, D. A.—Ouachita river, above Harrisonburg, not above Trenton.

WAGGAMAN'S, COL. PLANTATION.—Mississippi river, not above Bayou Sara.

WALMSLEY, WM.—Red river, above Grand Ecore, not above Shreveport.

WALMSLEY, T. C. (PANOLA).—Red river, above Grand Ecore, not above Shreveport.

WALCH, JOHN.—Black river, La.

WALTER'S, JOHN.—Red river, not above Alexandria.

WADE'S LANDING, *La*—Mississippi river, above Grand Gulf, not above Greenville.

WAGNER'S LANDING, *Tenn*—Tennessee river, not above Eastport.

WALBRIDGE LANDING, *Miss.*—Mississippi river, 1061 miles above New Orleans, above the mouth of the Ohio, not above Alton.

WALCONDA, *Mo.*—Missouri river, 314 miles above its mouth, above Jefferson City, not above Lexington.

WALLACE, LOUIS LANDING.—147 miles up Sunflower river.

WALLET, MRS. L.—Red river, above Grand Ecore, not above Shreveport.

WALLET, JOHN B.—Red river, above Grand Ecore, not above Shreveport.

WALKER & COLLINS.—Black river, La.

WALKER'S STORE.—Red river, above Shreveport, not above foot of Raft.

WALKER'S or WHITTAKER.—Red river, above Fulton, not above Lanesport.

WALKER, MRS. LANDING, *Ala.*—Tombigbee river, above Gainesville, not above Columbus.

WALKER, MRS. LANDING, *Ark.*—Mississippi river, above Grand Gulf, not above Greenville.

WALKER'S BEND, *Tenn.*—Mississippi river, 900 miles above New Orleans, above Memphis, not above the mouth of the Ohio.

WALKER, JACOB LANDING, *Ark.*—Red river, 265 miles above Shreveport, above Fulton, not above Lanesport.

WALKER'S LANDING, *Ark.*—Arkansas river, 176 miles above Napoleon, above Pine Bluff, not above Little Rock.

WALKER'S LANDING, *La.*—(Interior)—Shipping point at Bayou Sara.

WALKER, R. C. & Co. LANDING, *La.*—Black river, La.

WALLACE, *Ark.*—White river, above Batesville.

WALLACE CREEK, *Ark.*—White river, above Batesville.

WALNUT GROVE, *Ark.*—Arkansas river, 178 miles above Napoleon, above Pine Bluff, not above Little Rock.

WALNUT GROVE.—Bayou Macon, above Monticello.

WALNUT HILLS.—Mississippi river, 407 miles above New Orleans, above Grand Gulf, not above Greenville.

WALNUT HILLS, *La.*—Boyou Macon, 60 miles from its mouth, not above Monticello.

WALNUT POINT, *La.*—Mississippi river, above Grand Gulf, not above Greenville.

WALNUT PRAIRIE, or MRS. RUTY, *Texas.*—Red river, 365 miles above Shreveport, above Lanesport, not above Mound City.

WALNUT RIDGE, *Ark.*—White river, 129 miles from its mouth, below the junction of Black river.

WALNUT BEND.—Yazoo river, above Yazoo City, not above Leflore.

WALNUT GROVE.—Ouachita river, above Trenton, not above Alabama Landing.

WALNUT PLACE.—Tallahatchie river, not above Cassidy Bayou.

WALTER TAILOR LANDING, *Ala.*—Tombigbee river, not above Demopolis.

WALTER'S, WIDOW.—Red river, above Alexandria, not above Cane river.

WALTER, F. (ABNEY STELLA).—Red river, above Grand Ecore, not above Shreveport.

WAPSEPENECON RIVER, *Iowa.*—Mississippi river, 1547 miles above New Orleans, above second Rapids, not above Galena.

WAPETON.—Mississippi river, above Galena.

WARD, R. H.—Bayou Bartholomew, above Point Pleasant, not above Arkansas line.

WARD, LUM.—Bayou Bartholomew, above Point Pleasant, not above Arkansas line.

WARD.—Yazoo river, above Yazoo City, not above Leflore.

WARD, COL. S. C.—Red river, above Grand Ecore, not above Shreveport.

WARD'S LANDING, *Ala.*—Warrior river, not above Tuscaloosa.

WARD'S, DR. *Mo.*—Mississippi river, above Memphis, not above the mouth of the Ohio river.

WARD MOUND, *La.*—Bayou Macon, 42 miles from its mouth, not above Monticello.

WARDEN'S LANDING, *Texas.*—Red river, 290 miles above Shreveport, above White Oak Shoals.

WARDEN'S LANDING, *Ark.*—Red river, 291 miles above Shreveport, above Fulton, not above Lanesport.

WARDWORTH LANDING.—Red river, 55 miles above Shreveport, above Carolina Bluff not above Fulton.

WARFIELD, *Miss.*—Mississippi river, above Grand Gulf, not above Greenville.

WARE, D. H. LANDING, *Ark.*—Red river, 280 miles above Shreveport, above Fulton, not above Lanesport.

WARDLOW, G.—Ouachita river, not above Harrisonburg.

WARDLOW, J. B.—Ouachita river, not above Harrisonburg.

WARREN HOOKS' LANDING, *Texas.*—Red river, 323 miles above Shreveport, above Fulton, not above Lanesport.

WARREN'S LANDING, *Ala.*—Tombigbee river, not above Demopolis.

WARRENTON, *Miss.*—Mississippi river, 389 miles above New Orleans, above Grand Gulf, not above Greenville.

WARRENTON, *Ohio.*—Ohio river, 920 miles above its mouth, above Cincinnati.

WARRINGTON, *Ark.*—Mississippi river, above Greenville, not above Memphis.

WARRIOR, *Ill.*—Mississippi river, 1371 miles above New Orleans, above the first, not above the second Rapids.

WARRIOR RIVER, *Ala.*—Not above Tuscaloosa.

WARSAW, *Ind.*—Ohio river, 478 miles above its mouth, above Paducah, not above Cincinnati.

WARS, W. *La.*—Bayou Macon, 90 miles from its mouth, not above, Monticello.

WARSAW.—Ohio river, 533 miles above its mouth, not above Cincinnati.

WARSAW, *Ark.*—White river, 141 miles above its mouth, below the junction of Black river.

WARSAW, *Ala.*—Tombigbee river, above Gainesville, not above Columbus.

WARSAW, *Miss.*—Big Black river.

WASHINGTON, *La.*—Parish of St. Landry.

WASHINGTON, *Mo.*—Missouri river, 89 miles from its mouth, not above Jefferson City.

WASHAW.—Mississippi river, above Greenville, not above Memphis.
WARE.—Yazoo river, above Yazoo City, not above Leflore.
WARMACK'S.—Yazoo river, above Yazoo City, not above Leflore.
WARREN'S, GEN'L.—Arkansas river, above Pine Bluff, not above Little Rock.
WARREN'S LANDING.—Angelina river, Texas.
WARSAW, *Miss.*—154 miles up Big Deer Creek.
WASDER'S.—Red river, above Fulton, not above Lanesport.
WASHBURN.—Yazoo river, above Yazoo City, not above Leflore.
WASP LAKE.—Yazoo river, above Yazoo City, not above Leflore.
WATKINS, COL.—Arkansas river, above Pine Bluff, not above Little Rock.
WATKINS' LANDING.—137 miles up Bœuf river, above Thomas, Landing.
WATERS' FERRY.—Sabine river, Texas.
WATER, J.—Red river, not above Alexandria.
WATER FRONT.—Yazoo river, above Yazoo City, not above Leflore.
WATER VALLEY.—Yazoo river, above Yazoo City, not above Leflore.
WATSON, T. C.—Big Deer Creek, not above Yazoo City.
WATSON'S.—Yazoo river, above Yazoo City, not above Leflore.
WATSON'S PLANTATION (or PECAN POINT).—Red river, above Lanesport, not above Mound City.
WATSON'S.—Ouachita river, not above Harrisonburg.
WATSON, J.—Ouachita river, above Harrisonburg, not above Trenton.
WATT, WM. F.—Bayou Bartholomew, above Point Pleasant, not above Arkansas line.
WATTS' LANDING.—277 miles up Sunflower river.
W. B. McQUILLEN'S.—Big Deer Creek.
WASHINGTON, *La.*—Alabama river, 342 miles above Mobile, above Selma, not above Wetumpka.
WASHITA CITY, *La.*—Ouachita river, 322 miles from Old river, above Trenton, not above Alabama Landing.
WASHOOP, *Texas.*—Red river, 424 miles above Shreveport., above White Oak Shoals.
WATERLOO, *La.*—Mississippi river, 170 miles from New Orleans, not above Bayou Sara.

WATERLOO, *La.*—Red river, 665 miles from New Orleans, above Grand Ecore, not above Shreveport.

WATERLOO, *Tenn.*—Tennessee river, 243 miles above its mouth, not above Eastport.

WATKINS, MRS. LANDING, *La.*—Ouachita river, above Harrisonburg, not above Trenton.

WATERPROOF, *La.*—Mississippi river, 312 miles above New Orleans, above Bayou Sara, not above Grand Gulf.

WATERS' LANDING, *La.*—Red river, above Alexandria, not above Cane river.

WATERS' LANDING, *Mo.*—Mississippi river, above the mouth of the Ohio river, not above Alton.

WATERS', M. LANDING, *La.*—Red river, not above Alexandria.

WATER VALLEY, *Miss.*—Jackson railroad, 323 miles from New Orleans.

WATSON'S LANDING, *Texas.*—Red river, 416 miles above Shreveport, above Lanesport, not above Mound City.

WATSON'S, BEN. LANDING, *Ky.*—Mississippi river, above Greenville, not above the mouth of the Ohio river.

WATTENAW, *Ark.*—White river, 192 miles above its mouth, below the junction of Black river.

WAVERLEY, *La.*—Ouachita river, above Harrisonburg, not above Trenton.

WAVERLEY, *Mo.*—Missouri river, 311 miles from its mouth, above Jefferson City, not above Lexington.

WAVERLEY, *Tenn.*—Tennessee river, not above Eastport.

WAVERLEY, *Miss.*—Tombigbee river, above Columbus, not above Cotton Gin Port.

WAXFORD, *Ind.*—Mississippi river, above Galena.

WAXSHAW, *Miss.*—Mississippi river, above Greenville, not above the mouth of the Ohio river.

WAYNE, *Miss.*—San Francis river.

WAYNE CITY, *Mo.*—Missouri river, 393 miles above its mouth, above Lexington, not above Iatan.

WEAVER'S WOODYARD, *Ala.*—Alabama river, above Selma, not above Wetumpka.

WEBBER'S FALLS, *Ark.*—Arkansas river, 636 miles above Napoleon, above Fort Smith.

WEEDENS' LANDING, *Ala.*—Tombigbee river, above Demopolis, not above Gainesville.

WEGGENTERS' LANDING, *La.*—Black river, La.

WELCH'S LANDING, *La.*—Red river, not above Alexandria.

WELLS' LANDING.—Mississippi river, above Galena.

WELLS, R. W. LANDING, *Ala.*—Alabama river, not above Selma.

WELLSBURG, *Va.*—Ohio river, 927 miles from its mouth, above Cincinnati.

WELLSVILLE, *Ohio.*—Ohio river, 953 miles above its mouth, above Cincinnati.

WELLINGTON, *Ark.*—Arkansas river, 20 miles above Napoleon, not above Arkansas Post.

WELLINGTON, *Mo.*—Missouri river, 343 miles above its mouth above Lexington, not above Iatan.

WELTEN, *Ala.*—Tombigbee river, above Demopolis, not above Gainesville.

WELTEN, *La.*—Mississippi river, 445 miles above New Orleans, above Grand Gulf, not above Greenville.

WELTEN'S POND, *Miss.*—Mississippi river, above Grand Gulf, not above Greenville.

WENTZELL'S LANDING, *La.*—Ouachita river, above Harrisonburg, not above Trenton.

WESLEY CITY, *Ill.*—Illinois river, 170 miles above its mouth, above Beardstown, not above the mouth of Fox river.

WEST BUFFALO.—Mississippi river, above the first, not above the second Rapids.

WEST COLUMBIA, *Va.*—Ohio river, 748 miles from its mouth, above Cincinnati.

WEST FRANKLIN, *Ind.*—Ohio river, 175 miles from its mouth, above Paducah, not above Cincinnati.

WEST LEBANON, *Ind.*—Wabash river, above the rapids, not above Terre Haute.

WEST POINT, *Ark.*—Arkansas river, above Pine Bluff, not above Little Rock.

WEST POINT, *Ky.*—Ohio river, 369 miles from its mouth, above Paducah, not above Cincinnati.

WEST POINT, *Ark.*—Little Red river, 30 miles from its mouth, below the junction of White and Black rivers.

WEST POINT, *Ill.*—Illinois river, above Beardstown, not above the mouth of Fox river.

WEST UNION, *Ind.*—Wabash river, above the Rapids, not above Terre Haute.

WEST & MOORE'S LANDING, *Ala.*—Alabama river, not above Selma.

WEST WOOD PLACE.—Red river, above Grand Gulf, not above Shreveport.

WEST SIDE.—Ouachita river, above Harrisonburg, not above Trenton.

WESTMORELAND, MRS.—Bayou Bartholomew, above Point Pleasant, not above Arkansas line.

WESTEN, *Mo*,—Missouri river, 498 miles from its mouth, above Lexington, not above Iatan.

WESTEN, *Mo.*—Missouri river, above Iatan.

WESTPORT, *Ky.*—Ohio river, 418 miles from its mouth, above Paducah, not above Cincinnati.

WESTPORT, *Ind.*—Wabash river, above the Rapids, not above Terre Haute.

WESTPORT, *Miss.*—Tombigbee river, above Gainesville, not above Columbus.

WESTPORT, *Mo.*—Mississippi river, above Alton, not above the first Rapids.

WESTPORT, *Ala.*—Alabama river, above Selma, not above Wetumpka.

WEBB'S.—Bœuf river, above Thomas' Landing.

WEBB CITY.—Arkansas river, above Roseville, not above Fort Smith.

WEEPING WILLOW, *Miss.*—125 miles up Big Deer Creek.

WEBSTER'S LANDING.—Red river, above Grand Ecore, not above Shreveport.

WELCH'S CAMP.—Yazoo river, above Yazoo City, not above Leflore.

WELCOMSON.—134 miles up Bœuf river, above Thomas' Landing.

WELHAM PLANTATION.—Mississippi river, not above Bayou Sara.

WEISS BLUFF.—Neches river, Texas.

WELLS, J. Q. LANDING, *Miss.*—178 miles up Big Deer Creek.

WESTOVER.—Yazoo river, above Yazoo City, not above Leflore.

WEST, A. C. (STORE), *Miss.*—152 miles up Big Deer Creek.

WEBSTER'S, J. S. STORE.—Red river, above Grand Ecore, not above Shreveport.

WETUMPKA, *Ala.*—Alabama river, above Selma.

WHARHAPED.—Red river, above Lanesport, not above Mound City.

WHEELER'S.—81 miles up Bœuf river, above Thomas' Landing.

WHEELOCK, *Ind. Terr.*—Landing at Hodges, Red river, above Rowland and Mound City.

WHETSTONE, HOPE.—Bayou Bartholomew, above Point Pleasant, not above Arkansas line.

WHEELING, *Va.*—Ohio river, 911 miles from its mouth, above Cincinnati.

WHEELING or CANDY'S LANDING, *Ala.*—Warrior river, not above Tuscaloosa.

WHEELERSBURG, *Ohio.*—Ohio river, 659 miles from its mouth, above Cincinnati.

WHEELER'S, TOLAND, *Mo.*—Missouri river, 177 miles from its mouth, above Jefferson City, not above Lexington.

WHITE EARTH RIVER.—Missouri river, 1869 miles from its mouth, above Iatan.

WHITE, NORMAN LANDING, *La.*—Red river, not above Alexandria.

WHITE, MRS. LANDING, *La.*—Atchafalaya river, below Simmsport.

WHITE, J. K. LANDING, *La.*—Black river, La.

WHITE, J. O. LANDING, *Ala.*—Alabama river, not above Selma.

WHITE BLUFF, *Ala.*—Alabama river, not above Selma.

WHITE'S BLUFF, *Ala.*—Warrior river, not above Tuscaloosa.

WHITE CASTLE, *La.*—Mississippi river, not above Bayou Sara.

WHITE CLIFF, *Ark.*—Red river, 60 miles up Little river, above Carolina Bluff, not above Fulton, Ark.

WHITE CLOUD.—Missouri river, 625 miles from its mouth, above Iatan.

WHITE HALL, *La.*—Mississippi river, not above Bayou Sara.

WHITE OAK, *Ark.*—Arkansas river, 491 miles above Napoleon, above Norristown, not above Fort Smith.

WHITE POINT, *Mo.*—Missouri river, 191 miles above its mouth, above Jefferson City, not above Lexington.

WHITE RIVER.—Missouri river, 1408 miles from its mouth, above Iatan.

WHITE RIVER, *Ark.*—Mississippi river, above Greenville, not above Memphis.

WHITE OAK SHOALS, *Ark.*—Red river, 277 miles above Shreveport, above Carolina Bluff, not above Fulton.

WHITE BLUFFS.—Arkansas river, above Pine Bluff, not above Little Rock.

WHITE'S.—Ouachita river, above Trenton, not above Alabama Landing.

WHITE CLIFFS.—Little river, not above Hood's Landing.

WHITE HALL.—145 miles up Sunflower river.

WHITE HALL.—Ouachita river, above Alabama Landing, not above Camden.

WHITEHEAD.—Tallahatchie river, not above Cassidy Bayou.

WHITE HOUSE.—Yazoo river, not above Yazoo City.

WHITE OAK.—Bœuf river, not above Thomas' Landing.

WHITLY SLOUGH.—Yazoo river, above Yazoo City, not above Leflore.

WHITE, RUBE (BATES PLANTATION).—Red river, above Grand Ecore, not above Shreveport.

WHITE, RUBE LANDING, No. 1.—Red river, above Grand Ecore, not above Shreveport.

WHITE, R. (OLD PLACE).—Red river, above foot of Raft, not above Fulton.

WHITE, RUBE, No. 2.—Red river, above Grand Ecore, not above Shreveport.

WHITE LAND, *Miss.*—142 miles up Big Deer Creek.

WHITEHEADS' LANDING, *Ala.*—Tombigbee river, above Demopolis, not above Gainesville.

WHITESBURG, *Ala.*—Tennessee river, above Florance, not below Eastport.

WHITESTONES' LANDING, *Ala.*—Alabama river, above Selma, not above Wetumpka.

WHITAKER'S LANDING, *Ark.*—Red river, 310 miles above Shreveport, not above Fulton.

WHITTAKERS, CAPT.—Red river, above Lanesport, not above Mound City.

WHITIDE, ESTED.—Red river, above Grand Ecore, not above Shreveport.

WHITWORTH & PRAGUE, *La.*—Red river, above Grand Ecore, not above Shreveport.

WHITFIELD, N. LANDING, *Miss.*—Tombigbee river, above Columbus, not above Cotton Gin Port.

WHITSETT'S LANDING, *Ala.*—Tombigbee river, above Gainesville, not above Columbus.

WICKWIRE'S LANDING, *Ala.*—Tombigbee river, not above Demopolis.

WICKINS' LANDING, *Mo.*—Mississippi river, above the mouth of the Ohio river, not above Alton.

WIDOW WADDIE.—Red river, above Cane river, not above Grand Ecore.

WIGGINS LANDING.—Red river, not above Alexandria.

WIGGINTON, *La.*—Black river, not above Harrisonburg.

WIGGINS, TOM.—Bayou Bartholomew, above Point Pleasant, not above Arkansas line.

WIGGINTON LANDING.—Black river, La.

WILD WOOD LANDING.—149 miles up Sunflower river.

WILD CAT, *Ark.*—Arkansas river, 224 miles above Napoleon, above Pine Bluff, not above Little Rock.

WILD CAT, *La.*—Mississippi river, above Grand Gulf, not above Greenville.

WILD COW, *La.*—Black river, La.

WILD GOOSE BAYOU, *Ark.*—White river, 15 miles from its mouth, below the junction of Black river.

WILD WOOD, *Miss.*—Mississippi river, above Greenville, not above Memphis.

WILDERNESS, *Miss.*—Mississippi river, 482 miles above New Orleans, above Graud Gulf, not above Greenville.

WILKINSONVILLE, *Ills.*—Ohio river, 29 miles from its mouth, not above Paducah.

WILKINSON'S LANDING, *Mo.*—Mississippi river, 1117 miles from New Orleans, above the mouth of the Ohio, not above Alton.

WILKINSON'S LANDING, *Ark.*—White river, 288 miles from its mouth, below the junction of Black river.

WILKINSON'S LANDING.—Mississippi river, above Greenville, not above Memphis.

WILDERNESS.—Yazoo river, above Yazoo City. not above Leflore.
WILKINSON'S.—124 miles up Bœuf river, above Thomas' Landing.
WILLIAMS, WHITFIELD.—Red river, above Grand Ecore, not above Shreveport.
WILLIAMS.—Red river, above Shreveport, not above Carolina Bluff.
WILLIAMS, ALFRED LANDING.—Big Deer Creek.
WILLIAMS, W. (or HUNTER'S).—Red river, above Grand Ecore, not above Shreveport.
WILLIAMS, DR.—Red river, above Grand Ecore, not above Shreveport.
WILLIAMS, DANIEL, *Miss.*—176 miles up Big Deer Creek.
WILLIAMS' BRIDGE.—Deer Creek.
WILLIAMS, COL. or BANKHEAD'S.—Arkansas river, above Arkansas Post, not above Pine Bluff.
WILLIAMS, R. H. (OLD BATT PLACE).—Red river, above foot of Raft, not above Fulton.
WILLIAMS' LANDING.—Black river, La.
WILLIAMS, GEN —Arkansas river, above Arkansas Post, not above Pine Bluff.
WILLIAMS, J. H. GEN.—Red river, above Fulton, not above Lanesport.
WILLIAMS, R. W.—Ouachita river, above Harrisonburg, not above Trenton
WILLIAM'S, G. G.—Ouachita river, above Harrisonburg, not above Trenton.
WILLIAMS, M. E. MRS.—Bayou Bartholomew, above Arkansas line, not above Portland.
WILLIAMS (MORGAN).—Bayou Bartholomew, not above Point Pleasant.
WILLIAMS' LANDING.—278 miles up Sunflower river.
WILSON'S, GEO. LANDING, *La.*—Red river, 330 miles from New Orleans, not above Alexandria.
WILLIAMS LANDING, *La.*—Ouachita river, above Harrisonburg, not above Trenton.
WILLIAMS, S. LANDING, *La.*—Ouachita river, above Harrisonburg, not above Trenton.
WILLIAMS, H. LANDING, *La.*—Ouachita river, above Harrisonburg, not above Trenton.
WILLIAMS, C. LANDING.—Tombigbee river, not above Demopolis

WILLIAMS, JNO. LANDING, *La.*—Ouachita river, above Harrisonburg, not above Trenton.

WILLIAMS, H. R. LANDING, *Ala.*—Tombigbee river, not above Demopolis.

WILLIAMS LANDING, *Ala.*—Tombigbee river, above Demopolis, not above Gainesville.

WILLIAMS SAW-MILL, *La.*—Red river, not above Alexandria.

WILLIAMS, WM. LANDING, *La.*—Red river, above Grand Ecore, not above Shreveport.

WILLIAMS LANDING, *Miss.*—Yazoo river, above Yazoo City, not above Leflore.

WILLIAMS LANDING, *Miss.*—Mississippi river, above Grand Gulf, not above Greenville.

WILLIAMS, J. W. LANDING, *Ark.*—Red river, 178 miles above Shreveport, not above Carolina Bluff, not above Fulton.

WILLIAMS, B. K., *Texas.*—Red river, 335 miles above Shreveport, above Fulton, not above Lanesport.

WILLIAMS, J. W., *Ark.*—Arkansas river, 197 miles above Napoleon, above Pine Bluff, not above Little Rock.

WILLIAMS, L. E , *La.*—Black river, La.

WILLIAMS LANDING, *Miss.*—Yallabusha river, not above Grenada.

WILLIAMS, T. H. LANDING, *Ala.*—Alabama river, not above Selma.

WILLIAMS, A. LANDING, *Ala* —Alabama river, not above Selma.

WILLIAMS, J. LANDING, *Ala.*—Alabama river, not above Selma.

WILLIAMS LANDING, *Ala.*—Alabama river, above Selma, not above Wetumpka.

WILLIAMS LANDING, *Ark.*—Mississippi river, above Greenville, not above Memphis.

WILLIAMSBURG, *Miss.*—San Francis river.

WILLIAMSBURG, *Ky.*—Cumberland river, above Gainesboro.

WILLIAMSPORT, *La.*—Old river (Mississippi river), 250 miles above New Orleans, above Bayou Sara, not above Grand Gulf.

WILLIAMSPORT, *Ind.*—Wabash river, above the Rapids, not above Terre Haute.

WILLIAMSPORT, *La.*—Mississippi river, not above Bayou Sara.

WILLIS, J. H. (EAGLE BEND).—Mississippi river, above Grand Gulf, not above Greenville.

WILLIS, DR. LANDING.—Warrior river, not above Tuscaloosa.
WILLOW POINT, LOWER.—Red river, above Grand Ecore, not above Shreveport.
WILLOW POINT, *La.*—Red river, 567 miles from New Orleans, above Grand Ecore, not above Shreveport.
WILLOW GROVE (J. HUGHES), *La.*—Red river, above Grand Ecore, not above Shreveport.
WILLOW WATERS.—Mississippi river, 1210 miles above New Orleans, above the mouth of the Ohio river, not above Alton.
WILLOW POINT.—Mississippi river, above Grand Gulf, not above Greenville.
WILLOW POINT (or DR. McGEE).—Red river, above foot of Raft, not above Fulton.
WILLOW POINT.—Red river, above Grand Ecore, not above Shreveport.
WILLOW BEND (or MRS. ANN DICKERSON).—Red river, above Shreveport, not above foot of Raft.
WILMOT'S LANDING, *Miss.*—171 miles up Big Deer Creek.
WILSON, IKE LANDING.—148 miles up Sunflower river.
WILSON'S, B. C.—Black river, La.
WILSON'S, JOE.—Yazoo river, above Yazoo City, not above Leflore.
WILSON'S, MRS.—Bayou Bartholomew, above Point Pleasant, not above Arkansas line.
WILSON'S (or R. A. PUGH.—Bayau Bartholomew, above Arkansas line, not above Portland.
WILSONS & SCREWS.—Yazoo river, not above Yazoo City.
WILSON'S, B. C., *La.*—Black river, not above Harrisonburg.
WILSON'S LANDING, *Ala.*—Warrior river, not above Tuscaloosa.
WILSON'S BLUFF, *Ala.*—Warrior river, not above Tuscaloosa.
WILSON'S, L. J. LANDING.—Tombigbee river, not above Demopolis.
WILSON'S POINT.—Mississippi river, above Grand Gulf, not above Greenville.
WILSON'S LANDING, *Ark.*—Arkansas river, 566 miles above Napoleon, above Fort Smith.
WILSON'S, MRS. LANDING.—Mississippi river, above Greenville, not above Memphis.
WILSON'S LANDING, *La.*—Black river, not above Harrisonburg.

WILMINGTON.—Ouachita river, 423 miles from Old river, above Alabama Landing, not above Camden.

WINCHESTER, *Miss.*—Chicasaha river.

WINDHAM'S LANDING, *Ala.*—Tombigbee river, above Gainesville, not above Columbus.

WINONA, *Miss.*—Jackson railroad, 290 miles from New Orleans.

WINONA.—Mississippi river, above Galena.

WINNSBORO, *La.*—(Interior); shipping point at Chandler's Landing, Bayou Macon, not above Monticello.

WISCONSIN RIVER, *Wis.*—Mississippi river, 1672 miles above New Orleans, above Galena.

WISENEN LANDING, *La.*--Red river, 2 miles above Shreveport, not above Carolina Bluff.

WITTENBURG, *Mo.*—Missouri river, 1103 miles above New Orleans, above the mouth of the Ohio river, not above Alton.

WOLF BLUFF, *Ala.*—Warrior river, not above Tuscaloosa.

WOLF BAYOU, *Ark.*—White river, above Batesville.

WOLF RIVER, *Tenn*—Mississippi river, 739 miles above New Orleans, above Memphis, not above the mouth of the Ohio river.

WOLF RIVER.—Missouri river, 611 miles above its mouth, above Iatan.

WOOD'S LANDING, *La.*—Ouachita river, above Harrisonburg, not above Trenton.

WOODYARD'S LANDING, *Ala.*—Tombigbee river, not above Demopolis.

WOODLAWN (or RUSH BAYOU).—Red river, above Grand Ecore, not above Shreveport.

WOODLAWN, *La.*—Mississippi river, 95 miles above New Orleans, not above Bayou Sara.

WOODBOURNE, *La.*—Mississippi river, 162 miles above New Orleans, not above Bayou Sara.

WOODVILLE, *Miss.*—(Interior); shipping point at Bayou Sara, on the Mississippi river.

WOODVILLE, *Ala*—Chattahootchie river, not above Eufaula.

WOODCOOK, *Ala.*—Alabama river, not above Selma.

WOODS LOWER LANDING, *Ala.*—Alabama river, above Selma, not above Wetumpka.

WILSON'S, GEO.—Red river, not above Alexandria.
WILTON.—Mississippi river, above Grand Gulf, not above Greenville.
WILTON PLANTATION.—Mississippi river, not above Bayou Sara.
WILTON.—Yazoo river, not above Yazoo City.
WILTON.—Mississippi river, above Grand Gulf, not above Greenville.
WINN, BOB. ESTATE.—Red river, above foot of Raft, not above Fulton.
WINCHAL BAYOU.—Tallahatchie river, not above Cassidy Bayou.
WINTER QUARTERS.—Yazoo river, above Yazoo City, not above Leflore.
WINTERVILLE.—Mississippi river, above Grand Gulf, not above Greenville.
WISE, G. H. LANDING.—Red river, not above Alexandria.
WISE.—Black river, La.
WITTSBURG.—Arkansas river, above Little Rock, not above Norristown.
WITTSBURG (ST. FRANCIS CITY, ARK).—Above Philips Bayou.
WOLF CREEK AGENCY.—Missouri river, 2147 miles from its mouth, above Iatan.
WOMACK, WIDOW.—Bayou Bartholomew, above Portland.
WOOD PLANTATION.—Red river, above foot of Raft, not above Fulton.
WOODS' BLUFF, *Ala.*—Tombigbee river, not above Demopolis.
WOODS' UPPER LANDING, *Ala.*—Alabama river, above Selma, not above Wetumpka.
WOODSTREKS' LANDING, *Miss.*—Mississippi river, above Greenville, not above Memphis.
WOOD COTTAGE, *Ark.*—Mississippi river, above Greenville, not above Memphis.
WOODFORK, *Mo.*—Mississippi river, above Memphis, not above the mouth of the Ohio river.
WOODWARD'S LANDING, *Ark.*—Mississippi river, above Greenville, not above Memphis.
WOODFORK, *Ill.*—Mississippi river, above the mouth of the Ohio river, not above Alton.
WOODBERRY'S.—Yazoo river, above Yazoo City, not above Leflore.
WOODYARD.—Red river, above foot of Raft, not above Fulton.
WOODYARD.—Red river, above Grand Ecore, not above Shreveport.

WOOLEY'S LANDING, *Ala.*—Warrior river, not above Tuscaloosa.

WOODSTOCK.—Yazoo river, not above Yazoo City.

WOODSTOCK.—Tallahatchie river, not above Cassidy Bayou.

WOODSIDE.—Tensas river, La.

WOODWARD'S FERRY.—Red river, above Fulton, not above Lanesport.

WOOFOLK LANDING, *Miss.*—118 miles up Big Deer Creek.

WORK'S LANDING.—Neches river, Texas.

WORKINGER'S LANDING.—Black river, La., not above Harrisonburg.

WORLEY'S FERRY.—Bayou Bartholomew, above Point Pleasant, not above Arkansas line.

WORTHEY, DR. or SODA FOUNT.—Red river, above Shreveport, not above foot of the Raft.

WORTH, *Ark.*—White river, 430 miles from its mouth, above Batesville.

WRECK OF BIG HORN.—Bayou Bartholomew, not above Point Pleasant.

WRIGHT'S GIN.—Ouachita river, above Trenton, not above Alabama Landing.

WRIGHT'S LANDING.—Neches river, Texas.

WRIGHT'S LANDING. *Miss.*—80 miles up Sunflower river.

WRIGHT'S, NEWTON.—Red river, above Grand Ecore, not above Shreveport.

WRIGHT'S, T. G. & S. J. (PLANTATION AND STORE).—3 miles above Kiomittia, Texas.

WRIGHT'S LANDING, *Texas.*—Red river, 520 miles above Shreveport, above Mound City.

WRIGHT'S LANDING.—Mississippi river, above Greenville, not above the mouth of the Ohio river.

WRIGHT'S, JOHN LANDING, *Ark.*—Little Red river, 27 miles from its mouth, below the junction of White and Black rivers.

WRIGHT'S, JOHN LANDING, *Ark.*—White river, 190 miles from its mouth, below the junction of Black river.

WRIGHT'S, L. LANDING, *La.*—Black river, La., not above Harrisonburg.

WYANT.—Ouachita river, above Harrisonburg, not above Trenton.

WYALUSING.—Mississippi river, above Galena.

WYANDOTE, *Mo.*—Missouri river, 405 miles above its mouth, above Lexington, not above Iatan.

WYATT, *Miss.*—Tallahatchie river, above Belmont.

WYCHES (BRIER BEND).—Red river, above Grand Ecore, not above Shreveport.

WYESES BLUFF, *Texas.*—Neches river.

WYNN LANDING.—Red river, above Cane river, not above Grand Ecore.

WYNNES' BLUFF, *Ala.*—Warrior river, not above Tuscaloosa.

WYNN (FISHERS' PRAIRIE), *Ark.*—Red river, 176 miles above Shreveport, above Carolina Bluff, not above Fulton.

Y

YALLABUSHA RIVER, *Miss.*

YANKTON.—Missouri river, above Iatan.

YAZOO CITY, *Miss.*—Yazoo river, 102 miles from Vicksburg.

YAZOO RIVER, *Miss.*—Mississippi river, 404 miles from New Orleans.

YAMAR'S GIN.—123 miles up Bœuf river, above Thomas' Landing.

YATES, J. S. (or B. PLACE.—Red river, above Grand Ecore, not above Shreveport.

YATES, J. T. (WILLIAMS WHITFIELD).—Red river, above Grand Ecore, not above Shreveport.

YELLOW BLUFF,—Neches river, Texas.

YELL'S, GEN'L.—Arkansas river, above Pine Bluff, not above Little Rock.

YEARGIN'S LANDING, *Mo.*—Mississippi river, above Memphis, not above the mouth of the Ohio river.

YELLOW BLUFF, *Ala.*—Alabama river, not above Selma.

YELLOW CREEK, *Tenn.*—Cumberland river, not above Nashville.

YONGUE, HUGH LANDING, *La.*—Ouachita river, above Trenton, not above Alabama Landing.

YORK, *La.*— Mississippi river, above Bayou Sara, not above Grand Gulf.

YORK, *Ind.*—Wabash river, above Terre Haute.

YOUNG'S POINT, *Miss.*—Mississippi river, 412 miles above New Orleans, above Grand Gulf, not above Greenville.

YOUNG, J. G. LANDING, *Ala.*—Alabama river, not above Selma.

YOUNG, MACK LANDING, *Ark.*—Little Red river, 34 miles from its mouth.

YOUNG'S, DR. LANDING, *La.*—Ouachita river, above Trenton, not above Alabama Landing.

YOUNG'S, T. LANDING, *Ark.*—Little Red river.

YOUNG'S WOODYARD, *Miss.*—Mississippi river, above Grand Gulf, not above Greenville.

YOUNG'S, HY. LANDING, *La.*—Ouachita river, not above Harrisonburg.

YOUNG'S GIN.—Yazoo river, above Yazoo City, not above Leflore.

YOUNG'S.—Ouachita river, above Harrisonburg, not above Trenton.

YUBA DAM.—Tallahatchie river, not above Cassidy Bayou.

YUCATAW.—Mississippi river, above Grand Gulf, not above Greenville.

Z

ZACHARY, *Ala.*—Tennessee river, above Florence, not below Eastport.

ZAWALA, *Texas.*—Angelina river, above Bevilport.

ZENOR'S LANDING, *La.*—Black river, La., not above Harrisonburg.

ZACHARIE.—Bayou Bartholomew, above Point Pleasant, not above Arkansas line.

ZIMMERMAN'S SWELLY LANDING.—Red river, above Alexandria, not above Cane river.

ZOAR.—Yazoo river, above Yazoo City, not above Leflore.

www.ingramcontent.com/pod-product-compliance
Lightning Source LLC
LaVergne TN
LVHW061240100826
845148LV00008B/996

* 9 7 8 0 7 8 8 4 7 7 7 0 6 *